Research for What?

Making Engaged Scholarship Matter

a volume in
Advances in Service-Learning Research

Series Editor:
Shelley H. Billig
RMC Research Corporation, Denver

Advances in Service-Learning Research

Shelley H. Billig, Series Editor

Service Learning: The Essence of the Pedagogy (2002)
edited by Andrew Furco and Shelley H. Billig

Service Learning Through a Multidisciplinary Lens (2002)
edited by Shelley H. Billig and Andrew Furco

Deconstructing Service-Learning:
Research Exploring Context, Participation, and Impacts (2003)
edited by Janet Eyler and Shelley H. Billig

New Perspectives in Service Learning: Research to Advance the Field (2004)
edited by Andrew Furco and Shelley H. Billig

Improving Service-Learning Practice:
Research on Models to Enhance Impacts (2005)
edited by Susan Root, Jane Callahan, and Shelley H. Billig

Advancing Knowledge in Service-Learning:
Research to Transform the Field (2006)
edited by Karen McKnight Casey, Georgia Davidson,
Shelley H. Billig, and Nicole C. Springer

From Passion to Objectivity (2007)
edited by Sherril B. Gelmon and Shelley H. Billig

Scholarship for Sustaining Service-Learning and Civic Engagement (2008)
edited by Melody A. Bowdon, Shelley H. Billig, and Barbara A. Holland

Creating Our Identities in Service-Learning
and Community Engagement
edited by Barbara E. Moely, Shelley H. Billig, and Barbara A. Holland

Research for What? Making Engaged Scholarship Matter (2010)
edited by Jeff Keshen, Barbara A. Holland, and Barbara E. Moely

Research for What?

Making Engaged Scholarship Matter

edited by

Jeff Keshen
University of Ottawa, Canada

Barbara A. Holland
University of Sydney, Australia

and

Barbara E. Moely
Tulane University, New Orleans

Information Age Publishing, Inc.
Charlotte, North Carolina • www.infoagepub.com

Library of Congress Cataloging-in-Publication Data

Research for what? : making engaged scholarship matter / edited by Jeff
Keshen, Barbara A. Holland, and Barbara E. Moely.
    p. cm. — (Advances in service-learning research.)
    Consists of a selection of papers presented at the 9th conference of the
International Association for Research on Service-learning and Community
Engagement held in Ottawa, Canada, in 2009.
    Includes bibliographical references.
    ISBN 978-1-61735-165-5 (paperback) — ISBN 978-1-61735-166-2 (hardcover) —
ISBN 978-1-61735-167-9 (e-book)
    1. Service learning—Congresses. 2. Service learning—Research—Congresses.
I. Keshen, Jeff, 1962- II. Holland, Barbara A., 1950- III. Moely, Barbara E.
IV. International Association for Research on Service-learning and Community
Engagement. Conference (9th : 2009 : Ottawa, Ont.)
    LC220.5.R49 2010
    361.3'7—dc22

                                                          2010038052

Printed in the United States of America

CONTENTS

PART I
THEORY AND METHODOLOGY

PART II
SERVICE-LEARNING IN THE K-12 SETTING

ACKNOWLEDGMENTS

We would like to extend our appreciation to Sherril Gelmon, Gail Robinson, John Saltmarsh and Marshall Welch for their advice in planning and carrying out the 2009 conference. Jeff Keshen would like to acknowledge the invaluable assistance of Anne Millar, Barbara Alves, Kristina McDougall, and Denise Jeffrey in organizing the logistics of the conference and for excellent administrative support. We also appreciate the assistance of Stephanie O'Brien and Katie Houck at Tulane. Our thanks go out to the researchers who submitted papers, to the reviewers who so carefully assessed their work, and especially to the authors for their exceptional contributions and their respect for the tight deadlines necessary in preparing this volume.

INTRODUCTION

Jeff Keshen, Barbara A. Holland, and Barbara E. Moely

In October 2009, the 9th Conference of the International Association for Research on Service-learning and Community Engagement (IARSLCE) was held in Ottawa, Canada's national capital. It was a conference of firsts: The first time IARSLCE held its annual gathering outside of the United States and the first time that a major service-learning and community engagement conference took place in Canada. More than 300 delegates attended, from across North America, Latin America, Europe, Asia and Australia, to hear nearly 100 presentations.

The Ottawa conference provided a unique opportunity to highlight community service-learning (CSL) in Canada; in fact, nearly one third of the presentations were by Canadians. Most these Canadians spoke of newly launched initiatives. Although CSL programs presently exist at some 50 Canadian universities, or about two thirds of the national total, almost all these programs were created in the last 5 years. Although CSL programs are a recent addition to the Canadian university scene, service-learning as a pedagogical approach in higher education has long existed in Canada. Its roots trace back to the late-nineteenth century, are as old as similar U.S. initiatives, and link to the intensification of social problems associated with the rise of urban-industrial society. At the University of Toronto, Canada's flagship institution at the time, its president, Robert

Research for What? Making Engaged Scholarship Matter
pp. ix–xviii
Copyright © 2010 by Information Age Publishing

Falconer, underlined the importance of civic engagement as part of the development of ethical citizens and future leaders. In 1910, he told the graduating class, "Find the highest good by serving your fellows." Although few in number, female university students also became involved in community outreach activities, some of them carried out through new schools of social service (the forerunner of social work programs), the first of which was established in 1914 by the University of Toronto.

Canadian universities of the late-nineteenth and early-twentieth centuries were church affiliated and, in most cases, church financed. Numerous Christian denominations, particularly Protestant ones, became influenced by the Social Gospel movement, an activist Christian doctrine dedicated to building the "Kingdom of God on Earth" through a variety of outreach and relief measures. Besides religious-based motivation, community outreach by universities was buttressed in the early twentieth century by the rise of Progressivism and the modern social sciences, both of which emphasized that empirical analysis and the application of expert advice from emerging, and newly accredited, university-trained professions could bring greater efficiency, order, and uplift, particularly to urban centres confronting growing social challenges.

Several Canadian academics, a number of whom had migrated from England, were familiar with the work of the British economic historian, Arnold Toynbee of Balliol College. By the time of his death at only 36 years of age from meningitis, Toynbee had established an international reputation not only for his scholarship—on inequalities in the emerging industrial system and the importance of new trade unions—but also for establishing a settlement house in 1881. At Toynbee Hall, situated in London's notorious east end slum, university students conducted classes to educate the poor. This was an early expression of "engagement" with communities that may have influenced Canadian universities.

Similar engagement by Canadian universities started at the University of Toronto, which established a settlement house in the early 1890s. A driving force behind this initiative was William Ashley, who had studied at Balliol, knew Toynbee, and became the first recruit for the University of Toronto's new Department of Political Economy. After Ashley left for Harvard in 1892, his replacement, another British-trained academic, James Mavor, championed service as an integral component of university education. One of Mavor's students was William Lyon Mackenzie King, who, as prime minister for 22 years (between 1921 and 1948), became Canada's longest-serving national leader. His governments implemented legislation that formed the basis of the country's modern social welfare system. King was influenced by the pioneering and widely known social reformer, Jane Addams. While pursuing a postgraduate degree at the University of Chicago, he volunteered at Hull House, which was located in the Nineteenth Ward, Chicago's most notorious slum. There, Addams "recruited idealistic doctors, lawyers and academics" who worked to provide "better housing, cleaner water and elementary health services," as well as a "day nursery, library, [and] lecture program" (Gray, 1997, p. 135). Similarly, Canadian university students were encouraged during this time to work with inner city church missions and organizations such as the Young Men's Christian Association, where, for example, "football and gymnasium classes [were] conducted by popular university athletes, and were designed to exert a manly influence on the large number of neighbourhood boys who, it was assumed, would otherwise be amusing themselves in the streets" (Burke, 1996, p. 41).

Another milestone in the development of community engagement by Canadian universities occurred in 1928 at Nova Scotia's Catholic-affiliated St. Francis Xavier University, where the Antigonish Movement was established. Named for the area in which the university was situated, the Antigonish Movement was about getting the university involved in reversing regional economic decline, which had intensified after the First World War. Under the leadership of Father Moses Coady, St. Francis Xavier University established an Extension Department through which educators and students helped mobilize local communities to deal with problems. During the Great Depression, the reach of Antigonish Movement spread throughout Canada's Maritime region. By 1938, 2,390 local study groups were established with links to Antigonish educators; largely as a result of their recommendations and actions, there resulted "42 co-operative stores, 17 co-operative lobster canneries, 10 fish-processing plants, and 140 credit unions" (Alexander, 1997, p. 88).

Despite these strong roots, service-learning as a formal instructional strategy did not initially establish a presence in the modern, secular Canadian university system. One can postulate several reasons: There was no inspirational call from Canada's political leadership to citizens, and especially to young people, to provide service as part of a grand vision like the New Frontier or Great Society. Canada's version of the Peace Corps, named Katimavik, was not founded until 1977. Although Canada was an active member of the United Nations and a proponent of internationalism, it remained a self-proclaimed "middle power" and practiced "quiet diplomacy" rather than harbouring, as the United States did, ambitions of global stewardship, and therefore arguably did less to inspire and mobilize citizens. While Canada, like the United States, contained many examples of inequality and social injustice—such as the systemic poverty, racism and lower life expectancy faced by its Aboriginal peoples—its demographic breakdown did not lend itself as readily to producing mass campaigns for social justice, such as the Civil Rights movement that mobilized millions of African-Americans and their supporters in the United

States. Although sometimes overstated, governments in Canada, as compared to the United States, have played a more prominent role than grass roots community organizations in providing social support. While volunteerism in both countries remains low, there is a notable difference: According to the U.S. Department of Labor (2009), 63.4 million people, or 26.8% of the U.S. population, volunteered for an organization at least once a week during 2009, while the *Canada Survey of Giving, Volunteering and Participating* reports that, in 2007, only 11% of Canada's population provided over 80% of the country's total volunteer time (Statistics Canada, 2009). Besides more pronounced volunteerism in America upon which CSL has built a stronger foundation, there is a longstanding view of education, stretching back to Thomas Jefferson's insistence that it be universal, as being essential to bolstering democratic institutions and promoting social and individual progress. There is also the fact that since the 1960s the overwhelming majority of Canadian universities have become government-financed institutions; there are very few privately-funded or faith-based universities, and no Historically Black Colleges and Universities, institutions that appear in the United States to have made community service a more central component of the student experience. According to a 2008 report from Campus Compact, "Faith-based and historically black colleges and universities reported the highest levels of student service, with 61% of students participating in service and civic engagement," compared to a general average of 31% among students in all Campus Compact institutional members (Campus Compact, 2008, p. 2).

As late as the1990s, the only major university-based service-learning programs in Canada were at St. Francis Xavier University, where a program was created in 1996 as an outgrowth of the Antigonish Movement, and at the University of British Columbia, where a program emerged two years later, in large part because its president, Martha Piper, established community service as a priority for her mandate.

Recently, the J.W. McConnell Family Foundation, Canada's largest private charitable organization, has played a major role in catapulting CSL forward. Viewing this pedagogical approach as a means of transforming universities into community-builders, the foundation started its involvement in 1999 by providing a major grant to St. Francis Xavier University to expand its pioneering work in CSL. As part of that effort, St. Francis Xavier hosted a symposium in 2001 that brought together university professors, researchers and administrators, and representatives from the not-for-profit sector from across Canada who were involved or interested in CSL to share information and develop strategies to pursue funding and greater institutional buy-in. This coincided with increasing interest and recognition within academe of the importance of community-based research: In 1998, the Community-University Research Alliance funding program was introduced by the Social Sciences and Humanities Research Council of Canada (SSHRC). Over the following decade, the SSHRC funded over 100 projects, to an individual maximum of $1 million, that linked university researchers to more than 1,000 almost exclusively not-for-profit community organizations. In 2008, Community Based Research Canada was established. Housed at the University of Victoria, it is a nationwide network of several hundred academics, administrators, and community representatives whose goals include: "to build capacity for community-centered solutions ... uncover the root causes of complex issues facing communities ... and improve the lives of individuals and their communities." One of the challenges facing CSL in Canada is a tendency to lump it together with CBR (Community Based Research Canada, 2010). However, the joint contributions of these two initiatives, CSL and CBR, can contribute to broad-based and sustainable community engagement of universities.

Seeking to build upon the gathering of CSL practitioners at St. Francis Xavier University, similar colloquia were held in 2002 at the University of Guelph, in 2003 at the University of British Columbia, and in 2004 at the University of Ottawa. At the Ottawa gathering, delegates established the Canadian Association of Community Service Learning (CACSL). In 2007, it replaced the term *Association* with *Alliance* to reflect its decentralized structure, as the CASCL runs largely through the cooperation of volunteers and mainly as a clearing house for sharing information. With financial assistance from the McConnell Foundation, CACSL was initially housed at the University of Guelph and in 2007 moved to Carleton University in Ottawa, where it still resides.

In 2005, the McConnell Foundation announced a national competition providing up to $1 million dollars each to universities to build upon or to establish CSL programs. Ten institutions—the Universities of Alberta, British Columbia, Lakehead, Nippising, Ottawa, Sherbrooke, St. Francis Xavier, Trent, Trois-Rivières, and Wilfrid Laurier—received awards. The creation of these programs sparked the establishment of CSL at other universities and led to further success with fundraising: Community research projects were funded by SSHRC and the Canadian Council of Learning, while private sources funded CSL operations, such as an award of more than $2 million made by the Royal Bank of Canada to the University of Western Ontario in 2009.

The 2009 IARSLCE conference hosted by the University of Ottawa was a further affirmation of the impressive recent growth of CSL in Canada. It showcased Canadian CSL programs and research and made Canadians more aware of broader developments and cutting edge research in the field. In choosing the conference theme, "*Research for What? Making*

Inquiry Matter," local organizers and the national association sought to reaffirm the IARSLCE's raison d'etre, namely to demonstrate, through rigorous research, the impact of CSL on student learning, teaching, and community development. A select group of papers from the conference form the chapters in this volume. These chapters deal with research issues in service learning and community engagement, describing work done in Canada, the United States, and Singapore. While *quality* was the determining factor in selecting conference papers to publish, the editors sought out those that were innovative in using methodology and source material, that contributed to knowledge, and that, when taken together, portray engaged scholarship in a variety of contexts.

The papers in the first section of the volume focus on theory and methodology. In "Toward Understanding Reciprocity in Community-University Partnerships: An Analysis of Select Theories of Power," Lorilee Sandmann, Brandon Kliewer, Jihyun Kim and Anthony Omerikwa examine power relations in university-community interactions. They argue that university representatives, in interacting with community agencies, harbour the notion that they are the ones imparting knowledge and expertise, an attitude that too often results in community needs not being adequately heard and addressed. Partnerships thus become less effective, satisfying and sustainable. To better identify and understand the characteristics and consequences of unequal CSL relationships, and to prompt reflection on how to correct the situation, these authors turn to broader philosophical works on power written by Paulo Freire, Michel Foucault, and John Rawls.

The issue of valid measurement is the focus of Nicolas Bowman and Jay Brandenberger's paper on "Quantitative Assessment of Service-Learning Outcomes: Is Self-Reported Change a Reasonable Proxy for Longitudinal Change?" For many years, researchers and critics have complained about the heavy reliance on self-reported data in studies attempting to measure the impact of service-learning on students. These authors point out that self-reported data, obtained at one point in time, may be relatively easy to collect but has questionable validity in assessing changes in attitudes over time. This study of university students in service-learning courses discovered little correlation between six measures of self-reported attitude change and six corresponding measures of longitudinal attitude change. The authors find that while their study confirms that short-term self-reported data warrants doubt, quantitative approaches used over a longer period of time can provide accurate insights into student change, especially when multiple scales are used as a way of measuring students' self-estimation.

The next group of papers deals with service-learning in the K-12 environment. In their chapter on "Facilitating Transformation through Education: Promoting Teaching of Social Responsibility and Civic Education for Democracy," Janel Smith and Annie McKitrick explore the theory of transformational learning as a framework that can foster more inclusive learning environments and strengthen the ability of schools to build "an informed and socially responsible citizenry." Transformational learning, in their view, helps teachers move beyond factual knowledge to the wider use of critical reflection and interactions that promote deeper consideration of multiple points of view. They offer several examples of service-learning and other interactive school-community projects that demonstrate the power of transformational learning. In particular, they see transformational learning and service-learning as strategies for encouraging and promoting student learning around the concept of the social economy. They argue that as governments reduce or withdraw social supports, the community sector and social organization sectors are stepping into important policy spaces. Thus, they make the case for a greater emphasis on transformational learning strategies that will enhance civic capacities in students and an understanding of the social economy.

Nicole Nicotera, Inna Altschul, Andrew Schneider-Munoz, and Ben Webman's chapter on "Conceptual and Analytic Development of a Civic Engagement Scale for Preadolescents" addresses the need for age-appropriate measures of civic engagement for students in middle school and early adolescence, an age range that has received only limited attention to date in service-learning research. They describe steps taken to create and validate a measurement tool for this age group. The Pre-adolescent Civic Engagement Scale (PACES) that they developed includes a measure called "Foundation for Civic Ethics," in which students evaluate their own civic attitudes and skills/actions. The PACES includes a second measure, termed "Community Connection," that assesses students' civic actions in the context of their local communities. This new instrument is an important step toward understanding the meaning of civic engagement in pre-adolescents. The PACES will be useful for researchers interested in evaluating service-learning outcomes for adolescent learners, in looking at the influences of background or experiences, or in tracing development of civic attitudes from adolescence to later years.

A large-scale, mixed-methods study by Janet Eyler, Richard Bradley, Irwin Goldzweig, David Schlundt, and Paul Juarez examines "The Relationship Between the Quality of Service-Learning Interventions and Teen Seatbelt Use." The quality of the service-learning activity, evaluated on the basis of the K-12 Service-learning Standards developed by Billig (Billig & Weah, 2008), was shown to be important in determining outcomes: Service-learning course quality, as described by teachers, was related to motivation for and actual seatbelt use, as well as to a number of scales measuring aspects of personal development and school and community engagement. This well-crafted study constitutes a significant advancement in research design and identifies important and ongoing challenges for CSL researchers.

The next group of papers examines university-based service-learning as a component in the training of teachers who provide the principal feedback loop to the application of CSL in the K-12 setting. In their chapter on "Service-Learning and Preinternship Teacher Efficacy: A Comparison of Two Designs," Trae Stewart, Kay Allen, and Haiyan Bai investigate the contributions of service-learning to the perceptions of prospective teachers about their own effectiveness as educators. The study contrasts outcomes for pre-internship teacher education students who took part in service-learning that involved whole-class instruction with those who engaged in small-group tutoring, with the aim of identifying factors that contributed to students' growth over the semester. Their findings have important implications for how service-learning experiences can best contribute to the preparation of effective and confident K-12 teachers. In explaining the positive outcomes shown in both service-learning conditions, the authors emphasize the importance of student preparation for service, exposure to models of effective teaching, experience with authentic teaching tasks, and ongoing support from both campus and community sources.

Robert Shumer and Kim Chuan Goh's chapter on "Service-Learning in Singapore: Preparing Teachers for the Future," presents an ambitious program to incorporate service-learning into teacher training. Singapore's National Institute of Education mandates that every prospective teacher participate in a service-learning program that lasts as long as nine months and is designed to impart a defined set of values, skills and knowledge deemed to be in the national interest. In the "Group Endeavours in Service Learning" program, teacher trainees, working with young children and community agencies, plan and execute a service-learning program and then engage in structured reflection and the dissemination of results. Through observation and interviews, Shumer and Goh show positive impacts of this experience on teacher trainees' leadership skills, time management, social awareness and interpersonal skills, and on youth understanding and engagement. The implementation of mandatory service-learning for teacher trainees is possible in Singapore, the authors note, in that the education system is directed by a national authority, allowing broad changes that would be difficult to bring about in nations with a less centralized educational system.

The potential of a campus-wide themed initiative for service-learning is the focus of Connie Nelson and Mirella Stroink's chapter on "Benefits to Students of Service-Learning Through a Food Security Partnership Model." The authors describe a creative approach to service-learning and community engagement adopted at Lakehead University in Thunder Bay, Ontario, Canada. Courses from a number of different disciplines, each with service-learning options, are organized around the theme of food security. Campus-community relationships are developed in accordance with the five dimensions of a contextual fluidity partnership model, which characterizes reciprocal and mutually beneficial interrelationships between the university, community partners, and students. Positive changes in students' academic skills and civic attitudes were seen following participation in service-learning. The interdisciplinary approach around a conceptual theme, used at this university, provides all participants with a deeper understanding of the complex issues relating to food security in local, national and international contexts and sets the stage for mutually beneficial and sustained collaborations between campus and community.

A summary of an address given at the conference by Dwight Giles, the 2009 recipient of the IARSLCE Distinguished Research Award, serves as a conclusion for this volume. A pioneer in service-learning research and a practitioner for more than two decades, Giles weaves his own story into his description of major trends in the field, in his chapter, "Journey to Service-Learning Research: Agendas, Accomplishments, and Aspirations." Giles shows that although service-learning has achieved tremendous growth, and research in the field is increasing in sophistication, its appeal remains far more pronounced among female academics and those of color—arguably among those in academe who have been in the forefront of campaigns for greater inclusion and equality. He notes that many research issues have remained remarkably consistent over time, such as those concerning the most effective means of encouraging faculty involvement in CSL, the importance of structured reflection, and the necessity of reciprocity to achieve successful campus-community partnerships. He also points to research gaps, including the need for research on types of CSL placements that show the greatest impact on participants. And though Giles remains among the leading researchers on CSL, he cautions against an increasing trend of prioritizing CSL scholarship—publishing and obtaining research grants—over efforts to implement good practice. Turning to the theme of the 2009 conference, he reminds readers that in response to the question, *Research for What?* the answer should focus on identifying and supporting high quality CSL placements that bring demonstrated benefits to students, educators and the broader community. For, like the pioneers who established settlement houses more than a century earlier, service-learning is fundamentally about producing engaged citizenship and pursuing and using knowledge to improve society.

Through annual conferences and the *Advances in Service-Learning Research* series, the IARSLCE is supporting rigorous research on many aspects of engagement: Pedagogy, community partnerships, student learning, and program development. The Ottawa conference made it possible for researchers from Canada and the United States to share findings, models, and plans for future work, thereby enriching efforts in both nations. The IARSLCE aims to encourage the larger international movement in community engagement, in order to enrich both educational institutions and the communities they serve.

REFERENCES

Alexander, A. M. (1997). *The antigonish movement.* Toronto, Ontario, Canada: Thompson Educational.

Billig, S. H., & Weah, W. (2008). *K-12 service-learning standards for quality practice.* Retrieved from http://www.nylc.org/objects/publications/G2G2008_StdArticle.pdf

Burke, S. (1996). *Seeking the highest good: Social service and gender at the University of Toronto, 1888-1937.* Toronto, Ontario, Canada: University of Toronto Press.

Campus Compact. (2008). *Service statistics 2008: Highlights and trends from Campus Compact's annual membership survey.* Retrieved from http://www.compact.org/wp-content/uploads/2009/10/2008-statistics1.pdf

Community Based Research Canada. (2010). Retrieved from http://community researchcanada.ca/?action=who_are_we

Gray, C. (1997). *Mrs. King: The life and times of Isabel Mackenzie King.* Toronto, Ontario, Canada: Penguin.

Statistics Canada. (2009). *Canada Survey of giving, volunteering and participating.* Retrieved from http://www.statcan.gc.ca/cgi-bin/imdb/p2SV.pl?Function=getSurvey&SDDS=4430&lang=en&db=imdb&adm=8&dis=2

U.S. Department of Labor. (2009). *Volunteering in America.* Retrieved from www.nationalservice.gov/about/role_impact/performance_research.asp#VIA_2009

PART I

THEORY AND METHODOLOGY

CHAPTER 1

TOWARD UNDERSTANDING RECIPROCITY IN COMMUNITY-UNIVERSITY PARTNERSHIPS

An Analysis of Select Theories of Power

**Lorilee R. Sandmann, Brandon W. Kliewer,
Jihyun Kim, and Anthony Omerikwa**

Reciprocity and mutuality are fundamental values and inherent goals of community-engaged partnerships. However, authentic support for reciprocal relationships must incorporate an understanding of forms of power and differentials in power. With the work of major theorists and philosophers as its foundation, this chapter begins to provide the literature on community engagement a conceptual, theoretical, and philosophical analysis of power as it relates to reciprocity. It also features implications for community-engaged research and practice.

Research for What? Making Engaged Scholarship Matter
pp. 3–23
Copyright © 2010 by Information Age Publishing

UNDERSTANDING RECIPROCITY BY UNPACKING POWER

More than ever, universities and communities are establishing symbiotic relationships to work collaboratively in addressing societal issues. Boyer (1990) describes these relationships as community engagement. Such relationships between the university and the community are highly complex, with each partner having particular resources (Bender, 1988). How these resources are distributed and how the distribution is negotiated—specifically, reciprocity and mutuality—provide the context for this paper.

Reciprocity and mutuality are fundamental values and inherent goals of community-engaged partnerships. Yet one of the significant challenges that emerged from the 2006 Carnegie community-engaged classification applications was in the area of establishing reciprocal campus-community relationships. As Driscoll (2008) reports, "most institutions could only describe in vague generalities how they had achieved genuine reciprocity with their communities" (p. 41). Further analysis by Saltmarsh, Giles, Ward, and Buglione (2009) found that campuses that adopted Boyer's scholarship categories tended to frame community engagement as "application to" a community, instead of engagement "with" communities, an indicator of reciprocity.

Unpacking dimensions of power can be particularly relevant and helpful in understanding and supporting reciprocal community-university partnerships. Whenever entities interact they usually have some form of relationship through which power is apparent (Loomer, 1976). Operations of power inform how entities interact and establish the parameters of a relationship. Brookfield (2005) suggested that "power is co-extensive with the social body; there are no spaces of primal liberty between the meshes of its network" (p. 130). As Cervero and Wilson (2006) point out, power, interests, ethical commitment, and negotiation are central to engaged partnerships. Community-university partnerships are contextualized within various social structures that situate power. This means that engagement partnerships are informed by the same social, political and economic structures that impact other spaces of life.

Forms of power play a significant role in understanding and communicating reciprocal relationships in the context of engagement. In many ways the literature associated with engagement has failed to develop a theoretical lexicon of power. For example, Moje (2000) describes how power is produced and ascribed based upon forms of discipline that are present in her engaged research. Moje's description of power in her engaged research is not theory grounded. Likewise, Katrina Powell and Pamella Takayoshi (2003) identify some ethical issues associated with engaged research that can be interpreted as products of power. However, they also fail to ground their analysis of interpersonal dynamics of engagement in theory.

As a team of experienced and novice engaged scholar-practitioners, we too found ourselves seeking a deeper, richer understanding of attempts at achieving reciprocity and mutuality in partnerships we were studying. Most of these partnerships had obviously power differentials. This paper is part of our quest to draw from select theorists' understanding of power to address the theoretical limitations of the current engagement literature and illuminate power in the context of engagement. How does power influence reciprocity and mutuality in community-university collaborations? This paper reports on our exploration of this question and unpacks power through select theoretical perspectives in a relational framework related to engaged partnerships. Service-learning pedagogues and practitioners can benefit particularly from this analysis. Conversations within service-learning literature and practice approach discourses of power and reciprocity in general terms. The theories we discuss give scholars and practitioners explicit theoretical language to better discuss power and reciprocity. Furthermore, it provides consideration of power from diverse practical, political, and philosophical perspectives.

MODE OF INQUIRY

This is a challenging area of study as reciprocity, mutuality, and power are each complex concepts. Reciprocity can be defined as the negotiated process of working with a partner as opposed to doing something to or for a partner. Mutuality is a shared process that is collectively beneficial. Power will be defined variously by the select theorists. Moreover, the relationships between these concepts are continually changing. So to begin to provide a theoretical and conceptual understanding of power as it relates to reciprocity, we will draw from the work of three theorists and overlay these understandings of power across a multilevel and multidirectional framework that describes reciprocal relationships. Reciprocal relationships are bounded within socially constructed relationships and institutions. Therefore, to understand the nature of reciprocity, the elements of power (knowledge, positions, processes, and systems) that operate in and result from social relationships and institutions must be acknowledged.

For our inquiry, we have chosen three major theorists who offer distinct conceptualizations of power developed in a variety of contexts. We realize that the three theories do not represent an exhaustive perspective of power but they do situate power from important diverse perspectives.

Freire's ideas of power are practical and connected to predominant thought processes that explain the ways social groups are marginalized. Foucault's account of power is sociological and informed by discipline and human interaction. Finally, Rawls provides a philosophical account of power that is connected to determining the requirements of justice. By drawing from theorists with dissimilar perspectives who deal with power in diverse contexts, none specific to community-university partnerships, these three theories and our analysis provide an effective start point and unique approach to understanding reciprocity in an undertheorized arena of practice.

To inform our analysis of power as it operates within the concept of reciprocity, this research draws primarily upon the theoretical and philosophical work of Paulo Freire, (1970/2000, 1985, 1998) Michel Foucault, (1977, 1994, 1997) and John Rawls (1999a, 1999b). Freire's conceptualization of "critical consciousness" provides a theoretical understanding of how effective forms of dialogue can maintain high levels of reciprocity and maneuver through different forms of power. Michel Foucault understands power as spatially arranged and reinforced by forms of surveillance. Finally, John Rawls's account of what justice requires provides a lucent philosophical account of reciprocity and its relationship to power.

Each theory has been chosen for its specific understanding of power and will be viewed across the relational framework. Lazarsfeld and Menzel's (1969) relationship framework is used in this analysis. This framework is a useful social research tool that identifies analytical, structural, and global units of analysis. Of importance to this analysis is the structural or relational unit of analysis that describes the relational patterns among the entities in a given context (Books & Prysby, 1991). The understandings of power of the three theorists will be overlaid across this relational framework, which is characterized by four types of interactions illustrated in Exhibit 1.1: (a) individual-to-individual relationships, Quadrant 1; (b) individual-to-institution relationships, Quadrant 2; (c) institution-to-individual relationships, Quadrant 3, and; (d) institution-to-institution relationships, Quadrant 4. We present each theorist's conceptualization of power along with an analysis that applies it to parts of the Relational Engagement Framework as it informs our understanding related to reciprocity. Not all quadrants will be discussed for all theorists; we have developed those that are most salient. The individual levels can be understood as "people" associated with or independent of larger institutions. The "institutional" level is defined as the social constructions used to organize and give purpose to engagement activities.

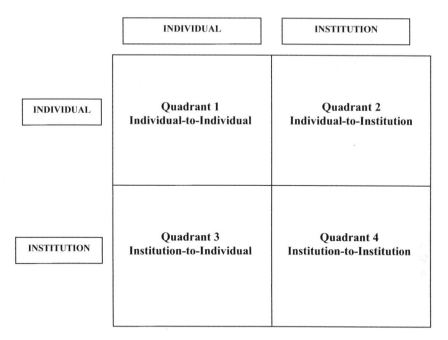

	INDIVIDUAL	INSTITUTION
INDIVIDUAL	Quadrant 1 Individual-to-Individual	Quadrant 2 Individual-to-Institution
INSTITUTION	Quadrant 3 Institution-to-Individual	Quadrant 4 Institution-to-Institution

Exhibit 1.1.   Relational engagement framework.

FREIRE'S PERSPECTIVE ON POWER

Freire's view of power includes both a dialectical and a phenomenological stance. Power is not viewed as either a negative or a positive force; instead, power is dialectical and thus exists everywhere people struggle. Giroux (1985) refers to Freire's notion of power as "more ubiquitous and ... expressed in a range of oppositional public spaces and spheres that traditionally have been characterized by the absence of power and thus any form of resistance" (p. xix). For example, school could be a place in which a positive form of power is exercised in terms of resistance.

Freire's concept of power is also phenomenological. That is, power is what normal people exercise daily; individuals construct the meaning of power based on their own experiences, which are influenced by knowledge, social relations, and cultural actions. For Freire (1985) power is not simply governmental authority such as an army or policy; rather, power is one type of domination that can be expressed as forms of power, technology, and ideology and which results in forms of knowledge, social relations, and cultural actions. This perspective on power implies that power is involved in the production and control of knowledge. Thus, social power determines what can be knowledge. Mayo (1999) points out that Freire's concept of power is influenced by Gramsci's (1971) notions of hegemony and war of position, which call for diverse forms of counter-hegemonic cultural activities. Thus, empowerment necessarily accompanies cultural actions.

Freire's educational thoughts are represented in *Pedagogy of the Oppressed* (1970/2000), originally published in 1970. This book begins with the assumption that no education is neutral. According to Freire, education is necessarily political, and its ultimate goals should be humanization and liberation. Humanization is the process of restoration of humanity to both the oppressors and the oppressed. Humanistic education is a "utopian project" (Freire, 1985, p. 113) involving both groups. Liberation is the condition through which dehumanization is overcome through a mutual process between the oppressors and the oppressed, which can result only from praxis. This notion of praxis, "the authentic union of action and reflection" (Freire, 1985, p. 87), is a dialectic relationship between reflection and action, influencing each other. For example, critical reflection of a relationship between teachers and learners could lead to finding that an unequal relationship exists; as a result, cultural action could be taken to change the relationship, and then further reflection follows. Dehumanization is a "concrete expression of alienation and domination" (Freire, 1985, p. 113). In order to achieve humanization and liberation, Freire suggests *problem-posing education* for the oppressed, an alternative to the *banking concept of education*, which oppresses students by forcing them to record, to memorize, and to repeat the given knowledge without reflective inquiry. With regard to problem-posing education, the student-teacher relationship needs to be reestablished as a mutual and co-evolutional relationship:

> Problem-posing education, which breaks with the vertical patterns characteristic of banking education, can fulfill its function as the practice of freedom only if it can overcome the above contradiction. Through dialogue, the teacher-of-the-students and the students-of-the-teacher cease to exist and a new term emerges: teacher-student with students-teachers. The teacher is no longer merely the one-who-teaches, but one who is himself taught in dialogue with the students, who in turn while being taught also teaches. They become jointly responsible for a process in which all grow. (Freire, 1970/2000, p. 80)

In this sense, both participants in education are not objects but subjects, and the role of educators is transformed from deliverers of knowledge to facilitators who learn *with* students and experience a dialectical process together.

Another key concept of Freire's (1970/2000) education theory is *conscientization*, "the process in which men, not as recipients, but as knowing subjects, achieve a deepening awareness both of the sociocultural reality that shapes their lives and of their capacity to transform that reality" (p. 106). Conscientization takes place through learning, specifically problem-posing education, and one aspect of problem-posing education is dialogue. When both teachers and students engage in reflective dialogue, cultural action and praxis can occur.

FREIRE'S RECIPROCITY AND THE
RELATIONAL ENGAGEMENT FRAMEWORK

Freire suggested the mutual educational relationship in terms of problem-posing education, and his theory and participation in social action greatly influenced participatory action research in Latin America (Torres, 1992). Although Freire did not use the term *reciprocity*, the process can be inferred from his dialectical concept of power and pedagogical theory. In this model, nobody should be oppressed through the university-community engagement process; like education, community engagement has humanization as its ultimate goal. In addition, Freire's critique of the higher education institution provides insights on building a mutual relationship. In the next section, the implications of Freire's ideas for multi-level mutual relationships are presented.

Power is by its nature exercised in two directions because it is dialectical. This characteristic applies in any quadrant of the relational framework. Additionally, student-teacher relationships described in Freire's works provide insights for mutual community engagement at the individual-to-individual level. Freire (1998) states:

> The democratic educator is also charged with teaching but, for this teacher, teaching is not the mechanical act of transferring to learners the profile of the concept of an object. Teaching is, above all, creating a situation in which the learners, who are epistemologically curious, will be able to appropriate the profound significance of the object so that, *in the act of learning it* they can *know it and understand it.* (pp. 66-67)

If the word *teacher* in the above paragraph is replaced with *faculty* and the word *student* is changed to *community*, it illustrates a mutual relationship at the individual level. Faculty members need to participate in engagement activities with critical reflection and to acknowledge themselves not as a practitioner of oppression but as subjects of engagement or learning.

Another insight into the individual-to-individual level is that both participants should recognize each other as knowledge creators who share equal power in creating knowledge. Reciprocity should be based on the assumption that inquiries are open to all and that all participants contribute to the resulting knowledge. In Freire's theory, equal power in creating and developing knowledge, which includes the contribution of indigenous knowledge, stems from the assumption of equal power in the teacher-student relationship and, in the case of engagement, in the faculty-community relationship.

Glass (2001) stated, "knowledge becomes founded on dialogue characterized by participatory, open communication focused around critical inquiry and analysis, linked to intentional action seeking to reconstruct the situation (including the "self") and to evaluate consequences" (p. 19) Partnership should be based on the idea that faculty are not ready-made knowledge deliverers and the premise that community members also act as knowledge creators. Ultimately, all participants should be subjects in community engagement to achieve a mutual relationship. Moreover, Freire (1970/2000) argues that "any situation in which some individuals prevent others from engaging in the process of inquiry is one of violence" (p. 85). Thus, in order to achieve high levels of mutuality and subjectivity, all interested parties should be included in collective decision making. This point leads to another: If individuals argue based on their authority, such arguments cannot be valid in the context of a mutual relationship (Freire, 1970/2000).

Freire further informs consideration of the institution-to-individual dimension of the Relational Engagement Framework. He often criticizes the university environment because it is "full of intolerance" (1998, p. 100). This results from characteristics of scholarship, namely, "Envy of the brilliance of others, fear of losing our small clique of admirers who are attracted by the knowledge that we supposedly illuminate, [and] our personal insecurity" (1998, p. 100). In this sense, to develop a mutual relationship and thus to support a reciprocal university-community partnership, a university should overcome these characteristics in a process that could result from *conscientization* (Freire, 1970/2000).

Also, there is an implication for evaluating process. Freire (1985) points out that evaluation should not be inspection because inspection makes educators objects of vigilance by a central organization. To build a mutual relationship at the institution-to-individual level, a university ought to build a process to eliminate its characteristics of pressing position and this process should result in an encouragement of engagement. Such a process would be attentive to whose culture is dominating when making decisions. Processes that share cultural context and make efforts to develop structural transformation can be useful in mitigating such dominance. Participatory action research is one such process that holds potential as a vehicle for supporting social change.

Through the above discussion, it can be concluded that in order to build a mutual relationship of community engagement, power must be exercised at the levels of both individual and institution. Reciprocity can be achieved if individuals develop a relationship based on Freire's problem-posing education. Reciprocity is undermined if it is assumed that universities represent a space of knowledge and that communities represent a space of ignorance. All participants should recognize themselves as subjects in engagement as well as being knowledge creators. Furthermore, institutions can contribute to the mutual relationship by developing and providing a democratic culture to faculty. When academic culture is changed, in terms of cultural action, more productive reciprocity can be developed.

FOUCAULT'S PERCEPTION OF POWER AS DISCIPLINE

The purpose of this section is to use specific elements of Michel Foucault's understanding of power in the context of engagement. The extension of his understanding of power begins to provide a basic conception of power as surveillance and discipline. This can be used to analyze forms of power operating at different levels of the Relational Engagement Framework.

While there is an assortment of secondary literature relating Foucault's understanding of power to the study of education and to education itself, (Gore, 1998; Green, 1998; Toll & Crumpler, 2004, among others) we rely on Foucault's original concentrations of power to inform our understanding. In *Discipline and Punish: The Birth of the Prison*, Foucault provides an account of how power is generated, produced, and regulated through torture, punishment, and discipline. Although the language is severe, as a poststructuralist theorist, Foucault gives meaning to power as it operates within the context of historical events and societal practices. His understanding of power as discipline and surveillance provides an appropriate theoretical grounding for engagement that was lacking in Moje and Powell's and Takayoshi's pieces.

Foucault suggests that observation is one way power is produced in social settings. Surveillance and observation regulate behavior and in turn channel forms of power. Political agents never truly know when they are being watched. As a result of the constant awareness of being "seen," political agents self-regulate their behavior to fit within predetermined social and cultural expectations. In this context, power is focused not only individually but collectively. Preconceived social norms and mores create spaces widely perceived as "normal." The approved space or behavior therefore regulates behavior and organizes power into dominant social, cultural, and political models. Foucault argues that "the perfect disciplinary apparatus would make it possible for a single gaze to see everything constantly" (Foucault, 1977, p. 173). Manifestations of observation/surveillance can present themselves while parties are attempting to communicate reciprocal engaged relationships. Both intentional and unintentional forms of surveillance/observation create forms of power that need to be accounted for when seeking reciprocity in engaged relationships.

Foucault refers to the power to regulate behavior through surveillance/observation as "normalizing judgment" (Foucault, 1977, p. 177). Thus forms of power are organized and reproduced by creating a standard of "normal" that is strictly regulated and controlled through defining and enforcing the "norm." Surveillance/observation is used as a vehicle to ensure that behavior fits within appropriate standards through both external and internal discipline. Marginalization occurs by self-identifying or being identified as deviant in relation to the norm. Power and privilege are immediately bestowed upon conforming political agents. Foucault argues that power is focused by differentiation of conforming and nonconforming behaviors and by strict regulation of the "norm." He demonstrates how surveillance/observation is related to power when he argues that "what is specific to the disciplinary penalty is non-observance, that which does not measure up to the rule, that departs from it" (Foucault, 1977, p. 178).

The external regulation of norms is both perceived and actual. As previously suggested, in some situations the power of "normalizing judgments" is ascribed to others. In other words, a subject can ascribe characteristics of the norm to others. In doing so, individuals create for themselves an identity that is based on the ideological "subject" and marginalized to a regulated position of power. This type of ascribed power is a particular threat to forming reciprocal university-community partnerships. These theoretical understandings of power can be extended to analyzing reciprocity across the Relational Engagement Framework.

FOUCAULT'S RECIPROCITY AND THE
RELATIONAL ENGAGEMENT FRAMEWORK

Engagement relations originating at the individual-to-individual level of the Relational Engagement Framework have limited amounts of power that are produced or ascribed through surveillance. In many ways, power differentials are not concentrated by surveillance. As a result, in Foucault's words, at the individual-to-individual level, forms of surveillance are not effective in producing or ascribing power. An inherent element of power as surveillance is differentials in power and a mechanism for discipline or the ability of another entity to negatively impact the observed. In many ways power at the individual-to-individual level will be ascribed to individuals. This point reinforces the limited effect of surveillance on producing power at the individual-to-individual level. In most situations, other individuals do not have enough power or perceived power to seriously influence others' actions through surveillance. This point highlights how the power of normalizing judgment is more helpful in understanding the operation of power at the individual-to-individual level.

Normalizing judgment does not require any differentials in power. The interesting element of normalizing judgment is that in most situations it is an indirect act of power. The ever-changing and free-flowing understanding of "normal" regulates subjects' behaviors. The normalizing power operates in two ways at the individual-to-individual level. First, normalizing behavior focuses power between individuals through requiring adherence to a particular range of conduct. This assumes, however, that one or more individuals do not conform to the expectations of normality and that the deviant subjects acknowledge that their behavior is outside the bounds of normality. The requirement of acknowledging "deviant" behavior highlights how power is ascribed: Deviant subjects must acknowledge that their situation or actions are defined as outside the norm. Indirectly or directly identifying the range of acceptability places deviant subjects in a situation such that they must yield to forms of power, and power is ascribed to those who meet the requirements of normality.

Normalizing power at the individual-to-individual level is defined by societal forces and not by particular individuals. As a result, individual interactions are forced to comply with standards of normality that are constructed not individually but collectively. Within the context of engagement this might mean that while reciprocity is defined at the individual-to-individual level, it is limited to protocols that conform to societal standards of normality. Individual subjects are forced to work within this range whether they want to or not. Thus a person's socioeconomic status, gender, race, or educational level can produce a power differential.

For the most part, an individual does not produce power through the surveillance of institutions. This is a result of disparities in power and influence. Generally, individuals lack the time, influence, and resources to monitor large institutions in any meaningful way. However, this does not mean it does not occur. It seems reasonable that individuals can generate power by maintaining large degrees of transparency and accountability in larger institutions. However, the power produced from individual "watchpersons" is in many ways in tension with the intent behind engagement. It is unlikely that relationships based upon the individual-to-institution model and designed to maintain reciprocity would be concerned about generating power this way. For the most part, individuals that produce power from regulating or observing institutions will do so in capacities other than engagement. However, within the context of "engaged" relationships, it is crucial to acknowledge the possibility of individuals generating power from large institutions. Relationships will be dysfunctional if power is being produced at the individual-to-institution level. This is particularly important to consider when operating within an environment that values and places authority in expertise.

Normalizing power regulates behavior by defining and enforcing a particular norm. Acknowledging nonconformity or deviance from the norm produces power. However, acting within the norm is not enough to organize power; one must have enough influence to have others recognize deviance. As a result, the production of power rests upon being able to illustrate deviance in others. The process of stigmatizing deviance within institutions can be subtle at times and other times more obvious. For example, when universities hit hard financial times, administrators' first response is often to cut programs that are not designed to bring in some type of revenue. The act of threatening to cut projects that do not generate revenue can discipline community-engagement programs to fit more neatly into a revenue-generating model. Profit/revenue generation becomes the norm and all other behavior is automatically signaled as deviant.

In most relationships designed to maintain elements of engagement, power is not produced in individuals at the individual-to-institution level. Individuals lack the influence needed to gain power to force larger institutions to comply with specific norms. In most circumstances it is more accurate to understand institutions as defining the norms that are used to define deviance and subsequently promote power. Individuals are really only able to enforce and help define norms by which institutions redirect power.

As previously suggested, how power is produced and ascribed is related to power differentials between the two subjects. Between the institution and the individual the disparity can be quite large. Institutions can have many resources and bureaucratic policies that intentionally or unintentionally give the impression of surveillance. Often these procedures are related to administrative transparency but still produce power. Individuals feel pressured to comply with the policies for fear of losing their association with the institution and its perceived benefits. As a result, power can be generated and transferred to the institution from the individual.

The power produced from this relationship can be created in one of two ways. First, the power can be created by and accumulated within the institution. The institution can deliberately design policies and operating procedures that disadvantage individuals in a way that creates a sense of power differential. For example, institutions can intentionally use their operating procedures to make it difficult for individuals to maneuver through the administrative and institutional culture. As a result, individuals actively surrender forms of power to the institution. Or, understood in another way, the institution is taking forms of power away from the individual by regulating certain forms of behavior within the bureaucratic structure.

Second, institutional policies or norms can lead individuals to ascribe power to the institution. In this case, specific policies and practices are employed to facilitate the operation of the institution. It is crucial to understand that such policies are not specifically designed to disadvantage individuals; they are most likely designed to ensure transparency or maintain "administrative efficiency." However, when the operation of these procedures creates difficulties for individuals, it results in individuals ascribing power to the institution. The affirmative act of granting power to the institution can go unseen and unnoticed by individuals and the institution alike.

The individual acting within the system regulates the norms created by the institution. As a result, an institution's power to regulate behavior is a very significant concern for communicating reciprocity. The expectations and procedures of institutions regulate and channel forms of power. However, it is not the mere existence of policies and expectations but the manner in which they are enforced upon individuals that situates power. In many situations norms develop around how individuals should interact and comply with institutional procedures. These informal and formal expectations create forms of power for the institution.

Institutions create expectations and routines that everyone within the organization begins to accept. In some situations it is conceivable to have an institutional culture that disciplines and regulates behavior in a way that is not supportive of effective community-engagement. In these cases institutional culture applies pressure up individuals to behave within accepted norms and expectations that are counter to sound community-engagement.

Although these normalizing expectations favor the institution, individuals can impact larger institutions. Individuals can slowly resist unsupportive institutions to create a culture of engagement. However, few individuals exert the leadership required to effectively change an institutional culture by themselves. Usually, this type of institutional culture change requires coalitions that are developed over time.

Power also derives from institution-to-institution relationships. Communities of institutions have a shared interest in maintaining common connections. If power is assumed by and ascribed to institutions at the institution-to-institution level, weaker institutions ascribe power to institutions with actual and perceived power. Power is ascribed across institutions chiefly through forms of surveillance. Similar institutions often have internal or common forms of regulation. These forms of regulation are premised as being accepted on equal terms. However, to receive the privileges and status associated with being a member of some community of institutions, an institution often must adhere to that group's common regulations and practices. Those institutions that maintain the standards or regulations are regarded as "compliant" and are asked to enforce these standards in their peer-group. As a result, weaker institutions can ascribe power to institutions that are asked to maintain the peer-group standards and operating procedures.

At the institution-to-institution level, power is generally ascribed through forms of surveillance. However, surveillance connected to enforcing regulations or operating approaches is connected to the production of power resulting from regulating and maintaining a standard of "normal." Institutions that observe and enforce institutional relationships can produce power by strictly regulating both formal and unofficial norms of operation. On the other hand, powerful institutions can diffuse power by relaxing some of the norms of operation and allowing other institutions to self-regulate their practices.

RAWLS'S PERSPECTIVE ON POWER AS JUSTICE

Philosopher John Rawls (1999a, 1999b) provides a third perspective on power and its relationship to reciprocity. The reciprocity inherent in Rawls's theory plays a crucial role in defining principles that are used to develop a just society, and as such can be used to analyze the philosophical requirements of reciprocity. Moreover, the basic design of his theory highlights the need for future inquiry into understanding what is required to realize justice in the context of engagement.

The first stage of Rawls's account occurs in what this paper will refer to as the "considered judgment phase." Once subjects define considered judgments, they are tested at the "original position." Considered judgments that achieve consensus, or what Rawls calls "reflective equilibrium," are used to define the principles of justice. The principles of justice that are generated at the original position stage are then used to define the requirements of justice. These principles are used to construct a just society, which Rawls refers to as a "well-ordered Society."

Considered judgments are the starting point at which the requirements of justice are discussed. Rawls (1999a) defines considered judgments as those rendered under conditions favorable to exercise the sense of justice, and therefore in circumstances where the more common excuses and explanations for making a mistake do not obtain. The person making the judgment is presumed, then, to have the ability, the opportunity, and the desire to reach a correct decision (or at least, not the desire not to) (Rawls, 1999a, p. 42).

Considered judgments can be understood as moral intuitions, rough estimations, or practical expectations of what principles would lead to the organization of a just society. Rawls identifies the value of deliberation and does not suggest these considered judgments will correct moral intuitions initially. For Rawls, considered judgments will be proposed and then evaluated behind the veil of ignorance in the original position. The original position is a hypothetical space in which political subjects think about the considerations of justice. In order to avoid biasing the considerations of justice, political subjects step behind what Rawls refers to as the "veil of ignorance." The following passage from *A Theory of Justice* (Rawls, 1999a) describes the informational restrictions of the veil of ignorance:

> Among the essential features of this situation [the original position behind the veil of ignorance] is that no one knows his place in society, his class position or social status, nor does anyone know his fortune in the distribution of natural assets and abilities, his intelligence, strength, and the like. I shall even assume that the parties do not know their conceptions of the good or their special psychological propensities. (p. 11)

Moving back and forth between moral intuitions and evaluation of them behind the veil will lead to "reflective equilibrium." Reflective equilibrium refers to the gauge that Rawls uses to determine that principles of justice are widely accepted by reasonable people and likely to produce a just society. Rawls (1999a) accurately acknowledges that "from the standpoint of moral theory the best account of a person's sense of justice is not the one which fits his judgments prior to his examining any conception of justice, but rather the one which matches his judgments in reflective equilibrium" (p. 43). Said in another way, once all reasonable and legitimate concerns are addressed, moral persons can confidently assume that principles of justice will produce just outcomes.

Rawls's conceptualization of justice is premised upon a traditional contractual theory method. Each subject that enters the original position agrees to follow certain procedures to define justice. Requiring subjects to agree to the process through which justice will be defined creates a moral obligation to accept the ultimate terms. However, this contractual obligation should not be confused with a legal obligation based on the authority of the state. Rawls specifically states that the "original position is purely hypothetical" (Rawls, 1999a, p. 19). For Rawls the original position is a theoretical device that people committed to justice can enter and exit as a means of defining moral relationships. Essentially, the original position is an intuitive tool that is helpful only to those committed to understanding and defining the requirements of justice.

Behind the veil of ignorance within the original position, subjects agree to define the requirements of justice without knowing their own abilities or their position in society. These informational restraints remove bias from the process so that individuals will accept the requirements of justice regardless of their natural and social endowments. Thus the deliberative processes will ultimately lead to principles of justice that will be accepted by everyone.

As defined by John Rawls, a well-ordered society is one "in which everyone accepts and knows that the others accept the same principles of justice, and the basic social institutions satisfy and are known to satisfy these principles" (Rawls, 1999a, p. 397). Essentially, a well-ordered society meets the requirements of justice and for all practical purposes is organized to be just. The well-ordered society develops from political subjects evaluating principles that they expect to produce just societal organizations. The political subjects make these considerations behind the veil of ignorance to avoid bias. This process results in unbiased principles that are used to develop the requirements of a just society or institution. As a philosophical construct that demonstrates what justice requires, the well-ordered society serves as a standard for measuring the degree of justice present in existing societies.

Rawls's understanding of reciprocity is related to defining the requirements of justice. His "Criterion of Reciprocity" includes an element of communication equality. Throughout the intricacies of his theory, he demonstrates a concern for reciprocal processes and outcomes. Much of his argument privileges elements of reciprocity and that logic can be extended to develop the philosophical elements of engagement.

Rawls argues that subjects operating within the original position will discuss the requirements of justice assuming reciprocal benefit. The well-ordered society rests on the assumption that its organizing principles will benefit not only the best off, but also the least-advantaged. Therefore, to ensure reciprocal outcomes, all participation in defining the requirements of justice must be on equal terms. Rawls constructs a notion of democratic equality that addresses unequal distributions of social endowments by allowing fair equality of positions (positions open to all) (Rawls, 1999a, p. 57). Democratic equality is the product of two assumptions: (1) an understanding of equality that allows for fair opportunity and (2) successful operation of the difference principle. The difference principle requires that a just society improve the positions of the least advantaged, but only by addressing unequal distributions of natural endowments (Rawls, 1999a, p. 65). It is crucial to note that Rawls understanding of lexical priority dictates that justice requires standards of liberty.

Critics suggest that language influences the definitions of justice; however, Rawls attempts to provide an account of "perfect procedural justice"

(Rawls, 1999a, p. 74) in which the structure of the theory will define the requirements of justice. This approach is in contrast to the view or assumption that justice is known, and that institutions can be arranged to meet the standards of justice (to each according to merit, virtue, and wealth, etc). Democratic equality and its two sub elements, fair equality of positions and the difference principle, are crucial in defining a relationship that can be used to articulate the requirements of justice. Although employed in the most general sense in Rawls's work, the idea of democratic equality and its two sub elements can be extended to analyze what justice requires for engaged university-community partnerships.

It is important to understand that this type of thinking in no way suggests that this theory will provide an account of "just" engaged learning, research, and partnerships. Before developing an account of what justice requires for engagement relationships, attention must be given to how the assumptions of democratic equality in the context of engagement will operate within the original position. The goal of this work is not to define the requirements of justice as they relate to engagement but to identify a theoretical gap within existing engagement literature.

RAWLS'S RECIPROCITY AND THE
RELATIONAL ENGAGEMENT FRAMEWORK

Although extremely complicated, Rawls's account of justice provides a systematic approach that includes both a specific and a general understanding of reciprocity. From one perspective, reciprocity can be understood narrowly within the operation of the original position, and this approach suggests that reciprocity dictates the development of reflective equilibrium. However, Rawls's procedural account of justice can be characterized as a reciprocal relationship between all just persons. As a result, simply applying Rawls's theory to the Relational Engagement Framework would be an incomplete analysis of the theory.

Under Rawls's theoretical arrangement, as individuals interact and define engaged relationships, their communication should be on equal terms. The process is procedural in the sense that the initial stages of communicating engaged relationships establish the basis for maintaining high levels of reciprocity. Rawls's approach attempts to acknowledge some forms of power by allowing only reasonable parties to define the elements of reciprocity. However, in order to capture the complexities of Rawls's procedural account of justice, the theoretical process of justice must be constructed within the context of engagement.

Rawls's account of justice has the potential to provide the engagement literature with a philosophical underpinning, particularly of reciprocity as an aspect of engagement. It operates as a systemic or meta-level theory to capture all elements of the Relational Engagement Framework. Significant philosophical inquiry can be devoted to defining the requirements of engagement relationships alone. Mechanistically applying Rawls's account of justice to the Relational Engagement Framework would be a disservice to the budding theoretical and philosophical literature surrounding engagement. Future research should definitely be devoted to outlining the philosophical requirements of justice as it relates to engagement.

THE WAY FORWARD

Rawls (1999a) depicts the requirements of procedural justice, and his theoretical underpinnings can be used to analyze the philosophical requirements of reciprocity. He hypothesizes that if the society is well ordered and without bias, "considered judgments" will aid in the achievement of consensus. The foregoing applies to engagement in scholarship as defined in university-community partnerships. The ideal reciprocity is achieved in engaged scholarship when there is quality communication, a state that Rawls refers to as reflective equilibrium and Freire (1970/2000) discusses as dialogue where all engaged individuals participate in the process as subjects. Foucault (1977, 1994, 1997) also underscores the importance of communication and conceptualizes power through discipline and surveillance. He asserts that observation does not require any differential in power but can be used to regulate behavior or normalize judgment. Additionally, Foucault's (1997) assertion that people should stop describing the effects of power in negative expressions like *exclude, repress,* and *censor* is arguably a way of championing reciprocity.

Our analysis of power and reciprocity represented as a Relational Engagement Framework offers an informed way of thinking deeply about issues of power and therefore has implications for the study and practice of service-learning and community engagement. The power analysis of each relationship and the concomitant varying definitions of mutuality and reciprocity can provide a basis for enhanced efforts toward more democratic and reciprocal community-engaged practices for both the community and the campus partners. In Exhibit 1.2, we offer a beginning, illustrative application of the theoretical and philosophical grounding of power and an understanding of the underlying relationships in the context of typical community-university partnerships as a way to explore how these might inform practice.

As importantly, this paper orients the study of service-learning and community engagement more broadly to grapple with new philosophical

	INDIVIDUAL	INSTITUTION
INDIVIDUAL	**Q 1 – Ascribed Power Based on Perceived Prestige** Individuals within the group defer to informal senior leader before making decision; group does not respond to informal leader's culturally insensitive remarks normalizing that behavior (Freire and Foucault analysis).	**Q 2 – Culture of Silence** Individuals within community group (as institution) respond to norms of operation, i.e., presence of informal leader outside official organization. Directional from the individual to the institution: Individuals ascribe power to the institution to permit an informal leader (Foucault analysis).
INSTITUTION	**Q 3 – Culture of Silence** Community group decides to hold all meetings at local facility. Community (as institution) organizes individuals on their terms as both community individuals and university individuals (Foucault analysis).	**Q 4 – Spatial Arrangements of Power** Holding the university-community partnership meetings at the community facility concentrates (community)/diffuses (university) power at the institutional level ■ Reality: Power differentials – in this example university is transferring flows of power to community, creating more reciprocal relationship ■ Small but significant 　■ Hosting 　■ Knowledge of building/area

Exhibit 1.2. Relational Engagement Framework: A practice application.

and theoretical complexities of the discipline. Further research is needed in defining the philosophical requirements of just community-university partnerships. So, in addition to suggestions for improved practice, further research questions have emerged. Representative questions include: From an epistemological standpoint, is it even possible to maintain authentic reciprocal relationships? How do the dynamics of race, gender, culture, authority, and class align to achieve reciprocity within the mission of community-university partnerships? Can maintaining high levels of reciprocity become an issue of justice? If so, how is one to define what justice requires within the context of service-learning and engaged scholarship? Also, how might one design empirical research based on power analysis? Hopefully this beginning discussion will spur continued scholarship around the issues of power in community-engaged partnerships.

REFERENCES

Bender, T. (Ed.). (1988). Afterword. In *The university and the city: From medieval origins to the present* (pp. 290-297). New York, NY: Oxford University Press.

Books, J., & Prysby, C. (1991). *Political behavior and the local context*. New York, NY: Praeger.

Boyer, E. L. (1990). *Scholarship reconsidered: Priorities of the professoriate*. Princeton, NJ: Carnegie Foundation for the Advancement of Teaching.

Brookfield, S. (2005). *The power of critical theory for adult learning and teaching*. Berkshire, United Kingdom: Open University Press.

Cervero, R. M., & Wilson, A. L. (2006). *Working the planning table: Negotiating democratically for adult, continuing and workplace education*. San Francisco, CA: Jossey-Bass.

Driscoll, A. (2008, January-February). Carnegie's Community-Engagement Classification: Intentions and Insights. *Change: The Magazine of Higher Learning, 40*(1), 38-41.

Foucault, M. (1977). *Discipline and punish: The birth of the prison* (1st American ed.). New York, NY: Pantheon Book.

Foucault, M. (1994). *Ethics: Subjectivity and truth*. New York, NY: New Press.

Foucault, M. (1997). *Society must be defended*. New York, NY: Picador.

Freire, P. (2000). *Pedagogy of the oppressed* (30th anniversary ed., M. B. Ramos, Trans.). New York, NY: Continuum. (Original work published 1970)

Freire, P. (1985). *Politics of education: Culture, power, and liberation*. New York, NY: Bergin & Garvey.

Freire, P. (1998). *Politics and education*. Los Angeles, CA: UCLA Latin American Center Publications.

Giroux, H. A. (1985). Introduction. In P. Freire (1985), *Politics of education: Culture, power, and liberation* (pp xi-xxv). New York, NY: Bergin & Garvey.

Glass, R. D. (2001). On Paulo Freire's philosophy of praxis and the foundations of liberation education. *Educational Researcher, 30*(2), 15-25.

Gore, J. M. (1998). Disciplining bodies: On the continuity of power relations In pedagogy. In T. S. Popkewitz & M. Brennan (Eds.), *Foucault's challenge: Discourse, knowledge and power in education* (pp. 231-254). New York, NY: Teachers College Press.

Gramsci, A. (1971). *Selections from the prison notebooks*. New York, NY: International.

Green, B. (1998). Born-again teaching? Governmentality, "grammar," and public schooling. In T. S. Popkewitz & M. Brennan (Eds.), *Foucault's challenge: Discourse, knowledge and power in education* (pp. 173-204). New York, NY: Teachers College Press.

Lazarsfeld, P. F., & Menzel, H. (1969). On the relation between individual and collective properties. In A. Etzioni (Ed.), *A sociological reader on complex organizations* (pp. 499-516). New York, NY: Holt, Rinehart & Winston.

Loomer, B. (1976). Two conceptions of power. *Criterion, 15*(1), 11-29.

Mayo, P. (1999). *Gramsci, Freire, and adult education: Possibilities for transformative action*. New York, NY: Zed Books.

Moje, E. (2000). Changing our minds, changing our bodies: Power as embodied in research relations. *International Journal of Qualitative Studies in Education, 13*(1), 1-18.

Powell, K., & Takayoshi, P. (2003). Accepting roles created for us: The ethics of reciprocity. *College Composition and Communication, 54* (3), 394-422.

Rawls, J. (1999a). *A theory of justice*. Cambridge, MA: The Belkin Press of Harvard University Press.

Rawls, J. (1999b). *The law of peoples; With "The idea of public reason revisited."* Cambridge, MA: Harvard University Press.

Saltmarsh, J., Giles, D., Ward, E., & Buglione, S. M. (2009). Rewarding community-engaged scholarship. In L. R. Sandmann, C. H. Thornton, & A. J. Jaeger (Eds.), *Institutionalizing community engagement in higher education: The first wave of Carnegie Classified Institutions. New Directions for Higher Education: No. 147* (pp. 25-36). San Francisco, CA: Jossey-Bass.

Toll, C., & Crumpler, T. (2004). Everything is dangerous: Pastoral power and university researchers conducting interviews. In B. Baker & K. Heyning (Eds.), *Dangerous coagulations? The uses of Foucault in the study of education.* New York, NY: Peter Lang.

Torres, C. A. (1992). Participatory action research and popular education in Latin America. *Qualitative Studies in Education, 5*(1), 51-62.

CHAPTER 2

QUANTITATIVE ASSESSMENT OF SERVICE-LEARNING OUTCOMES

Is Self-Reported Change a Reasonable Proxy for Longitudinal Change?

Nicholas A. Bowman and Jay W. Brandenberger

Service-learning research often relies on self-report measures of college student growth. Compared with longitudinal assessments, these measures are generally more cost-effective, require fewer human resources, and yield results more quickly. However, some evidence strongly questions the validity of self-reported gains as indicators of student outcomes. To explore these issues in the context of service-learning, the correspondence between 6 measures of self-reported attitude change and 6 corresponding longitudinal change measures was examined using a sample of 387 service-learning students. The results indicated that correlations between self-reported and longitudinal attitude change are generally low, regressions that predict the 2 types of outcomes yield strongly divergent results, and t tests using these 2 measures support disparate conclusions about the overall effectiveness of the service-learning course. Implications for practice and future research are discussed.

Research for What? Making Engaged Scholarship Matter
pp. 25–43

Service-learning faculty, practitioners, and researchers alike are interested in the learning and development that stem from students' experiences with service-learning. The easiest way to assess this growth is by simply asking these students how much they have gained on a variety of outcomes since the beginning of their course. Compared with conducting longitudinal assessments, this technique is cost-effective, requires minimal time and effort, and yields results quickly. This approach is used quite often to examine outcomes related not only to service-learning coursework (Gosen & Washbush, 2004), but also to the entire college experience (Gonyea, 2005). However, some research has cast serious doubt on the validity of college students' self-reported gains as a proxy for longitudinal learning and development (Bowman, 2010a, 2010b; Pascarella, 2001; Pike, 1993, 1999). This study explores the validity of service-learning students' self-reported gains on numerous attitudinal outcomes. More specifically, to what degree do students' estimates of their growth during service-learning coursework correspond with longitudinal gains on the same outcomes?

In this paper, we use the terms "self-reported gains" and "self-reported change" to denote students' perceptions of learning and development that occurred over some period of time. For example, a service-learning instructor may ask students to report what they have learned or how much they have grown during the semester; this would constitute one form of self-reported gains. Some national survey instruments, such as the National Survey of Student Engagement and the College Senior Survey from the Higher Education Research Institute, similarly ask students to self-report to what extent they have changed on numerous outcomes since starting college. In contrast, we use the terms "longitudinal gains" or "longitudinal change" to signify changes that are measured by comparing student attitudes, values, or skills at multiple points in time. For instance, a service-learning instructor might administer a survey of student attitudes or a critical thinking test at the beginning and the end of the course; the changes that occurred from the pretest to the posttest would be considered longitudinal gains. This definition differs from that of some other researchers, who suggest that longitudinal studies must consist of at least three waves of data (e.g., Coleman, 1981), but this term best reflects the type of pre-post change in which many service-learning constituents are interested.

Outcomes Assessment in Service-Learning

Research examining the impact of service-learning has expanded and progressed in recent years. Bringle, Phillips, and Hudson (2004), for example, provide a variety of research scales drawn from multiple contexts for use in service-learning research. Noting the limitations of early research built on single-item measures, they emphasize the importance of theoretically grounded studies and the use of well-validated multiple-item scales. However, the research methods used to study the student outcomes of service-learning continue to be flawed in multiple ways (Aronson et al., 2005; Bringle, 2003; Zeigert & McGoldrick, 2004).

In a thorough analysis of research on experiential learning, Gosen and Washbush (2004) examined 39 salient studies. Importantly, more than half of the experiential assessment studies used self-reported gains as indicators of student growth. While nearly all of the studies showed support for experiential engagement, the lack of rigorous research methodologies prompted the authors to suggest that "any conclusion about the effectiveness of these teaching approaches must be tentative" (p. 270). Given that service-learning presents challenges to mainstream pedagogies and accepted practices in higher education, research claims must be grounded in strong methodological approaches. An important step toward research credibility is moving beyond self-report measures toward more direct, longitudinal assessments of student outcomes—or, at a minimum, establishing a strong correspondence between commonly-used indicators of student development (e.g., self-reported gains) and more rigorous approaches.

Validity of College Student Self-Reported Gains

The available research suggests that students are fairly accurate when asked to estimate their *current* skills, abilities, and attitudes. For example, in one study (Berdie, 1971), the correlations between participants' self-assessments of general knowledge and their objectively tested knowledge of famous people were quite high, ranging from .47 to .74. Pohlmann and Beggs (1974) also observed high correlations between students' self-assessments of current academic subject knowledge and their scores on academic subject exams ($rs = .52$ to $.67$). Pike (1995, 1996) found a reasonably strong relationship between students' self-ratings of their existing academic skills and objective measures of those skills within a larger structural equation model. Furthermore, Greenwald and colleagues' (Greenwald, Poehlman, Uhlmann, & Banaji, 2009) meta-analytic review demonstrated a strong positive relationship between self-reported attitudes and objective behaviors, with the notable exception of attitudes toward socially sensitive topics (e.g., feelings about other racial groups).

In contrast, the correspondence between students' estimates of *changes* in their skills and abilities align quite poorly with longitudinal assessments of change. Bowman (2010b) found that correlations between self-reported and longitudinal gains in intrapersonal and interpersonal development are low (rs = .12 to .22), and the corresponding correlations for cognitive development are virtually zero (rs = −.01 to .03). These low correlations are generally apparent regardless of gender, race/ethnicity, and academic achievement (Bowman, 2010a). Moreover, when examining learning in a business simulation game, Gosen and Washbush (1999) also found that undergraduate business students' self-reported learning gains were virtually uncorrelated with corresponding longitudinal gains. Moreover, several studies have compared regression results of analyses that use self-reported gains to those that use longitudinal methods (Anaya, 1999; Bowman, 2010b; Whitt, Edison, Pascarella, Nora, & Terenzini, 1999). A close inspection of those results reveals that the relationship between a given independent variable and dependent variable varies substantially depending upon whether the dependent variable is measured via longitudinal versus self-reported gains.

Several dynamics may help explain the divergence between self-reported and longitudinal gains. First, students may form strong impressions about their overall growth, which then unduly affect their estimates of growth in specific domains. Pike (1999) has found substantial evidence for such "halo errors" in student judgments; these may account for over half of the explained variance in first-year students' self-reported gains (also see Pike, 1993). Second, students may respond to self-reported gain items in a socially desirable way. The effects of social desirability are apparent even when students are asked to report their SAT scores (Cole & Gonyea, 2010), and self-reported gains are positively correlated with a well-established social desirability scale (Bowman & Hill, 2010). Third, given the heavy cognitive demands required to estimate self-reported gains accurately, students may take mental shortcuts and provide answers that seem somewhat reasonable (Krosnick, 1991). Consistent with this view, Ross (1989) demonstrates that many people (including college students) use overly simplified strategies when attempting to assess how they have changed over time. Fourth, students may respond to the same item differently for reasons unrelated to their actual gains. For instance, some students habitually feel that they have gained a great deal (Pascarella, 2001), and people attach varied meanings to descriptors such as "a lot" or "some" (Pace & Friedlander, 1982), which are often used for measuring self-reported gains. A detailed discussion of these issues can be found in Bowman (2010b).

However, the greatest problem may be that students are simply unable to estimate their learning and development accurately. Over the past several decades, psychological research has demonstrated that people confidently report—and think they actually possess—a great deal of self-knowledge, but these reports are often quite erroneous (e.g., Nisbett & Wilson, 1977; Pronin & Kugler, 2007; Wilson, 2002). Estimating one's own learning and development is a special case of this general phenomenon. According to a review by Ross (1989), many people believe that skills and abilities increase over most of the lifespan, whereas they believe attitudes are fairly stable; people are often misled by these expectations, so they tend to overestimate their own skill development yet underestimate their own changes in attitudes (Conway & Ross, 1984; Goethals & Reckman, 1973; Markus, 1986; McFarland & Ross, 1987). More generally, people are not able to access various forms of self-knowledge, so they "fill in the blanks" with their lay theories of mental processes and lifespan development (see Wilson, 2002). Some have suggested that traditional-age college students are especially susceptible to subtle suggestions and other situational factors (Sears, 1986), which implies that they be more likely to provide erroneous self-reports.

Although numerous obstacles prevent accurate self-reporting of growth, an understanding and awareness of these difficulties can help researchers design more effective measures. For instance, self-reported gains on a particular outcome may generally be more accurate when a student is habitually motivated to attend to her development on that outcome (Bowman, 2010a). Thus, because reflection is an important component of most service-learning courses, service-learning students may be reasonable accurate when attempting to gauge their own changes in attitudes toward equality and social responsibility. Furthermore, framing student growth in terms of "changes" rather than "gains" may reduce socially desirable responding (i.e., it is socially acceptable for someone to "change" in multiple directions, but it is quite undesirable to report "losses" on an outcome). In addition, students' self-reports may become less accurate while taking a lengthy survey, so estimates of change or growth may be improved by administering a relatively brief questionnaire.

Present Research

The current study explores a specific instance of college students' self-reported growth, namely, the degree to which service-learning students' self-reported attitude changes during the semester correspond with longitudinal measures of change. This project expands upon the existing literature in several important ways. First, this research examines change solely over the course of students' service-learning experiences, whereas most studies of self-reported gains have examined change that occurs over at least a year. This analysis is of particular interest to service-learning constituents who are interested in simple, effective ways to assess student growth over a reasonably short period of time. Second, the outcomes of this study are attitudinal and value-based, which are among the most common types of developmental outcomes in service-learning research (Brandenberger, 2005). In contrast, previous studies of the validity of self-reported gains have primarily examined cognitive, academic, and/or interpersonal outcomes. Third, this study also examines whether conclusions about the effectiveness of a particular course or program (in this case, service-learning) vary depending upon the form of the relevant quantitative measure. Finally, in an attempt to increase the correspondence between measures of self-reported and longitudinal change, this study improves upon most commonly used self-report measures by administering a short survey (approximately 10 minutes), framing attitude shifts as "changes" instead of "gains" and "losses," and measuring outcomes that are highly relevant to service-learning experiences.

METHOD

Sample and Data Source

Participants were 387 students (71% female, 22% students of color, 64% freshmen and sophomores) that completed a one-credit service-learning course at a medium-sized Catholic university in the Midwest. Data were taken from students in several different courses, but all courses focused on issues of (in)equality and concern for the common good. Before the course, instructors requested that students complete an online survey. This survey contained six scales that measured students' entering attitudes and values, along with other items (e.g., demographics). All courses included a sustained community immersion experience that occurred during a scheduled break in the academic calendar. Depending on the course, the community immersion lasted from 2-7 days. After the final class session of the semester, the instructor or course coordinator asked students to complete a final survey. This posttest included the same six scales as the pretest, plus six items that asked students to report the extent to which their attitudes and values had changed since the beginning of the course; these items were designed to reflect the same constructs in the six scales. (Note that an additional scale regarding self-generating views of helping was included in both questionnaires, but no corresponding self-report item was included; for more information about this scale, see Bowman & Brandenberger, in press.)

Measures

Dependent Variables

The six outcome measures constitute a related set of attitudes and values pertaining to the recognition and denunciation of societal inequality and the importance placed on helping others. We have described this overarching construct as equality and social responsibility orientation (ESR; Bowman & Brandenberger, in press). *Situational attributions for poverty* conveys a belief that poverty is caused by societal factors (e.g., poor school systems); this six-item scale (Cronbach's alpha = .72) is adapted from a survey used by Feagin (1971). *Responsibility for improving society* assesses how much personal responsibility one feels for taking action to help others and the world; this seven-item scale (α = .84) is adapted from Nelson Laird et al. (2005). Four items from a scale by Pascarella and colleagues (Pascarella, Edison, Nora, Hagedorn, & Terenzini, 1996) were used to gauge *openness to diversity* (α = .83). An *empowerment view of helping* describes beliefs about whether people can overcome their problems with the assistance of others; this five-item scale (α = .63) was taken from Michlitsch and Frankel (1989). Two additional scales were reverse-coded for comparison with the self-reported change items. A short-form of the *social dominance orientation* scale was used (Pratto, Sidanius, Stallworth, & Malle, 1994); this eight-item scale (α = .83) measures people's preference for and acceptance of inequality among social groups. Finally, *belief in a just world* describes the belief that good things happen to good people, and bad things happen to bad people; Dalbert and colleagues' popular six-item version of this scale (α = .62) was used (Dalbert, Montada, & Schmitt, 1987). Each of these scales was then standardized with a mean of zero and a standard deviation of one, and the six standardized scales were averaged to create a combined measure of ESR orientation (α = .75).

Six items assessed self-reported changes in attitudes since the beginning of the course; responses were assessed on a seven-point scale (1 = *"I am now much less likely to agree"* to 7 = *"I am now much more likely to agree"*). These items were designed to capture the relevant longitudinal outcome as closely as possible; for example, the item corresponding to situational attributions for poverty was "I believe societal forces play a major role in causing poverty." A list of all constructs and phrasings for the corresponding self-reported change items is provided in Exhibit 2.1. These six self-reported change measures were averaged to create an index of self-reported change in ESR orientation (α = .85). To examine the direct correspondence between self-reported and longitudinal change, two separate measures of longitudinal change were computed: (1) a difference score (i.e., posttest minus pretest), and (2) a residual change score (i.e., posttest regressed on pretest). Scholars have divergent views on which measure is

Exhibit 2.1.   Overview of Scales for Longitudinal Measures and Phrasings for Corresponding Self-reported Change Items

Scale (and Source)	# of Items	Alpha (Time 2)	Self-Reported Change Item
Responsibility for Improving Society (adapted from Nelson Laird, Engberg, & Hurtado, 2005)	7	.84	"I feel responsible for making changes to improve society."
Situational Attributions for Poverty (adapted from Feagin, 1971)	6	.72	"I believe societal forces play a major role in causing poverty."
Empowerment View of Helping (Michlitsch & Frankel, 1989)	5	.63	"I think people can overcome obstacles with the assistance of others."
Openness to Diversity (adapted from Pascarella et al., 1996)	4	.83	"I value diverse cultures and perspectives."
Belief in a Just World (Dalbert et al., 1987)	6	.62	"I perceived widespread injustice throughout society."
Social Dominance Orientation (Pratto et al., 1994)	8	.83	"I think equality should be promoted."

Note: The last two scales were reverse-coded for comparisons to the self-reported change items.

most appropriate (e.g., see DuBois, 1957; Rogosa, Brandt, & Zimowski, 1982), so both of these were used.

Independent Variables

Several demographic variables were used; these included year in college (1 = freshman, to 5 = graduate student), gender (0 = female, 1 = male), race/ethnicity (0 = White/Caucasian, 1 = student of color), and family income (1 = less than $25,000/year, to 9 = $200,000 and above). In addition, two dummy-coded variables indicated whether students had taken one previous service-learning course or two courses or more; zero courses served as the referent group. Political conservatism was also measured (1 = very liberal, to 5 = very conservative).

Several experiences within the service-learning course were also included. Positive diversity experiences were measured with a five-item scale (α = .86) assessing the frequency of various interactions with "diverse people" (i.e., those differing from the participant "in race, social class, national origin, values, religion, or political views"). Negative diversity experiences were measured with four items (α = .87) regarding the

frequency of interactions with diverse people that were perceived as hurtful, unresolved, hostile, and/or threatening. The degree to which students' beliefs were challenged was measured with a four-item scale ($\alpha =$
.73). A single item measured a form of shared reflection (i.e., the degree
to which students discussed their service-learning experiences with people who were not taking the course). Finally, pretest values for all six ESR
orientation scales, along with the single combined measure of ESR orientation, were also used.

Analyses

Pearson correlations between each longitudinal change construct and
its corresponding self-reported change item were conducted. In addition,
correlations among the self-reported change measures and among the
longitudinal change measures were analyzed. *T* tests were also performed
to determine whether students' attitudes had changed over time: Paired *t*
tests were used to examine differences between the corresponding longitudinal pretest and posttest scores, and one-sample *t* tests were used to
examine whether the mean for each self-reported change measure differed significantly from 4.0 (i.e., "no change"). In addition, two ordinary
least squares multiple regression analyses were conducted; one predicting
ESR orientation at Time 2 and one representing self-reported change in
ESR orientation. Independent variables for both analyses included year
in school, gender, race/ethnicity, family income, previous service-learning
experience, positive and negative diversity experiences, belief challenge,
and student reflection. The analysis predicting the longitudinal outcome
also included ESR orientation at Time 1 as a predictor.

Limitations

Some limitations should be noted. First, each construct was measured
longitudinally with a multi-item scale, but self-reported change was
gauged with only one item. Although the self-report items have high face
validity, these do not capture the same depth and complexity as the multi-
item scales; this issue will be discussed later in more detail. Second, the
posttest occurred fairly soon after the courses ended (i.e., less than a
month). As a result, it is unclear whether the correspondence between
self-reported and longitudinal change in the context of service-learning
might differ over a longer period of time. Third, no control group is

included in the sample (i.e., students who did not take a service-learning course). Although the point of this study is not to examine the efficacy of service-learning, the inclusion of other students might have added variance in student growth, which could have affected the results.

RESULTS AND DISCUSSION

According to Cohen's (1988) frequently used guidelines, a correlation of .1 is considered low, .3 is medium, and .5 is high. By these standards, the correlations between longitudinal and self-reported change are generally low. As shown in Exhibit 2.2, when residual change scores are used to indicate longitudinal change, the median correlation between longitudinal and self-reported change is .19, and the correlations for two of the six change outcomes are not significantly different from zero. This correspondence is even weaker when difference scores are used: Three of the six correlations between self-reported and longitudinal change are not significantly different from zero, and the median correlation is only .09. The correlations for belief in a just world and social dominance orientation are among the lowest in the sample, which may be the result of the reverse coding of these two longitudinal scales. Nevertheless, the correlations for all measures suggest that self-reported change items are a poor proxy for longitudinal measures of change for a one-semester service-learning course, and this conclusion is consistent with previous research on gains during the first year of college. These correlations are somewhat higher than those reported by Bowman (2010b), which suggests that the

Exhibit 2.2.   Correlations Between Longitudinal Change and Self-Reported Change Items

Construct	Longitudinal Measure	
	Difference Score	Residual Change Score
Belief in a just world	.05	.10
Social dominance orientation	.07	.16**
Empowerment view of helping	.04	.08
Responsibility for improving society	.18***	.24***
Situational attributions for poverty	.13*	.28***
Openness to diversity	.12*	.23***
Median correlation	.09	.19

Note: *$p < .05$. **$p < .01$. ***$p < .001$.

attempted improvements in the validity of self-reported gain items may have been at least somewhat successful.

Importantly, the correspondence between self-reported and longitudinal change is higher for overall ESR orientation than for any of the six individual scales. Regardless of whether longitudinal change was indicated by residual change scores ($r = .32$, $p < .001$) or by difference scores ($r = .22$, $p < .001$), the correlations between self-reported and longitudinal change are best described as medium by Cohen's (1988) standards. Although this link is still far from perfect, these findings imply that multi-item self-reported change scales may constitute an important improvement upon single-item measures.

The correlations among the various self-reported change items suggest that a particular type of bias may be present. Halo error occurs when people allow their overall perceptions of growth or change to unduly affect their estimates of growth in specific domains (see Cooper, 1981). For example, a service-learning student who feels that her experience has been transformative may report that she has grown tremendously on virtually every outcome, even though her actual changes vary considerably across outcomes. The medium to high correlations in Exhibit 2.3 provide some evidence for halo error in the current sample; these correlations range from .31 to .68 (all $ps < .001$), and the median is .49. Intriguingly, the *lowest* correlation between disparate self-reported change measures (e.g., belief in a just world and openness to diversity) is higher than the *highest* correlation between self-reported change and longitudinal change *on the same outcome*! By themselves, these correlations do not conclusively

Exhibit 2.3.   Correlations Among Self-Reported Change Items

Self-Reported Change Item	BJW	SDO	EVH	RIS	SAP	OD
Belief in a just world (BJW)	—					
Social dominance orientation (SDO)	.48***	—				
Empowerment view of helping (EVH)	.31***	.46***	—			
Responsibility for improving society (RIS)	.43***	.63***	.45***	—		
Situational attributions for poverty (SAP)	.68***	.52***	.43***	.50***	—	
Openness to diversity (OD)	.38***	.56***	.49***	.52***	.43***	—
Median correlation	.49					

Note: *$p < .05$. **$p < .01$. ***$p < .001$.

demonstrate that students are making errors, because there may indeed be positive correlations among several student outcomes for "actual" growth. However, the correlations among the difference scores (median r = .13) and among the residual change scores (median r = .21) suggest that actual changes in these attitudes are weakly associated with one another; therefore, a substantial portion of the high correlations for self-reported change may be the product of halo error.

Regression analyses predicting a combined measure of all self-reported change items and another measure of all longitudinal change scales (i.e., ESR orientation) were conducted. As shown in Exhibit 2.4, both regression equations indicate that demographic and precourse factors are largely unrelated to either measure of attitude change. However, the pattern of significant predictors varies substantially across the two analyses. For example, political conservatism and negative diversity experiences are both significant, negative predictors of longitudinal change (βs = −.13 and −.10, respectively), but neither variable significantly predicts self-reported change (βs = −.02 and −.04, respectively). Moreover, positive diversity experiences and interpersonal reflection both positively predict self-reported change (βs = .20 and .19, respectively), but neither is significantly related to longitudinal change (βs = .04 and .07, respectively). In fact, the only independent variable that significantly predicts both types of outcome measures is belief challenge, but the magnitude of effect is much greater for predicting self-reported change (β = .26) than longitudinal change (β = .09). This lack of correspondence among predictors is similar to findings from previous studies (Bowman, 2010b; Whitt et al., 1999). Importantly, the independent variables that yielded the most divergent results are the college experiences, which suggests that the findings and implications that follow from service-learning studies may vary markedly depending upon how the outcome itself is measured.

In sum, measures of longitudinal and self-reported change are only loosely related to each other, and regression results differ substantially depending upon how the outcome is measured. However, if a practitioner or administrator simply wanted to assess the overall effectiveness of a program, then would it matter whether s/he measured self-reported or longitudinal change? Exhibit 2.5 provides some insight into this question. According to the self-reported change measures, students experienced significant and sizable "gains" (i.e., in the direction generally perceived to be desirable among service-learning professionals) on all six outcomes. The t values for the one-sample tests are greater than 18 for all outcomes, which implies that these results would be significant even within a very small sample. In contrast, on the longitudinal measures, students do not gain on belief in a just world, and they actually

Exhibit 2.4.   Multiple Regression Analyses Predicting Longitudinal and Self-Reported Change in Overall Equality and Social Responsibility (ESR) Orientation

Independent variable	Longitudinal Change		Self-Reported Change	
	B (SE)	β	B (SE)	β
Year in college	−.07 (.04)	−.06	−.07 (.06)	−.06
Gender	−.00 (.08)	−.00	.01 (.11)	.00
Student of color	−.06 (.11)	−.02	.06 (.14)	.02
Family income	−.01 (.02)	−.02	−.00 (.02)	−.00
One previous service-learning course	.17 (.09)	.07	.14 (.12)	.06
Two or more previous service-learning courses	.07 (.11)	.03	−.22 (.14)	−.08
Political conservatism	−.14 (.04)	−.13***	−.02 (.05)	−.02
Positive diversity experiences	.06 (.05)	.04	.25 (.07)	.20***
Negative diversity experiences	−.15 (.05)	-.10**	−.06 (.07)	-.04
Belief challenge	.11 (.05)	.09*	.33 (.06)	.26***
Interpersonal reflection	.06 (.03)	.07	.16 (.04)	.19***
Pretest ESR orientation	.64 (.04)	.63***		
R^2		.585		.237

Note: Standard errors are in parentheses. *$p < .05$. **$p < .01$. ***$p < .001$.

move in the "wrong" direction on social dominance orientation. Students did gain on the other four outcomes in the expected manner, but the relevant t-values were much more modest (all were less than 3.5). In other words, self-reported change measures provide a uniformly and extremely positive view of the attitudinal outcomes of service-learning, whereas the longitudinal outcomes paint a generally positive (yet much more conservative) picture. Clearly, the latter pattern of results seems much more reasonable than the former.

**Exhibit 2.5.   Attitude Change as Indicated by
Longitudinal and Self-Reported Change Measures**

Construct	Longitudinal Change		Self-Reported Change	
	Mean Change	t Value	Mean Change	t Value
Belief in a just world	.002 (.023)	.09	1.03 (.056)	18.50***
Social dominance orientation	−.091 (.031)	−3.01**	1.13 (.053)	21.24***
Empowerment view of helping	.072 (.024)	2.95**	1.16 (.055)	20.86***
Responsibility for improving society	.057 (.025)	2.31*	1.51 (.053)	28.17***
Situational attributions for poverty	.064 (.023)	2.76**	1.31 (.054)	24.46***
Openness to diversity	.086 (.025)	3.47**	1.32 (.056)	23.72***

Note: Standard errors are in parentheses. For the self-reported change items, one-sample *t* tests were conducted to determine whether the average response was significantly different from 4.0 (i.e., "no change"); therefore, the mean change values shown above are computed by subtracting 4.0 from the mean of each item. *p < .05. **p < .01. ***p< .001.

CONCLUSIONS AND IMPLICATIONS

When conducting research and assessment on service-learning, faculty, practitioners, and administrators are largely interested in at least one of three issues: (1) the overall impact of the course or program, (2) whether and how some students benefit more than others, and (3) student experiences or program characteristics associated with greater learning and development. The findings of this study suggest that, in all three circumstances, service-learning students' self-reported attitude change is a poor proxy for longitudinal attitude change. Instead of accurately indicating student growth, the self-reported change measures likely reflect students' subjective experiences with their coursework and immersion experiences. Interview data suggests many students find their service-learning experiences to be transformative and eye-opening (e.g., Eyler & Giles, 1999; Youniss & Yates, 1997). It is reasonable to assume that students who have these strong, positive reactions also perceived that their experiences substantially influenced many possible outcomes, that their experiences were challenging (generally in a good way), and that they spent a great deal of time reflecting on these experiences. Not coincidentally, these are the same types of biases present in the self-reported change measures. That is, compared with longitudinal assessments, self-reported change measures overestimate the overall impact of students' experiences, the association among changes on the various outcomes, and the positive effects of salient service-learning experiences (i.e., positive diversity experiences, belief challenge, and interpersonal reflection) on attitude change.

The most straightforward implication from this research is to use longitudinal assessments whenever possible for assessing service-learning outcomes. A number of useful and affordable online survey software programs are now available, and the data from pretest and posttest surveys can be easily linked using a student ID number or other identifier. However, as noted earlier, longitudinal assessments are often much more resource-intensive than one-time cross-sectional studies that use self-reported change items. Future research should examine ways of reducing the biases apparent in self-reported change measures. For example, some statistical adjustments may improve estimates, including controlling for social desirability (Bowman & Hill, 2010) and high school gains (to correct for some students' generalized predisposition to report large gains; see Pascarella, 2001). This study attempted to improve the correspondence between self-reported and longitudinal change by altering survey characteristics and the choice of outcomes. Despite the short period of time between the pretest and posttest, the correlations in this study were actually higher than in some previous research (Bowman, 2010b), which suggests that theoretically guided attempts to enhance these measures may be fruitful. Moreover, the correlations between self-reported and longitudinal change were highest when using multi-item measures of self-reported change (i.e., when examining changes in overall ESR orientation); this finding suggests that the use of several items to indicate change on a single construct may also help improve cross-sectional assessments of student growth. Some further evidence suggests that more advanced undergraduates' self-reported gains may be less prone to error than those of freshmen (Bowman & Hill, 2010; Pike, 1999), and first-generation college students may be particularly accurate at assessing their own learning and development (Bowman, 2010a). As a result, deciding whether self-reported change measures are appropriate may depend, in part, upon the specific population of interest.

Although this study casts doubt upon the validity of college students' self-reported change, these results do not imply that qualitative approaches for understanding students' perspectives or development over time are invalid. As noted earlier, students are often quite knowledgeable about their current skills and abilities (Berdie, 1971; Pike, 1995, 1996; Pohlmann & Beggs, 1974), so a longitudinal qualitative study can provide fascinating (and accurate) insights into changes in students' attitudes and perceptions. Moreover, because qualitative researchers do not necessarily take students' statements at face value, this methodology has the potential to identify areas in which students' self-perceptions differ from their actual characteristics. For instance, an entering first-year student may claim that she has a thorough understanding and appreciation for diversity; however, when asked to explain what she means by this, her response may indicate a relatively naïve perspective. A cross-sectional study that illustrates this disconnect would be useful in and of itself. Moreover, if the student were interviewed again years later, then she might also say that she has a thorough understanding and appreciation for diversity, but this statement may now be much more valid after she has attended college for several years. Thus, when used appropriately, students' voices clearly have an important place in examining student development.

In conclusion, as other researchers have suggested (Ewell & Jones, 1993; Gonyea, 2005), college student self-reported gains cannot serve as a substitute for well-validated, longitudinal measures of student growth. This study adds to the existing research by illustrating that self-reported attitude change does not constitute a reasonable proxy for longitudinal change in the context of a service-learning course and that the use of self-reported change indicators will likely lead to erroneous conclusions. Until valid cross-sectional measures and methods for assessing student learning and development are developed, service-learning researchers and practitioners would be best served by administering longitudinal surveys to assess the impact of their courses and student experiences.

REFERENCES

Anaya, G. (1999). College impact on student learning: Comparing the use of self-reported gains, standardized test scores, and college grades. *Research in Higher Education, 40*, 499-526.

Aronson, K. R., Webster, N. S., Reason, R., Ingram, P., Nolan, J., Mitchell, K., & Reed, D. (2005). Using randomized control field trials in service-learning research. In S. Root, J. Callahan, & S. H. Billig (Eds.), *Improving service-learning practice: Research on models to enhance impacts* (pp. 141-165). Charlotte, NC: Information Age.

Berdie, R. F. (1971). Self-claimed and tested knowledge. *Educational and Psychological Measurement, 31*, 629-636.

Bowman, N. A. (2010a). Assessing learning and development among diverse college students. In S. Herzog (Ed.), *New directions for institutional research: Vol. 145. Diversity and educational benefits* (pp. 53-71). San Francisco, CA: Jossey-Bass.

Bowman, N. A. (2010b). Can 1st-year college students accurately report their learning and development? *American Educational Research Journal, 47*, 466-496.

Bowman, N. A., & Brandenberger, J. W. (in press). Experiencing the unexpected: Toward a model of college diversity experiences and attitude change. *Review of Higher Education*.

Bowman, N. A., & Hill, P. L. (2010). *Measuring how college affects students: Validity and biases in college student self-reported gains*. Manuscript submitted for publication.

Brandenberger, J. W. (2005). College, character, and social responsibility: Moral learning through experience. In D. K. Lapsley & F. C. Power (Eds.), *Character psychology and character education* (pp. 305-334). Notre Dame, IN: University of Notre Dame Press.

Bringle, R. G. (2003). Enhancing theory-based research in service-learning. In S. H. Billig & J. Eyler (Eds.), *Deconstructing service-learning: Research exploring context, participation, and impacts* (pp. 3-24). Greenwich, CT: Information Age.

Bringle, R. G., Phillips, M. A., & Hudson, M. (2004). *The measure of service learning: Research scales to assess student experiences*. Washington, DC: American Psychological Association.

Cohen, J. (1988). *Statistical power analysis for the behavioral sciences* (2nd ed.). Mahwah, NJ: Erlbaum.

Cole, J. S., & Gonyea, R. M. (2010). Accuracy of self-reported SAT and ACT test scores: Implications for research. *Research in Higher Education, 51*, 305-319.

Coleman, J. S. (1981). *Longitudinal data analysis*. New York, NY: Basic Books.

Conway, M., & Ross, M. (1984). Getting what you want by revising what you had. *Journal of Personality and Social Psychology, 47*, 738-748.

Cooper, W. (1981). Ubiquitous halo. *Psychological Bulletin, 90*, 218-244.

Dalbert, C., Montada, L., & Schmitt, M. (1987). Glaube an die gerechte Welt als Motiv: Validnering Zweier Skalen. *Psychologische Beitrage, 29*, 596-615.

DuBois, P. H. (1957). *Multivariate correlational analysis*. New York, NY: Harper.

Ewell, P. T., & Jones, D. P. (1993). Actions matter: The case for indirect measures in assessing higher education's progress on the national education goals. *Journal of General Education, 42*, 123-148.

Eyler, J., & Giles, D. E., Jr. (1999). *Where's the learning in service-learning?* San Francisco, CA: Jossey-Bass.

Feagin, J. R. (1971). Poverty: We still believe that God helps those who help themselves. *Psychology Today, 6*(6), 101-110, 129.

Goethals, G. R., & Reckman, R. F. (1973). The perception of consistency in attitudes. *Journal of Experimental Social Psychology, 9*, 491-501.

Gonyea, R. M. (2005). Self-reported data in institutional research: Review and recommendations. In P. D. Umbach (Ed.), *New directions for institutional research* (Vol. 127, pp. 73-89). San Francisco, CA: Jossey-Bass.

Gosen, J., & Washbush, J. (1999). Perceptions of learning in TE simulations. *Developments in Business Simulation & Experiential Learning, 26*, 170-175.

Gosen, J., & Washbush, J. (2004). A review of scholarship on assessing experiential learning effectiveness. *Simulation and Gaming, 35*, 270-293.

Greenwald, A. G., Poehlman, T. A., Uhlmann, E. L., & Banaji, M. R. (2009). Understanding and using the Implicit Association Test: III. Meta-analysis of predictive validity. *Journal of Personality and Social Psychology, 97*, 17-41.

Krosnick, J. A. (1991). Response strategies for coping with the cognitive demands of attitude measures in surveys. *Applied Cognitive Psychology, 5*, 213-236.

Markus, G. B. (1986). Stability and change in political attitudes: Observed, recalled and explained. *Political Behavior, 8*, 21-44.

McFarland, C., & Ross, M. (1987). The relation between current impressions and memories of self and dating partners. *Personality and Social Psychology Bulletin, 13*, 228-238.

Michlitsch, J. F., & Frankel, S. (1989). Helping orientations: Four dimensions. *Perceptual and Motor Skills, 69*, 1371-1378.

Nelson Laird, T. F., Engberg, M. E., & Hurtado, S. (2005). Modeling accentuation effects: Enrolling in a diversity course and the importance of social engagement. *Journal of Higher Education, 76*, 448-476.

Nisbett, R. E., & Wilson, T. D. (1977). Telling more than we know: Verbal reports on mental processes. *Psychological Review, 84*, 231-259.

Pace, C., & Friedlander, J. (1982). The meaning of response categories: How often is occasionally, often, and very often? *Research in Higher Education, 17*, 267-281.

Pascarella, E. T. (2001). Using student self-reported gains to estimate college impact: A cautionary tale. *Journal of College Student Development, 42*, 488-492.

Pascarella, E., Edison, M., Nora, A., Hagedorn, L., & Terenzini, P. (1996). Influences on students' openness to diversity and challenge in the first year of college. *Journal of Higher Education, 67*, 174-195.

Pike, G. R. (1993). The relationship between perceived learning and satisfaction with college: An alternative view. *Research in Higher Education, 34*, 23-40.

Pike, G. R. (1995). The relationship between self reports of college experiences and achievement test scores. *Research in Higher Education, 36*, 1-21.

Pike, G. R. (1996). Limitations of using students' self-reports of academic development as proxies for traditional achievement measures. *Research in Higher Education, 37*, 89-114.

Pike, G. R. (1999). The constant error of the halo in educational outcomes research. *Research in Higher Education, 40*, 61-86.

Pohlmann, J., & Beggs, D. (1974). A study of the validity of self-reported measures of academic growth. *Journal of Educational Measurement, 11*, 115-119.

Pratto, F., Sidanius, J., Stallworth, L. M., & Malle, B. F. (1994). Social dominance orientation: A personality variable predicting social and political attitudes. *Journal of Personality and Social Psychology, 67*, 741-763.

Pronin, E., & Kugler, M. B. (2007). Valuing thoughts, ignoring behavior: The introspection illusion as a source of the blind spot bias. *Journal of Experimental Social Psychology, 43*, 565-578.

Rogosa, D. R., Brandt, D., & Zimowski, M. (1982). A growth curve approach to the measurement of change. *Psychological Bulletin, 90*, 726-748.

Ross, M. (1989). Relation of implicit theories to the construction of personal histories. *Psychological Review, 96*, 341-357.

Sears, D. O. (1986). College sophomores in the laboratory: Influences of a narrow database on social psychology's view of human nature. *Journal of Personality and Social Psychology, 51*, 515-530.

Whitt, E. J., Edison, M., Pascarella, E. T., Nora, A., & Terenzini, P. T. (1999). Inter-actions with peers and objective and self-reported cognitive outcomes across 3 years of college. *Journal of College Student Development, 40,* 61-78.

Wilson, T. D. (2002). *Strangers to ourselves.* Cambridge, MA: The Belknap Press of Harvard University Press.

Youniss, J., & Yates, M. (1997). *Community service and social responsibility in youth.* Chicago, IL: University of Chicago Press.

Zeigert, A. L., & McGoldrick, K. (2004). Adding rigor to service-learning research: An armchair economists' approach. In M. Welch & S. H. Billig (Eds.), *New perspectives in service-learning: Research to advance the field* (pp. 23-36). Green-wich, CT: Information Age.

PART II

SERVICE-LEARNING IN THE K-12 SETTING

CHAPTER 3

FACILITATING TRANSFORMATION THROUGH EDUCATION

Promoting Teaching of Social Responsibility and Civic Education for Democracy

Janel Smith and Annie McKitrick

This paper provides a foundation for understanding the conditions that facilitate transformative learning within education systems, with a view to encouraging and improving civic education for democracy. We explore definitions of transformative learning and examine the interconnections between processes of social change and transformative learning. Methods of teaching transformatively include service-learning, experiential education, and arts-based approaches. Finally, we give examples of ways in which transformative learning practices can be implemented into school curricula and/or degree programs.

As the nature of the state has changed dramatically over the last half century from "interventionist to facilitative" (Brock & Bulpitt, 2007, p. 2),

Research for What? Making Engaged Scholarship Matter
pp. 47–69
Copyright © 2010 by Information Age Publishing
All rights of reproduction in any form reserved.

there has been an increase in reliance on the private and "third" sectors[1] in areas relating to public policy (Barber, 1998; Florini & Simmons, 2000; Kaldor, 2005; Moulaert & Ailenei, 2005). Accompanying this change has been greater recognition of the potential roles and impacts that organizations in these sectors can have on policy development and implementation. Perhaps not coincidentally, we have witnessed a rise in the number of social movements and civic associations that coordinate across geographic borders and boundaries. Often these movements have formed in response to the failure of government to provide adequate levels of well-being to communities and individuals, providing viable alternatives and countering current institutional structures and relations of ruling.

In conjunction with these developments are events occurring at the "global" or transnational level most commonly associated with "globalization." The promotion of free market values and the increasing ease of movement of peoples, goods and ideas have been accompanied by threats to human security in the form of terrorism, intra- and intertate conflict, climate change, and peak oil concerns. Furthermore, concepts such as international human rights, ethical and "green" consumerism, and corporate accountability have taken on a resonance never before experienced. This has led to renewed discussion of what it means to live in a democratic society and the ideas surrounding active citizenry, responsible citizenship, civil society and civic associations.

Transformative learning is essentially about educating for citizenship, helping to mold, transform and inform learners about the values of active citizenship through approaches to educating and learning. It is "oriented towards the elimination of oppressive social relationships through the promotion of critical thinking and reflection, leading to transformative action" (Haughey, 2006, p. 298). This implies interconnectedness between the processes of social change and those of transformative learning. Sustained transformative and more inclusive learning environments can be fostered through an informed and socially responsible citizenry. One of the central purposes of this paper is to set out a vision for how education can act as a vehicle by which to transform society through increased use of transformative learning approaches. Such a strategy may prove to foster a greater understanding of the values and principles of the social economy, with the aim of making societies more socially just and equitable.

M. K. Smith (2001) argues that "one of the major tasks that education must perform in a democratic society 'is the proper preparation of young citizens for the roles and responsibilities they must be ready to take on when they reach maturity'" (p. 1). The underlying question concerns the *kind* or *type* of citizen it is believed will best foster an effective future democratic society. This is well discussed in Westheimer and Kahne's (2004) framework of three visions of citizenship: the personally responsible citizen, the participatory citizen, and the justice-oriented citizen. In their view, it is not sufficient to argue that educating about democratic values is as important as instruction on traditional academic subjects. What is required is consideration of the kinds of democratic values that are needed for democracy to flourish. Within the Canadian context, the importance placed on shaping future democratic citizens through education can be seen in the list of desired attributes that high school students should possess upon graduation, as listed by the British Columbia Ministry of Education. These are:

- the knowledge and skills required to be *socially responsible citizens* who act in caring and principled ways, *respecting the diversity of all people* and the *rights of others to hold different ideas and beliefs;*
- *the knowledge and understanding they need to participate in democracy as Canadian and global citizens,* acting in accordance with the laws, rights and responsibilities of a democracy;
- the *attitudes, knowledge and positive habits they need to be healthy individuals,* responsible for their physical and emotional well-being; and
- *the attitudes and competencies they need to be community contributors* who take the initiative to improve their own and others' quality of life (British Columbia Ministry of Education, 2004, italics added for emphasis).

These attributes are similar across other ministries of education throughout Canada and reflect a belief in the values of civic engagement and the establishment of an active citizenry towards the realization of a more just society. They are also reflected in the defining characteristics of transformative learning theory. However, they also raise important questions regarding political choices that frame what good citizenship is understood to be and how good citizens are to be characterized, choices that have consequences for the kind of democratic society produced (Westheimer & Kahne, 2004).

This paper provides a foundation for the development of an understanding of the conditions that help to facilitate transformation within education systems, with a view to encouraging and promoting teaching that builds social responsibility and active citizenship. Importantly, it is based on a conceptualization of transformation that is "oriented towards the elimination of oppressive social relationships through the promotion of critical thinking and reflection, leading to transformative action" (Haughey, 2006, p. 298). Drawing on transformative learning theory, we call upon educators, researchers and practitioners to reflect upon their own practice and to think critically about opportunities and challenges that exist for students to become more active, critical and responsible citizens. This includes taking greater responsibility for their own lifelong learning, participating actively in their community and taking actions that consider the long-term future and sustainability of economic, environmental and social dimensions. This work calls into question assumptions about the objectivity and neutrality of formal educational programs and systems, positing instead that schools are in fact contested sites for the production and reproduction of certain images, symbols, traditions and patterns of behavior that help to perpetuate social, political and economic arrangements and processes.

A review of definitions of transformative learning is first conducted in order to develop an understanding of the concept and its use within educational settings. Second, we connect transformative learning to educating for citizenship and sustainability as well as "alternative" public policy and social economy concepts. This emphasizes that civil, civic and citizen education are imperative to the development of the political, social and economic identity(ies) of a nation and to the deepening of democracy. Third, we explore some of the ways that transformative learning has been facilitated in schools. Fourth, we suggest ways that transformative learning practices might be implemented in the curricula of schools through a review of some current programs. Finally, we explore the role of each participant in the transformative learning process.

DEFINING TRANSFORMATIVE
LEARNING THEORY AND PEDAGOGY

Transformative learning is a process of seeking to "get beyond" a preoccupation with the attainment of factual knowledge in the classroom to recognize the potential to be transformed through learning in meaningful ways. It involves teaching learners to critically examine, question and consider assumptions, ways of making meaning, multiple points of view and values not only in the classroom but throughout their lives and interactions with others. There are a number of factors that influence transformative learning including the nature of critical reflection and relationships as well as the impacts of power, purpose and "life mission" (Taylor 2007, p. 175).

Indeed, recent studies have indicated that the "peer dynamics" of trust, nonhierarchical status, shared goals, authenticity and engagement in dialogue are vitally important to the transformative learning experience (Taylor, 2007). Brownlee, Purdie and Boulton-Lewis (2003) note that students' conceptions of learning, particularly learning as a meaning-making process, positively contribute to the likelihood that students will "engage in deep approaches to learning and actively construct and transform appropriate well-organised concepts" (p. 111). From their standpoint, transformative learning is a process of reflection, of helping us to construct and make meanings out of the information we acquire in relation to our prior knowledge and set of beliefs.

Similarly, for Taylor (2007), transformative learning theory "is a theory that is partly developmental, but even more it is about where 'learning is understood as the process of using a prior interpretation to construe a new or revised interpretation of the meaning of one's experience in order to guide future action'" (p. 173). According to Mezirow (2000; Mezirow & Associates, 1990), transformative learning attempts to explain "what happens in individual transformation. What changes in a cognitive/constructive notion of transformation is a meaning perspective, a habit of expectations that filters how we think, believe, and feel and how, what, when and why we learn" (Scott, 2006, p. 156). Mezirow & Associates link these "paradigm" shifts—that is changes in our belief structures and ways of making meaning—to transformative learning. They write that there is "a parallel between the profound, dramatic and far-reaching changes that at the disciplinary level are called *paradigm shifts* and at the personal level *transformative learning*" (p. 290). This also embraces Freire's (1970/1993) social-emancipatory approach to transformative learning that emphasizes the importance of social change in the transformative learning process (Cranton, 2006).

Moreover, transformative learning provides a medium in which to explore and deconstruct "the political economy of schooling," the state's policies toward education, the representation of particular histories and knowledge in texts, and the construction of student's subjectivity in learning (Grace, 2006, p. 134). It problematizes and calls into question the notion that schools are inherently "neutral places, relying on so called objective formal curriculum and evaluation systems, where some people are assumed to be 'naturally' suited and others are screened out" (Brigham, 2008, p. 45). Transformative learning theory attempts to "make sense of the nature of schooling and the contexts, power, and interests that influence it. It positions schooling as a form of cultural politics that 'always represents an introduction to, preparation for, and legitimization of particular forms of social life.' It critiques these cultural policies designed to protect exclusionary tradition and hierarchical social structures" (Grace, 2006, p. 133). Learning and education are seen as ways to both inform *and* be informed by social action toward the realization of social change. One of the primary goals of education is, therefore, the development of a more humane, responsible, and aware citizenry of empowered individuals acting collectively in order to transform current practices and relations of ruling that privilege certain groups above others.

TRANSFORMATIVE LEARNING AND EDUCATING FOR CITIZENSHIP

Transformative Learning connects to the notions of educating for citizenship and education for sustainability. Educating for citizenship is about *status* (i.e., being a member of a nation and community), *identity* (i.e., belonging and actually feeling like a member of a community), *civic virtues* (i.e., the values, attitudes and behaviors that are expected of a responsible citizen) and *agency* (i.e., the notion of citizens as social actors operating within and/or through social structures and relations of power) (Schugurensky, 2006, p. 69). Similarly, education for sustainability is an approach to education that recognizes education's primary role in constructing a sustainable future (Wooltorton, 2004). Education is seen as "essential for the development of new human perspectives that are embedded in the values of sustainability" (Wooltorton, 2004, p. 596). These human perspectives can in turn help to shape new notions of status, identity, civic virtues and agency.

The United Nations Educational, Scientific and Cultural Organization (UNESCO) approach to sustainable education asserts that education and democracy must be inexorably intertwined if a path toward greater sustainability is to be achieved (UNESCO, 2002). This links educating for sustainability directly to educating for citizenship. It must be recognized, however, that while educating for citizenship can be used as a transformative learning initiative to help create an environment in which democracy flourishes, it can also be used as a means of upholding the status quo and maintaining certain relations of ruling. From this perspective, transformative learning is viewed as constructivist in orientation. Transformative learning theory asserts that knowledge is socially and historically constructed, and encourages (self-) reflection in order that both individuals and communities define and construct their own understandings of status, identity, civic virtues and agency as well as what it means to live in a democratic society. This can be further visualized through Westheimer and Kahne's (2004) previously mentioned typology of visions of democratic citizenry that explains how variations in conceptions of citizenship reflect relatively distinct sets of political, theoretical and curricular goals, values and beliefs.

Challenges to transformative learning emerge from "resistors to change" on the part of learners, teachers and the institutional and community environments in which learning takes place. As Williams (2007) notes, "lengthy terms of employment for faculty and staff often result in substantial degrees of resistance to change.... Moreover, ritualistic and symbolic diversity planning efforts – which result in superficial and short-term gains—tend to crowd out initiatives that result in deep and sustained transformation" (p. 8). If schools are to overcome challenges associated with resistors to change they must focus on implementing change programs that are holistic and multidimensional. Therefore, "to create and sustain inclusive learning environments, institutions must attend to visible elements such as symbols and administrative structures, as well as invisible elements such as the unspoken priorities and subconscious attitudes of community members" (p. 9). Moreover, the roles of teacher, learner and the community must be taken into account in facilitating transformative learning.

Thompson (2002) calls attention to the work of Nussbaum in identifying three qualities that are essential for facilitating an active and engaged citizenry in today's world. These are "an ability to examine oneself and one's traditions critically; an ability to see beyond immediate group loyalties and to extend to strangers the moral concern we 'naturally' extend to friends and kin" and the development of what she calls 'the narrative imagination'—the ability to see unobvious connections between sequences of human actions" (p. 31). It follows that "if the intention is for children to be active citizens who act according to the values of democratic process, social justice and ecological sustainability" we must seek through our political system "to provide a cultural environment that models and demonstrates these values" (Wooltorton, 2004, p. 599).

In sum, transformative learning helps learners begin to reconceptualize of the world in different ways, challenging them to reflect upon assumptions, experiences and actions in their day-to-day lives. It is closely connected with educating on citizenry and democracy, "and democracy is inseparable from issues of equality, participation, and self-governance" (Schugurensky, 2006, p. 76). Therefore, education as a transformative experience helps to shape and define citizenship and is connected to democratic practice and social justice. It encourages the recognition that we share many common interests, that we must commit ourselves in turn to a consideration of those interests, and, therefore, the needs of others, if we are to realize those common interests. It also suggests that we must actively engage with, and seek to strengthen, relationships and movements that embody democratic values and encourage collective action. These definitions of transformative learning are particularly relevant with respect to how we conceive of student exposure to the social economy. The influence of concepts associated with the social economy, including the exploration of alternative career paths, democratic participation and active citizenry, would indeed help students to begin to understand and act in the world in different ways and critically reflect upon their preconceived notions, beliefs and ways of making meaning.

CONNECTING TRANSFORMATIVE LEARNING TO SOCIAL RESPONSIBILITY: "ALTERNATIVE" PUBLIC POLICY AND THE SOCIAL ECONOMY

Current discourse on the growing inequalities between income levels and employment opportunities in the public policy sphere rarely mention alternative political and economic models. This includes models of collective ownership of economic activities and organizational values that have a social goal embedded in its mission. For example, social economy initiatives "create new economic activity that responds to social goals, representing immeasurable cost savings to government. More importantly, the social economy meets what some call a 'triple bottom line' that takes into account financial, social and environmental impacts (Downing & Neamtan 2005, p. 10).

The potential of education rooted in transformative learning theory to open opportunities for learners to be exposed to 'alternative' public policy and social economy concepts as they relate to civic activism and social responsibility are encouraging. Here transformative learning implies "both structural changes in the psyches of the individual and in the structures of society" (Taylor, 2007, p. 184). The notion of working to instill an ethic of social responsibility through education is not new in the discourse surrounding adult education. Within adult education social responsibility has "been widely accepted as a self-evident goal achievable through learner empowerment, community development, citizen and global education, or participatory literacy" (Fenwick, 2008, p. 107). Many of the initiatives utilized to teach adult learners about social responsibility can be replicated in other education systems in order to teach about the concepts of social economy, civic activism and social responsibility.

The challenge comes in the need for educators themselves to be exposed to social economy and social responsibility discourses amidst a public policy environment that promotes individual, capitalistic and "get rich" approaches to living and participating in communities. Schugurensky and McCollum (2007) allude to this when they note that:

> Today, the typical textbook in North America does not even recognize cooperatives as a form of business organization. This is intriguing, to say the least, because of you go to the official website of Industry Canada, you will see that Corporations Canada includes business corporations, sole proprietor, partnership, not-for-profit organizations and cooperatives. Hence,

there is some incongruence between the Canadian business reality and what students are learning in schools (p. 4).

This suggests the impacts of public policy and the policy environment in determining what knowledge is taught to students and what knowledge is marginalized within the educational system. L. T. Smith (1999) addresses similar themes when she writes that often "what makes ideas 'real' is the system of knowledge, the formations of culture, and the relations of power in which these concepts are located" (p. 48). These are vital issues that we need to consider in assessing potential areas within the education system for the greater inclusion of socioeconomic forms of knowledge.

Schugurensky and McCollum (2007) conclude that "if we bring the social economy to the classroom, students could have the opportunity to examine different economic and business organizations.... Moreover, such inclusion can also help teachers to illustrate important issues in economics like workplace democracy, incentives and public goods, ... social accounting, and re-investments of capital" (p. 7). This highlights the utility of forging strategic alliances with like-minded allies within government and ministries of education, the private sector and among parents and concerned members of the community in order to promote teaching on the social economy on a more wide-scale basis.

METHODS OF TEACHING TRANSFORMATIVELY: SERVICE-LEARNING, EXPERIENTIAL EDUCATION, AND ARTS-BASED APPROACHES

Various programs and tools already exist to facilitate the introduction of transformative learning into education for greater social responsibility and civic engagement. This includes programs that adopt critical thinking and learning perspectives, emphasize self-reflection, encourage historical revisionism and question current structures, rules and regulations that are exclusionary to certain populations. It also involves the (re)interpretation of laws and social, political and economic structures through social lenses that examine power dynamics and relations of ruling. Among these are the revitalization of service-learning programs through experiential education and arts-based approaches that honor community-based practitioners/acteurs, parents, community members and educational institutions in the transformative learning process.

Faris (2008) defines service-learning as "the integration of formal learning (academic, vocational-technical, etc.) with student service in the voluntary or not-for-profit sector in Canada or abroad, *for academic credit*. It ... emphasizes—reflective thinking and reciprocal benefits to the student and the community/body involved" (p. 1, italics added). Similarly, service-learning is defined by Eyler and Giles (1999) as:

> a form of experiential education where learning occurs through a cycle of action and reflection as students work with others through a process of applying what they are learning to community problems and, at the same time, reflecting upon their experience as they seek to achieve real objectives for the community and deeper understanding and skills for themselves. In the process, students link personal and social development with academic and cognitive development. (p. 7)

Eyler and Giles (1999) summarize their observations stating that the service-learning model should "include a balance between service to the community and academic learning and that the hyphen in the phrase symbolizes the central role of reflection in the process of learning through community experience" (p. 4). Service-learning, thus, differs from volunteer work in that it includes a critical (self-) reflective component to the experience.

Service-learning is a growing movement utilized at both the K-12 and the post-secondary levels. The service-learning movement in the United States has a long history rooted in engaging youth in community development. Of particular interest are its ties to the Folk Schule of Sweden and social justice programs such as the Peace Corp and the War on Poverty. Currently service-learning aims to tie together both in-school and out-of-school programs for learners with the broad themes of civic engagement and community development. In Canada, this pedagogical approach has gained recent recognition in post-secondary institutions. It is also an approach that is reflected in the community service programs that are mandated by some of the provincial education ministries for high school graduation.

An example from the Learn and Serve America's National Service-Learning Clearinghouse website (2008) provides a good example of how the service-learning experience can be transformative rather than solely service oriented. It states:

> if school students collect trash out of an urban streambed, they are providing a service to the community as volunteers; a service that is highly valued and important. When school students collect trash from an urban streambed, then analyze what they found and possible sources so they suggestions for reducing pollution, they are engaging in service-learning.

This distinction is important as it differentiates the spirit and intention of service-learning from the requirement in some educational jurisdictions across Canada that stipulate that, in order to graduate, students must complete community volunteer hours. In British Columbia, for example, high school students are required to complete at least 30 hours of work experience and/or community service (British Columbia Ministry of Education, 2008).

These volunteer hours usually have no formal learning outcomes or an expectation of mutuality (reciprocity) included among its objectives. In most cases students in these types of volunteer programs end up contributing to projects that are useful to the organization (i.e., timekeeping at a tournament, stuffing envelops, helping special needs children, etc.) but do not allow them to fully understand the context of the work in which they are involved. The impact of their experience often depends more on community agency and the supervisor at the site of the volunteer activity, including their willingness to shape the volunteer experience so as to engage the learner, than in the directions given by the teacher supervising the volunteer placement. Furthermore, the community organization involved in the volunteer placement program can feel overburdened by the increased workload of having to train and supervise student volunteers and may not feel adequately supported by the academic institution with which they are affiliated. This can further hinder the volunteer placement process and experience for all those involved. It also runs counter to the vision of community-school based partnerships that aim to engage one another in the joint planning and execution of programs.

It must be noted that critiques of the service-learning model have resembled criticisms levied at volunteer-placement programs Too often, service-learning initiatives fall victim to both failing to fully educate learners on the notions of mutuality and civic association and overburdening volunteer organizations when adequate steps are not taken to ensure that collaborative dialogue is facilitated between schools and community organizations. Marullo and Edwards (2000) allude to this criticism when they write that they "focus on an important component of a broader transformational strategy by distinguishing between charity and social justice and discuss ways that through service-learning acts of charity—which typically end up reproducing the status quo—can facilitate the politicization of students and help them to become active promoters of a more just society" (p. 897). Therefore, it is important to ensure that, in service-learning initiatives, meaningful efforts are made to engage with community partners not only to address pressing social, economic, and political challenges but also to structure programs in ways that truly foster an ethic of mutuality and reciprocity.

Closely linked to service-learning is experiential education, which offers increased opportunity for facilitating transformative learning, teaching on social responsibility, citizenship, public policy, and the social economy, and for upholding a commitment to the principles of mutuality and reciprocity between schools and communities in service-learning programs. Experiential education initiatives represent a means of countering some of the challenges associated with the service-learning approach in order to enable the creation of a supportive educational environment in which transformative learning can occur. Experiential education has been defined as a learning model that "begins with the experience followed by reflection, discussion, analysis and evaluation of the experience. The assumption is that we seldom learn from the experience unless we assess the experience, assigning our own meaning in terms of our own goals, aims, ambitions and expectations" (Canadian Alliance for Community Service-Learning, 2007a). According to Kolb (1984) there are six key features of experiential education: (1) learner centered, (2) based on the premise that people learn best by doing, (3) occurs as a direct result of learner's participation in events and activities, (4) utilizes the learner's own reflection upon their experiences, (5) holistically addresses the cognitive, emotional, and (6) physical aspects of the learner and suggests that learning is active and dynamic. Experiential education emphasizes the importance of learning through experience, learning both within and outside the classroom, and embedding learning in one's own goals, beliefs and expectations.

Both experiential education and service learning use such methods as journaling, reflection, and open discussion about experiences. According to Kolb's (1984) model of experiential education, experience must always be followed by reflection as this helps to draw out new insights and discoveries that then deepen our conceptual schemas to perceive, organize, evaluate and develop understandings of events and experiences. Recent studies have revealed "the power of journaling and writing theses as providing a place for students to interject their own voice and a tangible product of the education experience. The written format potentially strengthens the analytical capability of transformative learning" (Taylor, 2007, p. 182). These tools provide learners with opportunities "through which students can record their actions and observations, as well their emotional and intellectual reactions to community experiences.... Through discussion, experiences are 'collectivized', allowing more voices to be heard and similarities and patterns among experiences to be identified" (Canadian Alliance for Community Service-Learning, 2007c). Through these methods learners can develop an ethic of social responsibility, transforming both their individual sense of themselves and their societal roles and responsibilities as an active citizen.

There are a number of innovative arts-based experiential teaching methods that can be utilized to teach about social responsibility, citizenship, public policy and social economy and promote greater transformative learning. These include painting, music and song-writing, photography, videography, designing ecologically sustainable landscapes, drama, and dance. The objectives of arts-based education are "to provide existing and potential audiences with the tools to understand, appreciate and enjoy the arts; it can provide direct experience of the arts as a means of personal and social development; or it can use education as a way of achieving specific organisational aims, such as attracting new audiences or supporting wider policy objectives" (Thompson, 2002, p. 29). Furthermore, "it is argued that enormous social benefits are to be derived from arts and cultural education, in terms of personal development, social cohesion and community empowerment, which can contribute to every area of social policy" (p. 38).

For students "coming together with others in cultural and educational activities, to define common, unfulfilled desires and needs, and to identify the forces that frustrate them, can be a powerful tonic for the imagination. This sense of common purpose and intention to make a difference is the stuff of social transformation—both in learning and in art" (Thompson, 2002, p. 31). It is conceivable to imagine that more "themed projects" like this could be created to teach social responsibility concepts such as social economy, social justice, community building, sustainable development, and empowerment. Arts-based approaches to learning can be "helpful for students that have been excluded from education for various barriers including age, gender and ethnic origin. The creative process 'transcend cultural differences' and helps people break out of their common patterns of framing the world" (Hartley, 2007, p. 15). Such projects encourage students to reflect on their own social, economic and political beliefs and how these impact their conceptions and understandings of the themes being explored through their work.

Community cultural development programs are another arts-based approach that explicitly encourages and sees the exploration of culture as a site for learning to take place. Community cultural development "not only privileges culture as a site for learning, but artists and arts practices as learning's facilitators" (Power, 1997, p. 173). Community cultural development "describes a range of initiatives undertaken by artists in collaboration with other community members to express identity, concerns, and aspirations through the arts and communications media, while building the capacity for social action and contributing to social change" (Imagining America, 2008). Community cultural development projects, therefore, possess an educational, mobilization and empowerment element that can help build community capacity and facilitate the growth of an active citizenry.

OPPORTUNITIES FOR ENHANCING
TRANSFORMATIVE LEARNING

There are a number of opportunities for enhancing the transformative learning environment in schools, thereby promoting greater knowledge and understandings of social responsibility, civic participation and alternative forms of social and economic organization such as those falling under the rubric of the social economy. Among these opportunities are encouraging granting foundations, programs and courses within academic institutions to incorporate service-learning and community-based initiatives into their structures. One such example is the work of the J.W. McConnell Family Foundation (n.d.) that offers funding for both service-learning and community-based projects for youth.

The McConnell Family Foundation has also funded the establishment of the Canadian Alliance for Community Service-Learning currently located at Carleton University. A key component of the Alliance's model of community service-learning is their approach to "Leadership for Social Change," which forms the raison d'etre for their involvement in community and their participation in service-learning (Canadian Alliance for Community Service-Learning, 2007b). This focus on fostering leaders who will work toward the realization of social change is of importance to the development of active citizenry that can make a real difference in communities. A number of universities including the University of British Columbia are now funded by the foundation to pursue the development of service-learning projects.

The McConnell Family Foundation awarded funds to the Canadian Community Economic Development Network (2007) for the development of community-based projects with youth and young adults. This initiative from the Foundation was in direct response to an evaluation of the Foundation's service-learning projects (Cawley, 2007). The project's central goal is "the development for intentional and meaningful learning opportunities to be integrated into Community Economic Development projects, increasing the capacity of the learner, the organization and the community to contribute to social change" (Backgrounder, 2008). Currently, CCEDNET is working closely with a group of CED organizations to provide training and support for integrating intentional learning into their CED work. This represents an enhanced opportunity to teach on the social economy, social change, and community development by engaging students in a transformative learning process. The resulting report and workbook can be found on both the CCEDNET and McConnell Family Foundation websites.

Through its Community Education Program (2008) and university and community-based partnerships, Simon Fraser University (SFU) in

Vancouver, British Columbia has sought to educate on concepts such as poverty, human rights, Aboriginal, immigrant and inner-city issues. The Program's mandate "is to support positive social change for socially excluded individuals and communities by creating access to education and other resources." Their "work is grounded in community-based projects which address critical needs identified by the community, and in which community members play active roles in decision making, implementation and evaluation" (Community Education Program, 2008). This program is founded on a number of beliefs and values that include beliefs that universities have a social responsibility to invest in communities, that SFU is capable of playing a strong role in the growth and health of our communities, that it is desirable to increase and widen access to higher education, and that education is a vital key in promoting positive social change.

The University of Alberta's Faculty of Arts has also taken steps toward educating on citizenship and to build linkages between the community and university by offering an "innovative classes on citizenship. It also offers a Community Service Learning program designed as a mutual exchange, in which the needs of the community and academic learning are considered and served" (Haughey, 2006, p. 305).

The University of Victoria's Office of Community Based Research (OCBR) is an example of a university-based initiative that aims to partner with the community to engage in research and learning activities that are of relevance and value to both the university and community. The OCBR is a "university-wide structure to facilitate research partnerships between the university and the community on issues of community priority" (Office of Community-Based Research, University of Victoria, 2008). Since its inception in 2007, OCBR has worked closely with First Nations organizations and the greater Victoria community on homelessness issues and developed a graduate level course on community-based research in partnership with the regional health authority.

The Clemente Program, a "radical humanities course for the poor and marginalized" is another program aimed at facilitating transformation and teaching of socioeconomic values in the classroom (Groen & Hyland-Russell, 2008, p. 152). Launched by Earl Shorris in 1995, this program has gained momentum and spread across Canada, the United States and Mexico. The programs "are directed at students experiencing both internal and external barriers to learning that include low self-esteem; a belief that education is not for them; negative histories with learning institutions; feelings of disenfranchisement; poverty; mental or physical illness; addictions; violence; and homelessness" (p. 152). In Canada, iterations of the Clemente Program include Storefront 101 in Calgary, Discovery University in Ottawa, and Humanities 101 at Lakehead University.

At the Forest School in Australia, students learn both about the social economy and environmental conservation through landscape art. The school grounds "are landscaped with children's gardens, buildings are ecologically designed, gardens are water efficient and use their own compost, and children engage in considerable environmental education through their daily work" (Wooltorton, 2004, p. 601). These arts-based approaches enable students to explore their values, beliefs, attitudes, and reflections and provide a medium for expressing them as students may lack the verbal skills in which to·do so since these feelings often operate at the subconscious level.

In Victoria, British Columbia, arts-based projects have also been put in place that enable transformative learning. In 2006, based upon the findings of a need assessment of impoverished women in Victoria carried out by Our Place Project an arts-based adult education and knowledge mobilization project was implemented (Clover & Craig, 2008). The 18-month project "provided a space for the women to explore collectively their own issues, ways of knowing and experiences and develop artworks based on these for public display.... The women participants came from diverse cultural backgrounds including Chinese, Métis, First Nations, South African and European" (p. 59). According to Clover and Craig's analysis, the outcomes of the women's participation in the project included building trust, bonding, new feelings of belonging and connectedness, the development of communication and critical reflection skills and capacities and a shift in perspective away from self-victimization to empowerment (pp. 60-61). These findings clearly reflect the values and objectives of transformative learning, social responsibility and the social economy and suggest the role of arts-based programs, such as the Our Place Project, in enhancing transformative learning.

PARTICIPANTS' ROLES IN TRANSFORMATIVE LEARNING

In cases where transformative learning is a goal of formal education, fostering an environment in which this type of learning process can occur is, ultimately, crucial. The creation of a learning community in which transformative learning can take place rests upon a number of key conditions and roles that must be adopted by teachers, learners, schools, communities and parents in order to facilitate transformative learning. This includes the commitment of all involved either directly or indirectly in the transformative learning program to the learning process, teamwork/collaboration, acceptance of differences and trust, respect and mutual support (Wooltorton, 2004). Below, we describe the various roles that the different practitioner/acteurs involved in the learning process can play in facilitating transformative learning.

Roles of the Teacher/Educator, Schools, and Professional Associations

The roles of the teacher include establishing an environment that builds trust and respect between teacher and learner both within and beyond the classroom. From this viewpoint the teacher is seen more as "coach" than "expert" (Olson & Raffanti, 2006). This is a core principle in fostering a transformative learning environment. It helps to create communities that encourage lifelong learning and where learners can feel safe engaging in self-reflection activities that include reflecting on previously held beliefs, assumptions and ways of making meaning as they participate in the transformative learning experience.

Teachers must find ways to help students "sustain the courage needed (e.g. living with the discomfort) and recognizing their own narrative while at the edge of their learning" (Taylor, 2007, p. 183). Cranton (2006) articulates five central characteristics that teachers should possess in order to teach transformatively: (1) have a strong sense of self-awareness, (2) be aware of the different preferences of learners, (3) develop a relationship with learners that fosters one's own ability to be genuine and open, (4) be aware of the constraints associated with teaching, and (5) engage in critical reflection and self-reflection on one's practice (p. 5). Teachers should take steps to display a willingness in their own lives to continue to learn from both the "learners" and "community" and demonstrate openness to experiencing and exploring challenges to their own belief systems. In this way, teachers become colearners in the classroom.

Schools must also reevaluate current structures that are in place, such as curriculum teaching guides and workshops/seminars that could help teachers to utilize more transformative learning-based techniques. Creating "faculty development opportunities to encourage such work, service-learning offices to support the work, and earmarked grants programs to allow the time for such collaborations to evolve are also needed" (Marullo & Edwards, 2000, p. 906). Schools are also implicated in the responsibility to provide a setting for students in which they are supported throughout their learning process. According to Marullo and Edwards, "the institution must provide not only material and logistical support to facilitate the students' service but also the supportive environment for the students to reflect on and analyze their volunteer work" (p. 909).

With respect to increasing transformative learning in the classroom through the curriculum, several steps can be taken by schools. The board of education can play an important leadership role in encouraging transformative education practices. Superintendents and trustees can support teachers and programs in schools, showcase transformative practices and highlight the work of students that reflect this approach.

Roles of the Learner

Similarly to the roles of the teacher, the learner also has a responsibility for cocreating an enabling environment in the classroom and community settings where transformative learning can occur (Taylor, 1998). Learning in this context is viewed not simply as the passive act of repetition and memorization, but instead it is advocated that the learner be an active participant in cocreating and coconstructing what a more just and democratic society might look like. Furthermore, learner creativity and curiosity should be encouraged, and learners have the task of finding ways to facilitate their own continued learning outside of the classroom by visiting libraries, galleries and museums, participating in community and extracurricular activities, keeping aware of current events and volunteering their time in their communities.

A number of researchers have paid attention to the role that the learner has in transformative learning. Billig has spearheaded a number of research studies on community service-learning and has developed a list of strategies for such programs that include the need to "maximize student voice in selecting, designing, implementing and evaluating the project" (Billig, 2000, p. 663).

Roles of Parents and Community Members

Learning within the formal education system operates not as a closed system but as a system heavily influenced by the impacts of community, media, parents and peers on learners. Parents "are implicated in the early political socialization of the younger generations. Thus, we contend that there is radical pedagogical potential in parenting" (Chovanec & Benitez, 2008, p. 53). One challenge in facilitating transformative learning is, therefore, to find ways to involve parents in positive ways in the learning process. The Parent Advisory Council can play crucial roles in informing parents and involving them in supporting students, schools and educators in teaching transformatively. Parent Advisory Council meetings can be a place of learning for parents and educators who share a common goal in the preparation of the student for life in society. Unfortunately, schools have faced strong financial challenges over the past decade, which has left

Parent Advisory Councils with a role in fundraising rather than in supporting transformative learning. Jurisdictions that have supported the community school movement have seen strong ties develop between school and community and these schools have provided opportunities for students to experience an environment that supports transformative learning with opportunity for volunteering, student leadership and engagement with community.

CONCLUSION

This paper has explored the use of innovative teaching methods to educate transformatively. These include practical, cooperative placements, service-learning, experiential education, arts-based approaches, and career training classes. This work has sought to raise awareness of creative models and to stimulate broad dialogue regarding methods for increasing transformational learning with the intention to educate on social responsibility, citizenship, and increased exposure to "alternative" public policy concepts and aspects of the social economy.

Strategies need to be in place that enable the different acteurs in the transformative learning process to address "difficult, self-explanatory topics and individual pedagogical topics such as infusing diversity into the curriculum or creating inclusive and learning-centered classroom environments" (Williams, 2007, p. 11). It is only by delving deeply into these "difficult" topics that collective action, a deepening of democracy and a more just society can be realized. Revitalizing service-learning programs through experiential and arts-based approaches to learning are two ways in which teachers *and* learners can work to transform the learning environment in ways that facilitate critical, (self-) reflection and the greater integration of social responsibility, citizenship, and social economy concepts into teaching and learning.

Further research and practice are required in order to broaden and advance knowledge on the potential for initiatives that encourage transformative learning to also facilitate teaching on the social economy and the transfer of social economy values and principles to learners. Equally important is the need to deepen explorations into the various roles that those outside of the formal education system, specifically parents, community members and community-based organizations, can play in encouraging and facilitating transformative learning and teaching on social economy values, practices and organizations. Though not addressed in this paper, the reciprocal nature of transformative learning theory that advocates for lifelong learning must also be acknowledged for the influence that learners can have on the informal learning of parents and community members about the social economy and its related institutions and partners. This represents an important area for future inquiry.

In the end, simply teaching on social responsibility and citizenship principles and values in the classroom is not enough. Unless learners come to understand the meanings and linkages of these concepts to their daily lives and within their communities the influence and impacts of such teachings will not be fully realized. Ultimately, "if we are to facilitate in schools some notion of an ethical culture to which an altered form of aesthetic education might powerfully contribute, it is important that the personal, social, and political implications of moral values for our lives and actions, in and out of school, become part of the curriculum" (Beyer, 2000, p. 85). This is the essence of transformative learning.

NOTE

1. The "third" sector refers to social and/or economic activity that can contain a political and/or activist character that occurs outside of both the public and private sectors. It is a unifying term that seeks to embrace the existing diversity of approaches and concepts that exists within the "third" sector that includes cooperatives, the voluntary sector, civil society and civic associations and networks, social economy organizations, and nongovernmental organizations.

REFERENCES

Backgrounder. (2008). *The Community Development Service Learning Initiative.* Retrieved from http://www.ccednet-rcdec.ca/?q=en/our_work/youth/emergingleaders/projects#cdsl

Barber, B. (1998). *A place for us: How to make society civil and democracy strong.* New York, NY: Hill & Wang.

Beyer, L. (2000). *The arts, popular culture and social change.* New York, NY: Peter Lang.

Billig, S. H. (2000). Research on K-12 school-based service-learning: The evidence builds. *Phi Delta Kappan, 81*(9), 658-664.

Brigham, S. (2008). *Seeing straight ahead with Pierre Bourdieu: Female immigrant teachers in an arts-informed research inquiry.* In J. Groen & S. Guo (Eds.) Canadian Association for the Study of Adult Education (CASAE) Conference Proceedings. 27th National Conference, Vancouver, BC. Retrieved from www.oise.utoronto.ca/CASAE/cnf2008/OnlineProceedings-2008/CAS2008-Brigham.pdf

British Columbia Ministry of Education. (2004). *Graduation portfolio assessment and focus areas: A program guide.* Retrieved from http://www.llbc.leg.bc.ca/public/PubDocs/bcdocs/368791/portfolio_p1_p2.pdf

British Columbia Ministry of Education. (2008). *Program guide for graduation transitions*. Retrieved from http://www.bced.gov.bc.ca/graduation/grad-transitions/

Brock, K. L., & Bulpitt, C. (2007). *Encouraging the social economy through public policy: The relationship between the Ontario government and social economy organizations*. Paper presented at the annual meeting of the Canadian Political Science Association, University of Saskatchewan, Saskatoon, Saskatchewan.

Brownlee, J., Purdie, N., & Boulton-Lewis, G. (2003). An investigation of student teachers' knowledge about their own learning. *Higher Education, 45*(1), 109-125.

Canadian Alliance for Community Service-Learning. (2007a). *Experiential education*. Retrieved from http://www.communityservicelearning.ca/en/documents/InformationSheets-ExperientialEducation-2007.pdf

Canadian Alliance for Community Service-Learning. (2007b). *Leadership for social change*. Retrieved from http://www.communityservicelearning.ca/en/documents/InformationSheets-Leadership-2007.pdf

Canadian Alliance for Community Service-Learning. (2007c). *Reflection tools for faculty*. Retrieved from http://www.communityservicelearning.ca/en/documents/InformationSheets-Reflection-2007.pdf

Canadian Community Economic Development Network. (2007). *The Community Development Service Learning Initiative*. Retrieved from http://www.ccednet-rcdec.ca/files/ccednet/Service_Learning_Backgrounder.pdf

Cawley, J. (2007). *Letter from the J.W. McConnell Family Foundation to the Canadian Alliance for Community Service-learning*. Retrieved from http://www.communityservicelearning.ca/en/documents/LetterCawleySept07_002.pdf

Chovanec, D.M. & Benitez, A. (2008). The Penguin Revolution in Chile: Exploring intergenerational learning in social movements. *Journal of Contemporary Issues in Education*, 3(1), 39-57.

Clover, D., & Craig, C. (2008). *Street-life's creative turn: An exploration of an arts-based adult education and knowledge mobilisation project with homeless/street involved women in Victoria*. Paper presented at Community-University Partnerships: Connecting for Change. The Third International Community-University Exposition (CUexpo 2008), University of Victoria.

Community Education Program. (2008). *Simon Fraser University*. Retrieved from http://www.sfu.ca/community/

Cranton, P. (2006). *Understanding and promoting transformative learning: A guide for educators of adults* (2nd ed). San Francisco, CA: Jossey-Bass.

Downing, R., & Neamtan, N. (2005). *Social economy and community economic development in Canada: Next steps for public policy*. Chantier de l'économie sociale, The Canadian Community Economic Development Network and Alliance Recherche Universités-Communautés en économie sociale.

Eyler, J., & Giles, D. E., Jr. (1999). *Where's the learning in service-learning?* San Francisco, CA: Jossey-Bass.

Faris, R. (2008). *Lifelong Learning Communities homepage*. Retrieved from http://members.shaw.ca/rfaris/

Fenwick, T. (2008). *What is 'responsibility' in social responsibility? Tensions in workplace learning*. Paper presented at the Thinking Beyond Borders: Global Ideas,

Global Values Conference, Online Proceedings of the Canadian Association for the Study of Adult Education.

Florini, A. M., & Simmons, P. J. (2000). What the world needs now? In A. M. Florini (Ed.), *The third force: The rise of transnational civil society* (pp. 1-16). Washington, DC: Carnegie Endowment for International Peace.

Freire, P. (1970/1993). *Pedagogy of the oppressed*. New York, NY: Herder and Herder.

Grace, A. P. (2006). Critical adult education: Engaging the social in theory and practice. In T. Fenwick, T. Nesbit & B. Spencer (Eds.), *Contexts of adult education: Canadian perspectives* (pp. 128-139). Toronto, Ontario, Canada: Thompson Educational.

Groen, J., & Hyland-Russell, T. (2008). *Authenticity: Honouring self and others in practice*. Paper presented at the Thinking Beyond Borders: Global Ideas, Global Values Conference, Online Proceedings of the Canadian Association for the Study of Adult Education.

Hartley, L. (2007). *Sprouting seeds in the field of transformative learning theory*. Ginger Group. Retrieved from http://www.gingergroup.net/pdf/Transformative_Learning_Paper.pdf

Haughey, D. J. (2006). Not waving but drowning: Canadian University Extension for Social Change revisited. In T. Fenwick, T. Nesbit, & B. Spencer (Eds.), *Contexts of adult education: Canadian perspectives* (pp. 298-306). Toronto, Ontario, Canada: Thompson Educational.

Imagining America (2008). *What is community cultural development?* Retrieved from http://curriculumproject.net/glossary.html

J.W. McConnell Family Foundation. (n.d.). Retrieved from http://www.mcconnellfoundation.ca/

Kaldor, M. (2005). The idea of global civil society. In G. Baker & D. Chandler (Eds.), *Global civil society: Contested futures*. New York, NY: Routledge.

Kolb, D. A. (1984). *Experiential learning: Experience as the source of learning and development*. Englewood Hills, NJ: Prentice Hall.

Learn and Serve America's National Service-Learning Clearinghouse. (2008). *What is service-learning?* Retrieved from http://www.servicelearning.org/what-service-learning

Marullo, S., & Edwards, B. (2000). From charity to justice: The potential of university-community collaboration for social change. *American Behavioral Scientist*, 43(5), 895-911.

Mezirow, J. (2000.) Learning to think like an adult: Core concepts of transformation theory. In J. Mezirow (Ed.), *Learning as transformation: Critical perspectives on a theory in progress* (pp. 3-34). San Francisco, CA: Jossey-Bass.

Mezirow, J., & Associates. (1990). *Fostering critical reflection in adulthood*. San Francisco, CA: Jossey-Bass.

Moulaert, F., & Ailenei, O. (2005). Social economy, third sector and solidarity relations: A conceptual synthesis from history to present. *Urban Studies, 42*(11), 2037-2053.

Office of Community-Based Research, University of Victoria. (2008). Retrieved from http://web.uvic.ca/ocbr/index.html

Olson, M. M., & Raffanti, M. A. (2006). Leverage points, paradigms, and grounded action: Intervening in educational systems. *World Futures*, 62(7), 533-541.

Power, L. (1997). *Community cultural development in British Columbia*. Re-thinking Community, Culture, Solidarity and Survival. CASAE Proceedings, Mount Saint Vincent University, Halifax, pp. 169-174.

Schugurensky, D. (2006). Adult citizenship education: An overview of the Field. In T. Fenwick, T. Nesbit, & B. Spencer (Eds.), *Contexts of adult education: Canadian perspectives* (pp. 68-80). Toronto, Ontario, Canada: Thompson Educational.

Schugurensky, D., & McCollum, E. (2007). *The representation of the social economy in high school textbooks*. Building and Strengthening Communities: The Social Economy in a Changing World Conference Proceedings. Victoria: Centre international de recherches et d'information sur l'économie publique, sociale et coopérative (CIRIEC).

Scott, S. M. (2006). A way of seeing: Transformation for a new century. In T. Fenwick, T. Nesbit, & B. Spencer (Eds.), *Contexts of adult education: Canadian perspectives* (pp. 153-161). Toronto, Ontario, Canada: Thompson Educational.

Smith, L. T. (1999). *Decolonizing methodologies: Research and Indigenous Peoples*. London, England: Zed Books.

Smith, M. K. (2001). *Education for democracy*. Retrieved from http://www.infed.org/biblio/b-dem.htm

Taylor, E. W. (1998). *The theory and practice of transformative learning: A critical review*. Information Series No. 374. Columbus, OH: ERIC Clearinghouse on Adult, Career, and Vocational Education, Center on Education and Training for Employment, College of Education, the Ohio State University.

Taylor, E. W. (2007). An update of transformative learning theory: A critical review of the empirical research. *International Journal of Lifelong Learning*, 26(2), 173-191.

Thompson, J. (2002). *Bread and roses: Arts, culture and lifelong learning*. Leicester, United Kingdom: NIACE.

United Nations Educational, Scientific, and, Cultural Organization. (2002). *Education for sustainability, from Rio to Johannesburg: Lessons learnt from a decade of commitment*. Johannesburg, South Africa: Author.

Westheimer, J., & Kahne J. (2004). What kind of citizen? The politics of educating for democracy. *American Educational Research Journal*, 41(2), 237-269.

Williams, D. A. (2007). Achieving inclusive excellence: Strategies for creating real and sustainable change in quality and diversity. *About Campus*, 12(1), 8-14.

Wooltorton, S. (2004). Local sustainability at school: A political reorientation. *Local Environment*, 9(6), 595-609.

CHAPTER 4

CONCEPTUAL AND ANALYTIC DEVELOPMENT OF A CIVIC ENGAGEMENT SCALE FOR PREADOLESCENTS

**Nicole Nicotera, Inna Altschul,
Andrew Schneider-Munoz, and Ben Webman**

This paper presents the conceptual basis and statistical assessment of the Pre-Adolescent Civic Engagement Scale (PACES), a civic engagement measure developed for use with middle childhood and early adolescent young people. We expand the current work on civic engagement measures by contributing a parsimonious measure that has been subjected to more rigorous statistical assessments than other measures developed for preadolescents. Results of factor analyses, both exploratory and confirmatory, conducted with 2 samples ($n = 136$; $n = 151$) of children and youth (aged 7 to 14 years), yielded an 11-item, 2-component scale assessing *foundation for civic ethics* and *community connection* among preadolescents.

Traditional definitions of civic engagement center on age-related behaviors such as participation in electoral processes and attendance at public meetings (Camino & Zeldin, 2002). However, community service and civic

Research for What? Making Engaged Scholarship Matter
pp. 71–89
Copyright © 2010 by Information Age Publishing
All rights of reproduction in any form reserved.

engagement programs are deemed beneficial for young people, who are often too young to vote and have not yet developed skills for participation in public meetings (Balsano, 2005; Bolland, 2003; Driskell, 2002; Flanagan & Faison, 2001; Ginwright & Cammarota, 2007; Lerner, Dowling, & Anderson, 2003; Nicotera, 2008; Yates & Youniss, 1996). The perceived benefits of community service and civic engagement for preadolescents arise from the theoretical link between participation in civically oriented activities and community service and positive youth development (Flanagan, 2003; Flanagan & Faison, 2001; Lerner et al., 2003). For example, Yates and Youniss' (1996) review of 44 studies of adolescents and young adults who performed community service report that service was related to positive social development in areas such as agency, self-esteem, and personal competence. Advancement in the measuring of civic engagement has allowed for the growth of empirical evidence connecting civic engagement to positive youth development (e.g., Baldi et al., 2001; Flanagan, Syvertsen, & Stout, 2007; Johnson, Johnson-Pynn, & Johnson, 2007; Keeter, Jenkins, Zukin, & Andolina, 2003; Reinders & Youniss, 2006; Shiarella, McCarthy, & Tucker, 2000; Torney-Purta, Lehman, & Oswald, & Schulz, 2001). However, the majority of empirical evidence that supports this link between civic engagement and positive youth development is aimed at adolescents (ages 14-17) and young adults (ages 18 to 24).

In contrast, aside from a few preliminary studies (Nicotera, 2008; RMC Research Corporation, 2005, 2006; Wilson, Dasho, Martin, Wallerstein, Wang, & Minkler, 2007), there is a dearth of similar empirical evidence for preadolescents.[1] Instead, assertions that community engagement promotes positive development in preadolescents tend to be anecdotal (e.g., Driskell, 2002; Ginwright & Cammarota, 2007). For example, based on his international work, Driskell (2002) observes that children who play an active part in community development "increase their self-esteem and sense of self and pride, [as well as] learn about democracy, develop acceptance for diversity of people and ideas, develop a sense of caring for their local environment and a civic outlook" (p. 35). The few empirical studies and anecdotal assertions suggest encouraging outcomes that warrant further research with this younger population. However, more evidence is needed to fully assess the effects of civic participation among preadolescents. Development of civic engagement measures aimed at this younger population is essential to establishing this evidence.

Concepts and measures related to civic engagement among adolescents and young adults have received substantial scholarly attention. Various researchers (Flanagan et al., 2007; Keeter et al., 2003; Moely, Mercer, Illustre, Miron, & McFarland, 2002; Reinders & Youniss, 2006; Shiarella et al., 2000) have made inroads to measures of civic engagement for use with this age group (ages 14 to 24 years), while others have focused on developing conceptual frameworks of civic engagement (Atkins & Hart, 2003; Borden & Serido, 2009; Flanagan et al., 2007; Lerner et al., 2003). Although some of the components of civic engagement covered in these frameworks focus on constructs that are less applicable to preadolescents, such as following sociopolitical issues in the news media and writing opinion letters to local media outlets, other concepts that emanate from this work provide a useful lens for considering civic engagement among preadolescents. For example, attitudes and skills that promote tolerance for diversity of ideas, a willingness to help others, and an awareness of one's community are all components of civic engagement as conceptualized and measured among adolescents and young adults that can be applied to younger youth. This existing body of work serves as a basis for developing a conceptual framework and measure of civic engagement for use with preadolescents.

Conceptualizing Civic Engagement for Preadolescents

As previously noted, conceptualizations of the civically engaged young person tend to be geared toward adolescents and young adults (Golombek, 2006; Jans, 2004). Civic engagement measures that do encompass preadolescents tend toward an emphasis on civic knowledge about government and democracy taught in schools (e.g. National Assessment of Educational Progress [NAEP], 1998) as opposed to attitudes, skills, and actions that may lead to age-appropriate civic participation in this younger population. However, a number of scholars emphasize more general frameworks for civic engagement that extend beyond civic knowledge.

We have reviewed frameworks that focus specifically on the development of attitudes, skills and actions that underlie civic engagement (e.g., Atkins & Hart, 2003; Flanagan, 2003; Lerner et al., 2003). While these models were generally developed with older youth in mind, they can be applied to preadolescents who need to develop the attitudes, skills, and actions that form a foundation for future civic participation. We summarize the concepts derived from these models in terms of civic attitudes and civic skills/actions in Exhibit 4.1. Civic skills and actions are considered together since they are often intertwined, in that actions are often a demonstration of skills. Civic attitudes are addressed separately from skills and actions because one can have the skills necessary to take action, but lack the civic attitudes that would lead one to put those skills into action.

**Exhibit 4.1.   Conceptual Summary of Attitudes
and Skills/Actions for Civic Engagement**

Scholars	*Attitudes*
Atkins and Hart (2003)	• a sense of connection to a geographically located and bounded community such that proximity is a basis for interaction among the people who reside within it • a sense of the rights and responsibilities associated with the well-being of one's community of location
Flanagan (2003)	• positive influence of family tendencies toward social responsibility • the elements of a civic ethic or social trust include self-transcendence, compassion, and caring for others within an ethos that one's own enhancement is connected to the well-being of others and vice versa • Unlearning stereotypes
Lerner et al. (2000)	• in the American milieu, values for "equity, democracy, social justice, and personal freedom" (p. 176) • the "five C's" of positive youth development: competence, confidence, character, social connection, and caring
Pittman, Irby, Tolman, Yohalem, and Ferber (2003)	• "the growing recognition of one's impact on one's surroundings and responsibility to others" (p.10)

Scholars	*Skills/Actions*
Torney-Purta (2002)	• ability to "be comfortable participating in respectful discussions of important and potentially controversial issues" (p. 203)
Lerner et al. (2003); Torney-Purta (2002)	• acting in the interests of others with whom one shares community, "transcendence of self-interest" • "Extending rights to others, especially to disenfranchised or marginalized populations (p. 206)
Pittman, Irby, Tolman, Yohalem, and Ferber (2003)	• "the ability and opportunity to work collaboratively with others for a common goal" (p.10)
Flanagan (2003) Lerner et al. (2003); Torney-Purta (2002)	• Young people contributing to and benefiting their communities • Young people acting as leaders in efforts to enhance social justice and the social life of their communities
Flanagan (2003)	• Participation in activities that require working together with a heterogeneous group of peers through which they develop trust, unlearn stereotypes, and begin to see the interrelatedness of their fortunes with the fortunes of others

The conceptualization of civic engagement as comprised of civic attitudes, skills and actions is echoed in Flanagan and Faison's (2001) definition of civic attachment. Their definition includes (1) a sense of one's importance as a member of a community and (2) the desire to contribute to the well-being of that community, as well as the skill/action of having a voice in relation to community concerns. Pittman, Irby, Tolman, Yohalem, and Ferber's (2003) approach also combines civic attitudes, skills and actions, as they suggest that "civic development and engagement [include] the growing recognition of one's impact on one's surroundings and responsibility to others as well as the ability and opportunity to work collaboratively with others for a common goal" (p.10).

The framework presented in Exhibit 4.1 is aligned with Jans' (2004) recommendation that, in order to be useful for considering preadolescents' abilities for participation in civic life, definitions of civic engagement must incorporate attitudes and skills for connecting and contributing to one's community on various levels. Similarly, Camino and Zeldin (2002) suggest that more age-inclusive conceptualizations of civic engagement should consider the development of agency or actions taken to influence decisions within a group or collaborative effort. The broader perspective on civic participation and engagement described in this section may serve as a response to calls for conceptualizations of civic engagement that include preadolescents (Golombek, 2006).

In summary, the civic engagement framework presented in Exhibit 4.1 suggests that *civic attitudes* seen in preadolescents are comprised of (1) a sense of connection to one's community of location and the notion that belonging to a community comes with rights and responsibilities for its health (Atkins & Hart, 2003), and 2) social trust and a civic ethic that require persistent faith in others "on the basis of what they can be sometimes" (Flanagan, 2003, p. 169). Key *civic skills/actions* among preadolescents include 1) the capacity to see beyond one's own self interest (Lerner et al., 2003), such as "extending rights to others especially to disenfranchised or marginalized populations" (Torney-Purta, 2002, p. 206); (2) the capacity to remain in relationship with others, even when controversial issues arise (Atkins & Hart, 2003); (3) playing an active role to make changes in one's school or neighborhood, and 4) willingly assisting peers, even when it takes time away from one's own self interests (Flanagan 2003). On the basis of this review, we developed a working definition of civic engagement that is inclusive of preadolescents: *A sense of connection to and responsibility for others with whom one shares a geographic locality* (Atkins & Hart, 2003) *combined with collaboration and participation* (Flanagan, 2003; Lerner et al., 2003; Lerner, Fisher & Weinberg, 2000; Pittman et al., 2003) *that foster connection and responsibility across multi-*

cultural differences (Flanagan 2003; Lerner et al., 2003; Torney-Purta, 2002).

Existing Measurement Tools

Instruments for measuring civic engagement in older adolescents and young adults that may be conceptually appropriate for use with younger youth are reviewed below. Although we are aware of the work of many scholars who have developed measures for older youth, presenting all such measures is beyond the scope of this paper (e.g., Ammon, Furco, Chi, & Middaugh, 2002; Andolina, Keeter, Zukin, & Jenkins, 2003; Education Commission of the States (ECS, n.d.); Flanagan et al. (2007); Keeter et al., 2003; Moely et al., 2002; NAEP, 1998; National Center for Learning and Citizenship, 2004; Shiarella et al., 2000; Torney-Purta et al., 2001; Torney-Purta & Vermeer, 2004).

Below, we describe measures that are consistent with the conceptual frameworks for development of civic attitudes, skills, and actions among preadolescents. Then, we discuss two measures developed specifically for preadolescents and describe how our study furthers this work. Flanagan et al. (2007) developed a measure for seventh through 12th graders that consists of 14 general areas of civic engagement, each of which is assessed through a number of subscales. Four of their subscales address civic attitudes: (1) trustworthiness of elected officials (e.g., elected officials listen to citizens; care about citizens more than money); (2) civic accountability (e.g., active involvement in my community is my responsibility); (3) government responsiveness to "the People" (e.g., government does not care about ordinary people); and (4) unconditional support for government policies (e.g., newspapers should not criticize the government). Three subscales are specific to skills and actions: (1) competence for civic action (e.g., write an opinion letter, create a plan to address a community problem); (2) political voice (e.g., contact or visit government representative); and (3) critical consumer of political information (e.g., try to decide if a news story is just telling one side of a story).

Moely and colleagues (2002) created a measure called the Civic Attitudes and Skills Questionnaire, which was tested on undergraduate college students. This instrument covers six general areas: civic action, interpersonal and problem solving skills, political awareness, leadership skills, social justice attitudes, and diversity attitudes. Andolina and colleagues (2003) developed the 19-item Index of Civic and Political Engagement, which has been used with adolescents as young as 15 years, as well as with adults. The index is concerned with four broad conceptual areas: "(1) civic indicators (e.g., community problem solving, regular volunteering, active member of group or association, participation in fund raising); (2) electoral indicators (e.g., regular voting, campaign contributions); (3) indicators of political voice (e.g., contact elected officials or print media, protesting, boycotting); and (4) indicators of attentiveness (e.g., following public affairs, regular reading of news papers)" (p. 5).

The Education Commission of the States (ECS, n.d.) has compiled what may be one of the most encompassing databases for measuring civic engagement in students of grades 3 through 12. The database incorporates items from various sources available for public use via the Civic Assessment Data Base. Publications related to these items suggest that they cover four broad areas of civic engagement: civic dispositions, civic knowledge, civic thinking skills, and civic participation skills (Torney-Purta & Vermeer, 2004). Civic dispositions refer to respect and support for others, laws, social norms, and basic democratic values. Civic knowledge includes items that query respondents about (1) the structure and principles of democracy and government and their foundations, (2) the roles that citizens play in formal institutions, and (3) the roles played by individuals in a civil society or democracy. Civic thinking skills are delineated as the ability: (1) to read and understand information about the government and issues in the media, (2) to differentiate between fact and opinion, and (3) to articulate abstract concepts such as democracy. Civic participation skills are described as those that allow one to (1) analyze public issues and to understand conversations related to issues that arise during election times, (2) use leadership skills to motivate groups to act, and (3) use communication skills to resolve conflicts that arise in group processes. (ECS, n.d.; Torney-Purta & Vermeer, 2004). Custom surveys can be created from the ECS data base. However, the majority of the items represent age-bound abilities, with only a few of the items geared toward the capacities of preadolescents.

A thorough search of print and web-based literature uncovered two civic engagement instruments specifically designed to be developmentally appropriate for preadolescents (Chi, Jastrzab, & Melchior, 2006; Furco, Muller, & Ammon, 1998). To varying degrees, these measures incorporate the broader, developmentally inclusive conceptualization of civic engagement already discussed. These measures provide a sound foundation for furthering research in this area. The first measure was developed by the Center for Information and Research on Civic Learning and Engagement (Chi et al., 2006). It includes the same categories as the ECS database, but specifically articulates them for use with elementary school-age children beginning in kindergarten. The goal of Chi and colleagues was to develop a framework for the acquisition of civic competence that includes basic knowledge about democracy, but also encompasses more foundational attitudes, skills, and actions such as making choices and accepting the results of those choices, acknowledging one's capacity to impact others, and recognizing that following rules benefits the safety of others beyond the self. Their items lean more toward knowledge, attitudes, skills, and actions that are developmentally appropriate for preadolescents. For example, at the most basic level, civic knowledge includes comprehension of the concept of "community" and what it means to be a member of a community, why rules and laws exist, and recognition of multicultural differences. At this most basic level, civic thinking skills include the capacity to recognize differences between self and others including how others might feel or think, the ability to describe one's actions and the reasons for taking those actions, and being able to present one's own ideas and support those ideas with evidence. Civic participation skills are translated for these younger youth as the ability for self-management and for following group norms, the ability to listen while others speak and wait one's turn to speak or to take turns in general, and the ability to work together with same-age children to solve conflicts without fighting. Finally, positive civic dispositions of preadolescents encompass the demonstration of respect and empathy for others, willingness to help others out, following rules, and paying attention in the classroom. The knowledge, skills, and attitudes associated with each conceptual area increase from this foundation as young people age across the elementary school grades. Chi and colleagues' (2006) four conceptual areas are assessed with a total of 55 items, some of them adapted from existing instruments, that were tested in a national pilot study with approximately 500 young people. Their work provided information on internal consistency of each scale. All but two of the subscales had Cronbach alpha scores between .64 and .78 when four outlier items were removed. This work provides a solid conceptual base, but no data reduction or factor verification techniques, such as exploratory and confirmatory factor analysis, were applied to the survey items.

A second measure for preadolescents, developed by Furco et al. (1998), uses ten items to assess civic engagement. The items group into three categories that the authors label as connection to community ($\alpha = .53$; feel I am a part of the community, I know a lot of people in my community), civic awareness ($\alpha = .53$; helping others is important), and civic efficacy ($\alpha = .59$; feel like I can make a difference in the community). The measure's overall reliability is .76. The three conceptual categories identified by Furco and colleagues are similar to the broad categories noted by Chi and her colleagues (2006), but place less emphasis on basic civic knowledge about democracy and government.

In sum, the measures for civic engagement reviewed here emphasize a broad range of civic knowledge, attitudes, skills, and actions. This range is consistent with Youniss et al.'s (2002) continuum approach to measuring civic behaviors of young people. This approach suggests that civic engagement covers an array of knowledge and action from political participation/knowledge (e.g., voting and understanding the political process of democracy) to political actions (e.g., protesting) to community service (e.g., serving one's neighborhood, school, or religious institution). For example, researchers studying outcomes in a school setting, where young people are gaining academic knowledge about the origins of democracy and how it works, may elect to apply measures with greater emphasis on traditional civic knowledge or the political participation/knowledge part of the continuum. In contrast, researchers who are interested in the outcomes of service learning and community youth-led organizing, where the emphasis is on hands-on learning, may choose measures that are geared toward assessment of civic attitudes, skills, and actions that may result from community service (Youniss et al., 2002).

The Pre-Adolescent Civic Engagement Scale (PACES) developed and assessed in this study aims to evaluate civic engagement outcomes that result from hands-on involvement in service learning and youth-led organizing. It includes items geared toward assessing attitudes, skills and actions related to the community service sector of the Youniss and colleagues (2002) continuum, and builds on previous work, especially that of Chi et al. (2006) and Furco and colleagues (1998). Our study furthers this area of research by applying data reduction and factor verification to develop a more psychometrically sound measure.

METHOD

Participants

A survey was administered to a group of children and young adolescents in a northeastern U.S. city by City Year (Sample 1). Collaboration between the first author and City Year allowed for administering the survey to a second sample of youth in a US city in the mountain west (Sample 2). The combined samples consist of 287 young people aged 7 to 14 years (Sample 1 $n = 136$; Sample 2 $n = 151$). The combined samples include a nearly equal numbers of boys and girls from a range of racial and ethnic backgrounds. The majority of the respondents were young people of color with a small minority of Euro-Americans represented. All respondents lived in low-income urban neighborhoods. Sample 1 represents administrative data collected by City Year Boston. Therefore, specific demographics of this sample are not available. However, the two co-authors formerly associated with City Year confirm that participants were in grades 6 -8 and resemble the gender, social class, and ethnicities noted above. The first author collected the demographics for Sample 2 when she administered the survey. The average age in this second sample is 10. Five years and gender is nearly equal (52% boys). The majority of Sample 2 is Latino (70%) with 18% African American, 8% Euro American, and 4% Asian American.

Procedure

Participants in Sample 1 completed the paper and pencil survey independently, while participants in Sample 2 completed the survey in one-to-one settings. For example, participants in Sample 1completed the survey within the context of a group of peers and were given directions to ensure that they understood that the survey was not a test and did not contain right or wrong answers. Youth in Sample 2 heard similar directions, but completed the survey with a familiar person who was either the first author or one of her trained research assistants, all of whom had other contact with the youth through volunteering at the after-school program they attended. Survey questions were read out loud and each participant used a pencil to circle the desired response to each item. Surveys were delivered in English, as all participants used English as their predominant language.

Although survey administration differed between the two samples, the Cronbach alpha's for the two components of PACES (described below) were similar for the two samples (α = .765 & .711 for Sample 1, and α = .799 & .659 for Sample 2) indicating the integrity of the measure across these different types of survey administration.

Initial Survey

A 39-item survey was created to assess a range of civic engagement attitudes, skills and actions. The items were compiled and developed by a team of City Year researchers in consultation with a panel of national experts on youth civic engagement (Research and Systematic Learning, n.d.; Schneider-Munoz, Webman, & Sarvey, n.d.). The resulting items, with Likert-type responses, were comprised of questions from various "nationally recognized surveys in the public domain" (Schneider-Munoz et al., n.d), as well as questions posed in existing City Year surveys. The City Year Research and Systematic Learning team intended the survey items to represent categories suggested in the literature (civic attitudes and skills), with the addition of categories not directly addressed in the literature (values and transformation).

RESULTS

Data Analyses

Preliminary principal component analyses were conducted on the 39 survey items to assess the viability of a measure with civic and social development subscales of attitudes, skills, values, and transformation as proposed during survey development (Research and Systematic Learning, n.d.; Schneider-Munoz et al., n.d.). Unfortunately, the pattern of youth responses did not correspond to the categories originally proposed by the City Year team. Consequently, exploratory factor analyses were utilized to identify a factor structure represented by the survey items. The first data sample ($n = 136$) was used for this purpose, because it included youth who were involved in City Year programming and for whom the survey was originally intended.

To identify the optimum number of factors, parallel analysis (Horn, 1965) and minimum average partial correlation (MAP) tests (Velicer, 1976) were conducted in SPSS 16.0 as described by (O'Connor, 2000). These two techniques produce less biased estimates of the number of factors than more widely used eigenvalues greater than one and scree plot techniques (Zwick & Velicer, 1986). For example, both parallel analysis and MAP identified a three-factor solution as optimal, while up to seven factors were shown to have eigenvalues greater than one. In subsequent exploratory factor analyses, we focused on two, three and four factor solutions.

Exploratory Factor Analyses

Exploratory factor analyses (EFA) were conducted in Mplus 5.1 using maximum likelihood estimation and geomin rotation. An oblique rotation was used to account for the likely correlations between factors, and, indeed, significant interfactor correlations were identified. The following strategies were used to simplify factor structure in the EFA process: (1) items with no significant loadings on any factor were removed; (2) items with significant but low loadings on multiple factors were removed; (3) emerging factors were assessed for thematic consistency and thematically inconsistent items were removed. Exploratory factor analyses resulted in the identification of three possible models, with two, three and four factors each.

Confirmatory Factor Analyses

Confirmatory factor analyses (also in Mplus 5.1) were applied to the second sample ($n = 151$) as a means of assessing the three possible models identified in the EFA. Youth in the second sample were geographically distant from the first group and were not involved with City Year, thus providing a good test of the robustness of the measure. CFA models were assessed using chi-square, the comparative fit index (CFI), the root mean square error of approximation (RMSEA), and the standardized root mean residual (SRMR) to evaluate fit between models and the observed data, with cutoff values of .95 for CFI and .06 for RMSEA and SRMR establishing good fit (Hu & Bentler, 1999).

The CFAs with Sample 2 identified one well-fitting model among the three models that had been identified in the exploratory factor analyses. The two-factor model has an excellent fit to the data ($\chi^2(43) = 48.056$, $p = .275$; CFI = .986; RMSEA = .028; SRMR = .052). Conceptually, the two factors represent measures of attitudes, skills, and actions, with the first one labeled *foundation for civic ethics* and the second labeled *community connection*. The eleven items comprising the two factors appear in Exhibit 4.2 along with corresponding Chronbach alpha's for each of the samples and factor loadings from the CFA. A discussion of how this civic engagement measure fits within the conceptual framework presented earlier appears in the next section.

Exhibit 4.2.   Components of the Civic Engagement Scale for Preadolescents

Factor 1—Foundation for Civic Ethics α =.765 (Sample 1); α =.799 (Sample 2)	*Factor Loadings* *(Sample 2)*
I should be the one to help	1.000
I like doing something to help in my neighborhood.	0.987
I let others know I want to help.	0.763
I like doing activities with other people.	0.724
I like to help other people even if it is hard work.	0.488
It's important to take care of people who are in need of help.	0.470
Factor 2—Community Connection α =.711 (Sample 1); α =.659 (Sample 2)	
I participate in projects that help my neighborhood.	1.000
When I help out in the neighborhood I make friends.	0.814
As I get older, I plan to help my neighborhood, family, or school.	0.703
People in my neighborhood take care of me.	0.697
If I had to take time away from one of my favorite activities to work on a project that makes my neighborhood a better place, I would.	0.584

DISCUSSION

The eleven items in the Pre-Adolescent Civic Engagement Scale (PACES) form two subscales that cover a range of civic attitudes and civic skills and actions as outlined in our literature review. The foundation for civic ethics subscale addresses civic attitudes and skills/actions that form the basis for future civic involvement, and can be viewed as values, preferences, and actions aimed at the general world. The community connection subscale encompasses actions on the part of youth or community members that reflect a place-based commitment, placing civic attitudes and civic skills/action within the context of one's community of location or neighborhood.

Items representing the foundation for civic ethics component include attitudes related a civic ethic or social trust as described by Flanagan (2003) as well as by Lerner and colleagues (2000) caring element of the five "C's" (e.g., I like to help other people even if it is hard work). Another item, "I like doing activities with other people" addresses the social interactive element of the five "C's" (Lerner et al., 2000). Pittman and colleagues (2003) conceptualization of civic engagement as including "a sense of responsibility to others" is addressed with items like, "It is important to take care of people who are in need." Finally, this component also assesses a skill/action related to another element of the five "C's", competence (e.g., I let others know I want to help).

The second component, community connection, addresses civic attitudes and skills/action within the context of one's own neighborhood. For example Atkins and Hart's (2003) conceptualization of civic engagement as encompassing "connection to a geographically-located and bounded community" is summed up in items assessing attitudes such as "People in my neighborhood take care of me" and "As I get older I plan to help my neighborhood, family, or school." A third item, "If I had to take time away from one of my activities to work on a project that makes my neighborhood a better place, I would" addresses Atkins and Hart's characterization of civic engagement as inclusive of a sense of the rights and responsibilities associated with the well-being of one's community of location. Items assessing skills/action such as "I participate in projects that help my neighborhood" address several scholars' characterization of civic engagement as including contributions that benefit one's community (Flanagan, 2003; Lerner et al., 2003; Torney-Purta, 2002). Finally, another item, "When I help out in the neighborhood I make friends" addresses Pittman and colleagues (2003) view that civic engagement includes "the ability and opportunity to work collaboratively with others for a common goal" (p. 10).

The two components of PACES—foundation for civic ethics and community connection—most likely work in tandem. For example, the elements of civic ethics alone are not likely to turn into civic engagement without a meaningful connection to a site of action. On the other hand, a connection to a community of location on its own is not likely to lead specifically to civic engagement without the foundation for a civic ethic. Thus, these two components together form the necessary raw materials to support future civic engagement. Foundation for civic ethics and community connection are indicative of preadolescents' developing civic capacities, and may be predictive of future civic engagement in the form of community participation and service.

We recognize that the items used in this scale may be seen as representing the notion of a charity approach to civic engagement rather than a social change orientation (Morton, 1995), conceptualizations often applied to adults or older adolescents. The nature of the PACES items is justified on the basis of several important points. The first point addresses the developmental phase of preadolescents for whom PACES is intended. PACES items reflect the foundational seeds of thriving (Lerner, Brentano, Dowling, & Anderson, 2002) that are required for becoming adolescents with an orientation toward "promoting equity, democracy, social justice, and personal freedom (p. 22). This process is further described by Lerner and colleagues (2002; Lerner, Freund, De Stefanis, & Habermas, 2001; Lerner & Spanier, 1980):

Developmentally emergent and contextually mediated successful regulation of positive person-context relations ensures that individuals have the nurturance and support needed for healthy development. Simultaneously, such regulation produces, for society, people having the mental and behavioral capacities—the inner and outer lives—requisite to maintain, perpetuate, and enhance socially just, equitable, and democratic institutions" (Lerner et al., 2002, p. 27).

Secondly, preadolescent cognitive processes tend to be concrete, with limited capacity for abstract reasoning (Piaget, 1952). Therefore, they would not be likely to provide reliable and valid data when reading and responding to more abstract items about social justice and equity. At these younger ages, the beginning of the ability to understand a social justice orientation is likely to arise from concrete hands-on activities, accompanied by hands-on analysis and verbal discussions. Researchers and practitioners can gain a glimpse into evolving verbal abilities to consider these more abstract ideas from qualitative studies on preadolescents and civic engagement. For example, concrete activities to foster preadolescent civic engagement and peer-to-peer group conversations about the evidence gathered from such activities suggest the beginning ability to understand the concept of helping within a social justice orientation. In one such study, the theme *getting along* emerged and "was indicated in the data by examples of positive social skills in action as well as recognition among the children of the need for respecting differences in both ideas and cultures" (Nicotera, 2008, p. 237). The following quote from an 8-year-old child in this study represents the level of social justice orientation one might expect in younger youth:

> It's, um, easy to work with other people. Because, because, they're just, they're just, um, people.... They're the same, they're like us but they're like, they might be a different color from us and you can't, and I'm like you can't, like, just say.... Say they wanna be your friend. And they're like ah, I was wishin', um, would you like to be my friend? You can't just say no because they're a different color from you. Even if you're a different color you could just be friends with them, instead of making fun of their color and stuff.

In another study (Nicotera & Matera, 2010) that engaged preadolescents in hands-on neighborhood assessment along with neighborhood action days, an 11 year old wrote the following to accompany the photo she took of a vacant lot in the neighborhood:

> Here I see a paint barrel and shopping carts pushed over. What is really happening here is trash is destroying our world. I could convince people to not throw garbage there too. We could go and pick up the trash.

This quote demonstrates the beginning capacity of preadolescents to consider, in very concrete terms, an adult idea that a social justice orientation to helping requires thinking globally and acting locally.

In conclusion, the range of attitudes, skills, actions, and knowledge that have been considered in relation to the development of capacity for civic engagement is sizeable. Youniss and colleagues (2002) suggest that it is important to consider this entire range, from political knowledge to involvement in civil society. The developmental trajectory associated with the expansion of civic engagement capacity (Hart, 2002) suggests that civic attitudes, skills and actions are likely to be more relevant for preadolescents, rather than knowledge about and participation in democratic processes. While it is important for young people to develop knowledge regarding democratic processes, such as following political issues and how a bill becomes a law, this knowledge is more indicative of classroom-based learning. When assessing the civic engagement of preadolescents engaged in service learning or community participation, it is more relevant to measure civic attitude, skills, and actions.

Civic attitudes, skills, and actions, as operationalized in PACES, can be assessed at multiple ages as youth participate in service learning either in school or during out of school time. The two components, foundation for civic ethics and community connection, are consistent with the conceptual approaches of civic engagement scholars (Atkins & Hart, 2003; Flanagan, 2003; Flanagan & Faison, 2001). In fact, the two capacities are interrelated; in order to develop the belief that one should act on behalf of the well-being of a collective (e.g., civic ethic), a child must also develop the sense of belonging to that collective (e.g., connection to a collectivity).

The first goal of our ongoing research was to create a parsimonious measure that would make it feasible to evaluate the development of civic capacity among preadolescents. The current study provides the conceptual basis for the PACES and a preliminary assessment of the scale using two independent samples. The results further the excellent work of other scholars (Chi et al.,2006; Furco et al., 1998) who focus on measures for preadolescents. In addition, other research with PACES demonstrates that it is predictive of academic positive youth development (Altschul & Nicotera, 2010). However, the work to date is limited by the lack of criterion validation, the cross-sectional nature of the data, and the relatively small sample size. Further testing of the Pre-Adolescent Civic Engagement Scale via full psychometric procedures with larger samples and in conjunction with criterion measures is needed to demonstrate its utility for assessing preadolescents' developing civic capacities.

NOTE

1. In this paper we refer to middle childhood ages and early adolescent ages as preadolescence.

REFERENCES

Altschul, I., & Nicotera, N. (2010, January). *Connecting civic engagement with positive academic development in adolescents*. Paper presented at the Society for Social Work Research Conference, San Francisco, CA.

Ammon, M., Furco, A., Chi, B., & Middaugh, E. (2002, March). *Service learning in California: A profile of the CalServe service learning partnerships (1997-2000)*. Berkeley, CA: University of California, Berkeley: Service Learning-Research and Development Center.

Andolina, M., Keeter, S., Zukin, C., & Jenkins, K., (2003). *A guide to the index of civic and political engagement*. Retrieved from http://www.civicyouth.org/Core_Indicators_page.htm

Atkins, R., & Hart, D. (2003). Neighborhoods, adults, and the development of civic identity in urban youth. *Applied Developmental Science, 7*, 156-164.

Baldi, S., Perie, M., Skidmore, D., Greenberg, E., Hahn, C. & Nelson, D. (2001). *What democracy means to ninth-graders: U.S. results from the International IEA Civic Education Study*. Washington, DC: U.S. Government Printing Office.

Balsano, A. (2005). Youth civic engagement in the United States: Understanding and addressing the impact of social impediments on positive youth community development. *Applied Developmental Science, 9(4)*, 188-201.

Bolland, J. (2003). Hopelessness and risk behavior among adolescents living in high-poverty inner-city neighborhoods. *Journal of Adolescence, 26*, 145-158.

Borden, L., & Serido, J. (2009). From program participant to engaged citizen: A developmental journey. *Journal of Community Psychology, 37(4)*, 423-438.

Camino, L., & Zeldin, S. (2002). From periphery to center: Pathways for youth civic engagement in the day to day life of communities. *Applied Developmental Science, 6(4)*, 213-220.

Chi, B., Jastrzab, J., & Melchior, A. (2006). *Developing indicators and measures of civic outcomes for elementary school students.* Retrieved from http://www.civicyouth.org/PopUps/WorkingPapers/WP47chi.pdf

Driskell, D. (2002). *Creating better cities with children and youth.* London, England: Earthscan.

Education Commission of the States. (n.d.). *Civic competency categories.* Retrieved from http://www.ecs.org/QNA/docs/Civic_Competency.pdf

Flanagan, C. (2003). Trust, identity, and civic hope. *Journal of Applied Developmental Science, 7(3)*, 165-171).

Flanagan, C., & Faison, N. (2001). *Youth civic development: Implications of research for social policy and programs.* Ann Arbor, MI.: Society for Research in Child Development.

Flanagan, C., Syvertsen, A., & Stout, M. (2007) *Civic measurement models: Tapping adolescent's civic engagement.* Retrieved from http://www.civicyouth.org/PopUps/WorkingPapers/WP55Flannagan.pdf)

Furco, A., Muller, P. & Ammon, M. (1998). *Civic responsibility survey for K-12 students engaged in service-Learning.* Retrieved from http://cart.rmcdenver.com/instruments/civic_responsibility.pdf

Ginwright, S., & Cammarota, J. (2007). Youth activism in the urban community: Learning critical civic praxis with community organizations. *International Journal of Qualitative Studies in Education, 20(6)*, 693-710.

Golombek, S. (2006). Children as citizens. *Journal of Community Practice, 14(1/2)*, 9-28.

Hart, R. (2002). *Children's participation.* London, England: Earthscan Publications.

Horn, J. L. (1965). A rationale and test for the number of factors in factor analysis. *Psychometrika, 30(2)*, 179-185.

Hu, L., & Bentler, P. M. (1999). Cutoff criteria for fit indexes in covariance structure analysis: Conventional criteria versus new alternatives. *Structural Equation Modeling, 6(1)*, 1-55.

Jans, M. (2004). Children as citizens: Towards a contemporary notion of child participation. *Childhood: A Global Journal of Child Research, 11*, 27-44.

Johnson, L., Johnson-Pynn, J., & Johnson, T. (2007). Youth civic engagement in China: Results from a program promoting environmental activism. *Journal of Adolescent Research, 22(4)*, 355-386.

Keeter, S., Jenkins, K., Zukin, C., & Andolina, M. (2003, March). *Three measures of community-based civic engagement: Evidence from the youth civic engagement indica-*

tors project. Paper presented at the Child Trends Conference on Indicators of Positive Development, Washington, DC.

Lerner, R., Brentano, C., Dowling, E., & Anderson, P. (2002). Positive youth development: Thriving as the basis of personhood and civil society. *New Directions for Youth Development, 95,* 11-33.

Lerner, R., Dowling, E., & Anderson, P. (2003). Positive youth development: Thriving as the basis of personhood and civil society. *Applied Developmental Science, 7*(3), 172-180.

Lerner, R., Fisher, C., & Weinberg, R. (2000). Toward a science for and of the people: Promoting civil society through the application of developmental science. *Child Development, 71,* 11-20).

Lerner, R., Freund, A., De Stefanis, I., & Habermas, T. (2001). Understanding developmental regulation in adolescence: The use of the selection, optimization, and compensation model. *Human Development, 44,* 29-50.

Lerner, R., & Spanier, G. (1980). *Adolescent development: A life-span perspective.* New York, NY: McGraw-Hill.

Moely, B., Mercer, S., Illustre, V., Miron, D., & McFarland, M. (2002). Psychometric properties and correlates of the civic attitudes and skills questionnaire (CASQ): A measure of students' attitudes related to service learning. *Michigan Journal of Service Learning, 8*(2), 15-26.

Morton, K. (1995). The irony of service: Charity, project and social change in service-learning. *Michigan Journal of Community Service Learning, 2*(1), 5-18.

National Assessment of Educational Progress. (1998). *Civics framework for the 1998 National Assessment of Educational Progress.* Retrieved from http://www.nagb.org/pubs/civics.pdf

National Center for Learning and Citizenship. (2004). *Developing citizenship competencies from kindergarten through grade 12.* Denver, CO: Education Commission of the States.

Nicotera, N. (2008). Building skills for civic engagement: Children as agents of neighborhood change. *Journal of Community Practice, 16*(2), 221-242.

Nicotera, N., & Matera, D. (2010, January). *Building civic leadership through neighborhood-based afterschool programming.* Paper presented at the conference of Society for Social Work Research, San Francisco, CA.

O'Connor, B. P. (2000). SPSS and SAS programs for determining the number of components using parallel analysis and Velicer's MAP test. *Behavior Research Methods, Instruments & Computers, 32*(3), 396-402.

Piaget, J. (1952). *The origins of intelligence in children.* New York, NY: International Universities Press.

Pittman, K., Irby, M., Tolman, J., Yohalem, N., & Ferber, T. (2003). *Preventing problems, promoting development, encouraging engagement: Competing priorities or inseparable goals?* Washington, DC: The Forum for Youth Investment, Impact Strategies. Retrieved from www.forumfyi.org

Reinders, H., & Youniss, J. (2006). School-based community service and civic development in adolescents. *Applied Developmental Science, 10*(1), 2-12.

Research and Systematic Learning. (n.d.). *Survey measure of youth civic engagement and social development.* City Year, Boston, MA: Unpublished survey questionnaire.

RMC Research Corporation. (2005, October). *Public achievement evaluation report*. Minneapolis, MN: Center for Democracy and Citizenship, Humphrey Institute of Public Affairs.

RMC Research Corporation. (2006, October). *Public achievement evaluation report*. Minneapolis, MN: Center for Democracy and Citizenship, Humphrey Institute of Public Affairs.

Schneider-Munoz, A., Webman, B., & Sarvey, J. (n.d.) *Civic youth development index: Survey guide*. Civic Leadership Department, City Year, Inc.: Unpublished white paper.

Shiarella, A., McCarthy, A., & Tucker, M. (2000). Development and construct validity of scores on the community service attitudes scale. *Educational and Psychological Measurement, 60*(2), 286-300.

Torney-Purta, J. (2002). The school's role in developing civic engagement. *Applied Developmental Science 6*(4), 203-212

Torney-Purta, J., Lehman, R., Oswald, H., & Schulz, W. (2001). *Citizenship and education in twenty-eight countries: Civic knowledge and engagement at age fourteen.* Retrieved from http://www.wam.umd.edu/~jtpurta/

Torney-Purta, J., & Vermeer, S. (2004). *Developing citizenship competencies from Kindergarten through 12th grade: A background paper for policymakers and educators*. Denver, CO: Education Commission of the States. Retrieved from http://www.ecs.org/html/projectsPartners/nclc/docs/DevelopingCompetencies.pdf

Velicer, W. F. (1976). Determining the number of components from the matrix of partial correlations. *Psychometrika, 41*(3), 321-327.

Wilson, N., Dasho, S., Martin, A., Wallerstein, N., Wang, C. & Minkler, M. (2007). Engaging young adolescents in social action through photovoice: The Youth Empowerment Strategies (YES!) project. *Journal of Early Adolescence, 27*(2), 241-261.

Yates, M., & Youniss, J. (1996). A developmental perspective on community service in adolescence. *Social Development, 5*(1), 85-111.

Youniss, J., Bales, S., Christmas-Best, V., Diversi, M., McLaughlin, M., & Silbereisen, R. (2002). Youth civic engagement in the twenty-first century. *Journal of Research on Adolescence, 12*(1), 121-148.

Zwick, W. R., & Velicer, W. F. (1986). Comparison of five rules for determining the number of components to retain. *Psychological Bulletin, 99*(3), 432-442.

CHAPTER 5

THE RELATIONSHIP BETWEEN THE QUALITY OF SERVICE-LEARNING INTERVENTIONS AND TEEN SEATBELT USE

Janet Eyler, L. Richard Bradley, Irwin Goldzweig, David Schlundt, and Paul Juarez

The Teen Service-Learning Project (TSLP) tests the potential of peer-to-peer, student-designed and implemented service-learning projects to increase seatbelt use among urban high school minority youth. The present study focused on the relationship between the quality of the service-learning interventions and student knowledge, attitudes, and behaviors related to seatbelt use. The quality of the service-learning intervention was positively associated with increased driver and passenger seatbelt use, greater motivation for drivers and passengers to use seatbelts, and reduction of perceived barriers to seatbelt use among African Americans. From the perspective of service-learning participants, the quality of the service-learning experience and reflection using discussion were significant predictors of personal development, school and community engagement, and safety related outcomes.

Research for What? Making Engaged Scholarship Matter
pp. 91–118
Copyright © 2010 by Information Age Publishing
All rights of reproduction in any form reserved.

91

African American and Hispanic young people suffer disproportionate risk of preventable death and injury in motor vehicle crashes due to lower rates of seatbelt usage. A 1999 Meharry Medical College (MMC) report found a disparity in seatbelt use between African Americans and the overall population and concluded that an increase in the use of seatbelts among African Americans could: (1) save 1,300 African American lives each year; (2) prevent 26,000 African American injuries annually, and (3) save $2.6 billion in societal costs each year. The disparities in seatbelt use among African Americans are confirmed in studies by Wells and Williams (2002) and Briggs et al. (2006). Research by MMC documents that young African American and Hispanic males are at the highest risk of preventable death and injury due to low rates of seatbelt use (Schlundt, Easley, & Goldzweig, 2005). Statistics released by the CDC indicate that African American students (13.4%) and Hispanic students (10.6%) were more likely than White students (9.4%) to rarely or never wear seatbelts (2006).

In response to the 1999 Meharry report and a 2002 report and recommendations by a national Blue Ribbon Panel appointed by the U.S. Department of Transportation, the Meharry-State Farm Alliance (MSFA) was formed in 2002 to decrease preventable deaths and injuries among African Americans due to motor vehicle crashes by promoting appropriate and consistent use of seatbelts and child safety seats. The MSFA has conducted research focused on seeking to better understand cultural barriers—such as knowledge, attitudes, and behaviors of African Americans—related to the observed lower rates of use of driver and passenger restraints in this population, as compared to observed rates of use among White Americans, with the objective of increasing use of driver and passenger restraints among African Americans.

The MSFA supports high schools across the country in developing programs to increase seatbelt use among students and in their communities with an emphasis on urban schools with large minority populations. Early programs involved student research on the pros and cons of primary seatbelt enforcement legislation, developing persuasive speeches and presentations by students, physicians and legislators to student groups. The impact of these programs, which generally involved one way communication to groups of students during assemblies, was limited. The limited effect of these programs led to the MSFA Teen Service-Learning Project (TSLP).

The TSLP was designed to explore the potential of service-learning as an intervention to increase seatbelt knowledge, awareness and usage among teens in selected high schools. Juarez, Schlundt, Goldzweig, and Stinson (2006) outlined a conceptual framework linking service-learning and seatbelt safety campaigns, suggesting that "a peer-to-peer (service-learning) approach" could be an effective alternative to traditional public health education campaigns or stand-alone law enforcement campaigns. Ownership or student involvement in the actual design of the service-learning project is central to this effect and is well established as a powerful element of effective service-learning (Morgan & Streb, 2003).

Quality service-learning programs meet these requirements by linking academic learning with student voice (ownership) to meaningful service that meets real community needs (e.g., increasing seatbelt use among African Americans). High-quality service-learning has also been proven to promote the development of resiliency, defined as the ability of adolescents to overcome the negative effects of risk exposure (Fergus & Zimmerman, 2005). Therefore, providing youth with experiences that build personal resources such as self-confidence and interpersonal connections and skills may be an effective strategy for addressing the disparities in seatbelt use among African American teens, many of whom attend urban high schools and are considered to be "at risk," not only academically, but also personally.

Numerous studies point to the positive impacts of engaging young people in service on reducing risk taking behavior (Benson, 1993; Follman, 1998). Duckenfield and Swanson (1992) found that service-learning is an effective strategy for the prevention of substance abuse and dropping out of school. Conrad and Hedin (1982, 1987, 1989, 1991) and Weiler, LaGoy, Crane, and Rovner (1998) found that students engaged in service gain in social and personal responsibility and sense of educational competence. Eyler and Giles (1999), Melchior (1999) and Berkas (1997) found that students engaged in high quality service-learning programs showed an increase in the degree to which they felt aware of community needs, believed they could make a difference and were committed to serve now and later. Follman (1998), Melchior (1999), Melchior and Bailis (2002), Meyer and Billig (2003), and Meyer, Billig, and Hofschire (2004) found that service-learning was positively associated with impacts such as attendance, school engagement, attitudes toward school, motivation, and improved achievement scores.

A pilot project (Bradley et al., 2007), implemented in 2005/2006, supported the view that a service-learning approach that engaged students in the design and implementation of these projects could increase observed seatbelt use by students and help develop leadership skill and civic engagement in student participants.

The current research builds on the pilot study and takes it to a new level. The project continues to use observations of actual seatbelt use as a behavioral outcome measure but has developed a new measure of service-learning quality and uses this assessment to test the impact of service-learning quality on use of seatbelts by students in the school community. It measures the impact of quality on changes in surveys assessing seatbelt related attitudes, knowledge and behavior in the student community. The study also replicates the pilot study of links between service-learning experiences and personal development outcomes for service-learning participants who design and implement the projects. Four primary research questions are examined in the TSLP:

1. Does a peer-to-peer service-learning project in a high school increase seatbelt use among students?
2. Is increased seatbelt use related to service-learning quality?
3. Does service-learning quality affect knowledge, attitudes and reported behaviors of students in the school community?
4. Do the characteristics of the service-learning experience affect the personal development, civic engagement and safety-related knowledge and behavior of service-learning students?

METHOD

Research Design

A quasi-experimental, pretest/posttest design was used to assess the impact of service on student knowledge, awareness and seatbelt usage. During Years 1 to 4, students and teachers from 22 largely urban high schools participated. The schools were located in Arizona, Arkansas, Florida, Illinois, Michigan, Ohio, South Carolina, and Tennessee.

Data Collection Procedures

Two surveys were developed: The "Teen Seatbelt Usage Survey" and the "Teen Service-Learning Survey." The first survey was administered pre-/postproject to students directly involved in the service-learning project and also to a sample of the general student body, that is, the community for which the service was performed. This survey looked at student attitudes about and awareness of the importance of seatbelt use and self-reported seatbelt use. The second survey was administered postproject only to students involved in the service-learning project and assessed their level of involvement in project design and implementation (student voice and quality of the service-learning experience), hours of service (duration/intensity), frequency and type of reflection, and overall attitudes about service (school engagement, civic engagement, and personal development).

Actual rates of seatbelt use were assessed through direct pre-/postproject observations of student and adult drivers and their passengers entering and leaving school parking lots and/or drop off areas before and after school, using hand-held personal digital assistants that contained software designed and used for similar studies conducted by MMC. Data recorded included information on vehicle type and driver/passenger gender, seatbelt use of driver and front seat passenger, age and ethnicity. Schoolwide survey data were collected at the same time as the parking lot observations.

Assessing Service-Learning Quality

Because one of the key research questions in the TSLP has always been how the quality of the service-learning experience impacts students directly involved in the project and their peers, looking for methods to assess quality in relation to outcomes has been at the forefront of the research. During the pilot year of the project, researchers relied on pre-/postproject observations of seatbelt use and results of a pre-/poststudent surveys. Postproject data were collected from teachers on variables such as curriculum connections, hours of preparation, service and reflection, and observed changes among students directly involved in projects. In Years 1 to 3 of the project, researchers also conducted postproject interviews with teachers to gather additional anecdotal information. Based on this information, researchers assigned a service-learning implementation "quality rating" between 0 (no activities) to 3 (exemplary service-learning activities with strong and obvious curriculum links, evidence that the project lasted enough for in-depth exploration of the issues and school-wide implementation activities aimed at changing student attitudes and behaviors related to seatbelt use, ongoing reflection and school-wide implementation activities aimed at changing student attitudes and behaviors related to seatbelt use).

The release of the *K-12 Service Standards for Quality Practice* (Billig & Weah, 2008) made it possible for researchers to take a new approach. The Standards include meaningful service, curriculum links, challenging reflection activities, diversity, youth voice, reciprocal partnerships with the community, progress monitoring, and duration and intensity. Of these, current research suggests that standards 1, 2, 3, and 8 have the strongest impacts on student and community outcomes.

A brief overview of some of the research supporting these standards follows:

1. **Meaningful Service:** Furco (2002) found that students who were most highly influenced by their service experiences were engaged

in service activities that challenged them to some degree and/or ones in which they had responsibility and interest. Conversely, when students were engaged in service activities they described as "useless," "meaningless," "boring," or "pointless," their feelings of empowerment were very low. Billig, Root, and Jesse (2005) found that service that was perceived as meaningful prompted students to be more committed to their service-learning project and acquire greater knowledge and skills.

2. **Link to Curriculum:** Billig et al. (2005) found that using service-learning to teach content standards or curricular objectives was among the strongest predictors of all academic outcomes. Kirkham (2001) found that almost 98% of teachers who linked service-learning to curriculum reported that students learned more than what they would have through regular instruction. Students' grades improved and absenteeism decreased. Billig and Brodersen (2007) reported that teachers who aligned their service-learning activities with standards had students who scored higher on measures of academic efficiency and engagement than those who did not.

3. **Challenging Reflection Activities:** Billig et al. (2005) found that service-learning experiences that featured cognitively challenging activities and reflection were associated with students being more likely to value school, feel more efficacious, engage in school and enjoy subject matters, and acquire more civic knowledge and more positive civic dispositions. Marzano, Pickering, and Pollock (2001) found that the strongest effect sizes for school improvement occurred when teachers engaged in integrated strategies, such as teaching similarities and differences, perspective taking, and non-linguistic representation, as part of classroom instruction. Many of these strategies are associated with cognitive challenge and represent a type of reflective activity.

4. **Diversity:** Spring, Dietz, and Grimm (2007) found that youth from economically disadvantaged communities were likely to volunteer so that they could gain skills for school or work. Weah, Simmons, and McClellan (2000) found that service-learning can help students go beyond personal perspectives to learn the perspectives of others and provide structured opportunities for them to reflect on and discuss concerns about race, culture, or other differences, and a way for practicing respect for diversity.

5. **Youth Voice:** In a peer-to-peer project centered on seat belt use, Bradley et al. (2007) found that when high school students had ownership of the development and presentation of the service project, they showed increases in self-confidence, personal efficacy,

interpersonal skills and communication, and critical thinking. Student involvement was also found to be a predictor of increased school and community engagement. Fredericks, Kaplan, and Zeisler (2001) found that when youth are not actively involved in service-learning experiences they become dissatisfied with their experiences. They feel discouraged, alienated, not respected, and believe their contributions are not important.

6. **Reciprocal Partnerships:** In a review of 18 service-learning programs funded by the W. K. Kellogg Foundation, Billig (2002) found that reciprocal partnerships were seen as one of seven critical success factors in institutionalizing service-learning. Similar findings were reported by Ammon, Furco, Chi and Middaugh (2002) in a 3-year study of CalServe programs.

7. **Progress Monitoring:** Safer and Fleischman (2005) reported that when teachers implement student progress monitoring, students learn more, teacher decision making improves, and students become more aware of their own performance. Billig et al. (2005) found that service-learning assessment and program evaluation, including progress and process monitoring, were related to students' enjoyment of subject matters, civic knowledge, and efficacy.

8. **Duration and Intensity:** Spring, Dietz, and Grimm (2005) found that the number and types of quality service experiences were correlated to outcomes in the areas of civic engagement. Billig and Brodersen (2007) found that the duration of service-learning activities was positively related to valuing school, civic engagement, social responsibility, and locus of control.

At the beginning of Year 4, Meharry researchers created a tool for evaluating the quality of service-learning practice (Bradley, 2003), based on the new "K-12 Service-Learning Standards and Indicators." Following each standard, indicators for that standard were listed. After completion of project activities, teachers were asked to rate themselves on a scale of 1 to 4, with 1 = "Does not meet the requirements of this standard" and 4 = "Represents an exemplary level of practice." For each standard, teachers were also asked to give examples of activities they and their students implemented. The principle field investigator then talked with each teacher—in person where possible or by phone—to gather additional information. Mean scores for each standard were then calculated, and an overall mean score obtained to index service-learning quality at each site. This made it possible to evaluate the extent to which project outcomes were related to service-learning implementation quality.

Data Analysis Strategy

Linear models have been used for decades to analyze data from obser-vational and experimental research studies (Raudenbush & Bryk, 2002; Seal, 1967; Ware, 1985). In recent years, hierarchical linear models (HLM) have emerged as a flexible and powerful way to study the impact of context on individuals, and to model how contextual factors are associ-ated with changes in individuals over time (Hofmann, 1997; Raudenbush & Bryk, 2002; Singer, 1998). These models initially gained widespread use in educational research where they were used to understand how classroom and school characteristics were associated with student perfor-mance (Lee, 2000).

HLM begins with nested data structures. For example, children in a school are nested in a classroom setting, while classrooms are nested in schools. Measurement strategies are used to capture the characteristics of students (e.g., age and gender), classrooms (e.g., class size, teacher train-ing), and schools (e.g., percent of children receiving free lunch, No Child Left behind status). In some cases, one of the levels of nesting in a HLM may represent repeated observations (longitudinal or repeated cross sec-tions) of people over time (Verbeke & Molenberghs, 2000). The different degrees of nesting in a HLM are referred to as levels, and are usually numbered starting with the most deeply nested level.

Exhibit 5.1 is a diagram illustrating the nesting structure used to ana-lyze the school service learning data. There were three levels of data col-lection: Level 3 represents the 22 separate schools that were included in the project. School characteristics were measured using publicly available data on whether the school was in a state with a primary or secondary seatbelt law, the ethnic composition of the schools, school size, and pro-portion of the student body qualifying for free lunch. At each school, Level 2 represents the timing of data collection. Each data collection could be characterized as pre (beginning of a school term) or post (end of a school term). For the preobservations, a quality of service-learning qual-ity score of zero was assigned. For the post observations, a service-learning quality score (1-4) was assigned. For schools that participated during more than one year, a second variable was created to represent the cumu-lative quality of the service learning intervention. Level 1 represents indi-viduals nested within times and schools. For seatbelt observations, these were drivers and passengers of vehicles observed at parking lot entrances and exits. For the surveys, these were the individual students completing the surveys.

Building hierarchical linear models begins at Level 1 with a model of individual differences. Here a regression or logit (binary data) regression model is used to predict some outcome (e.g., wearing a seatbelt) with a

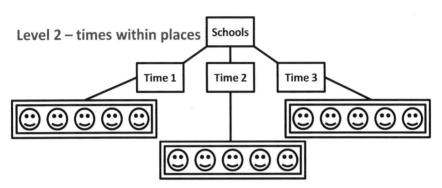

Exhibit 5.1.   Three-level hierarchical model to evaluate service-learning.

linear combination of demographic and/or other individual difference measures. The model has an intercept and slope parameters. Models are then created to understand how the intercept parameter of the Level 1 equation varies across the levels of the nesting variable (e.g., seatbelt use varies over time or between schools). The between-unit variations in the intercept parameter are modeled using linear equations as a function of the variables measured at the second or third level of the model. Models can also be created to represent how slope parameters (measures of the strength and direction of association) vary across nesting units. For example, the association between driver race/ethnicity and seatbelt use may be stronger in some types of schools than others. The measures of school characteristics and intervention quality are used to model the between-unit variations in the slope parameters. The two kinds of models are sometimes referred to as "intercepts as outcomes" and "slopes as outcomes" models (Cuddy, Swanson, Dillon, Holtman, & Clauser, 2006).

RESULTS

Impact of Individual Characteristics and Service-Learning Quality on Observed Driver Seatbelt Use

A total of 30,367 vehicles was observed and coded using the PDAs. Exhibit 5.2 gives an overview of the results, showing driver seatbelt use by time period and ethnicity. While this ignores the quality of service-

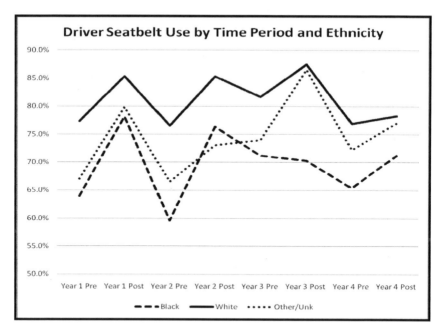

Exhibit 5.2.   Driver seatbelt use by time period and ethnicity.

learning, it does show a clear increase in seatbelt use in the post service-learning observations compared to the pre service-learning observations. Exhibit 5.2 also shows the disparity in seatbelt use between White and Black drivers.

Exhibit 5.3 presents the results of the HLM analysis of observed driver seatbelt use. The rows of the table represent the intercept and the predictor variables. The column labeled Level 1 displays the odds-ratios of the predictor variables at the level of individual drivers. Higher rates of seatbelt use were observed for older drivers, SUV drivers, and females. Lower rates of seatbelt use were observed for young drivers, pickup truck drivers, Black and Other/Unknown drivers, males, and drivers with a male passenger in the front seat. The Level 3 model showed that seatbelt use declined as the percent of students eligible for free lunch in the school increased, and that seatbelt use was higher in schools where there is a primary state seatbelt law. After controlling for Level 1 and Level 3 effects, there was a Level 2 effect for intervention quality. Each increment in intervention quality was associated with a *12% increase* in the odds of observing a driver wearing a seatbelt. There were no slopes as outcomes effects that were included in this model.

Exhibit 5.3. HLM Analysis of Observed Driver Seatbelt Use

Predictor	Level 1	Level 2 Intervention	Level 3 % Free Lunch	Level 3 Primary Law
Intercept	1.83***	1.12**	0.99**	1.44*
Age	1.23***			
Pickup	0.68***			
SUV	1.08*			
Van	1.18			
Female	1.60***			
Black	0.60***			
Other	0.87**			
Alone	0.99			
Male passenger	0.76**			

Note: Odds ratio for each included parameter is shown in the table.
*p < 0.05. **p < 0.01. ***p < 0.001.

Impact of Service-Learning Quality on Student Attitudes and Beliefs: The Teen Seatbelt Usage Survey

Next, using data from the Teen Seatbelt Usage survey, researchers looked at the effect of service-learning quality on changes in knowledge, attitudes, and self-reported behaviors of students in the school community. This pre-/postproject survey asked students to create their own anonymous code so that they could be linked. Since less than 10% could be matched on pre-/postsurvey forms, data were analyzed as repeated cross sections. A total of 6,875 usable surveys were completed.

Students were asked to respond to a series of questions, using a scale from 1 (*strongly disagree*) to 4 (*strongly agree*). The survey included: 3 questions related to driver seatbelt use, 13 questions related to driver motivations to use their seatbelts, 4 questions related to passenger seatbelt use, 7 questions related to passenger motivation to use their seatbelts, 13 questions related to barriers to seatbelt use, 6 items related to intervention awareness, demographic information (age, gender, ethnicity), and driver status (whether or not driver had a license). The groupings of items were used to form scales by summing the ratings.

Self-Reported Driver Seatbelt Use. Items measuring driver seatbelt use were added together to create a scale which had a coefficient alpha of 0.86. The results of the HLM regression analysis used to predict drivers' reports of seatbelt use are presented in Exhibit 5.4. Compared to females,

males reported higher rates of seatbelt use (the opposite of the observed data) while Blacks reported lower rates than Whites. At Level 3, the percent of students with free lunch in a school was associated with lower self-reported seatbelt use. Although they were not statistically significant, the model included two slopes as outcomes effects for the intervention—an effect for male gender, and another for African American ethnicity. After controlling for the Level 1 and Level 3 effects, there was a significant positive association between the cumulative intervention variable and self-reported seatbelt use. This shows that the more intervention a school received, the higher the reported levels of driver seatbelt use.

The passenger seatbelt use scale had a coefficient alpha of 0.89 and the results of the HLM analysis are included in the bottom half of Exhibit 5.4. The Level 1 and Level 3 effects were similar to those shown (above) for drivers. At Level 2, there was a positive association between intervention quality and self-reported seatbelt use for passengers. No slopes as out-

Exhibit 5.4.   HLM Analysis of Driver and Passenger Self-Reported Seatbelt

		Level 2		Level 3
	Level 1	*Intervention*	*Cumulative Intervention*	*Free Lunch*
Drivers				
Intercept	+++		+	--
Age	0			
Male	+++	0		
Black	-	0		
Hispanic	0			
Other	-			
		Intervention	*Cumulative Intervention*	*Free Lunch*
Passengers				
Intercept	+++	+		--
Age	0			
Male	+++			
Black	---			++
Hispanic	0			
Other	0			
Driver	++			

Note: Negative association: -p < 0.05, --p < 0.02, ---p < 0.001. Positive association: +p < 0.05, ++p < 0.01, +++p < 0.001. Included but not significant: 0.

comes parameters were included in the passenger model at Level 2. For reported seatbelt use, both drivers and passengers were responsive to intervention quality, with passengers showing an immediate response, and drivers showing an increase as a function of repeated intervention efforts in the school.

Motivations for Seatbelt Use. Examples of motivations for seatbelt use were: "I always wear my seatbelt because I might get a ticket if I don't" and "I always wear my seatbelt because my parents expect me to." The motivation items for drivers had a coefficient alpha of 0.91. Motivations for seatbelt use among passengers included parental expectations, setting an example for friends, habit, avoiding injury, friends wearing theirs, knowing someone who was injured or killed because they were not wearing their seatbelt, and wanting to be safe (coefficient alpha = 0.88). Exhibit 5.5 shows the results of the HLM analysis for driver and passenger motivations.

Exhibit 5.5.   HLM Analysis of Driver and Passenger Motivation for Seatbelt Use

	Level 1	Level 2		Level 3
		Intervention	Cumulative Intervention	Free Lunch
Drivers				
Intercept	+++	+		--
Age	0			
Male	+++			
Black	-			
Hispanic	0			
Other	-			
		Intervention	Cumulative Intervention	Free Lunch
Passengers				
Intercept	+++	+		--
Age	0			
Male	+++			
Black	---			++
Hispanic	0			
Other	0			
Driver	++			

Note: Negative association: -p < 0.05, --p < 0.02, ---p < 0.001. Positive association: +p < 0.05, ++p < 0.01, +++ p < 0.001. Included but not significant: 0.

For the questions about driver motivation, males reported more reasons to wear seatbelts than females, and Blacks reported fewer reasons. At Level 3, the percent of students in the school receiving free lunch was negatively associated with motivations to use seatbelts. There was a positive association between intervention quality at Level 2 and driver motivation to use seatbelts. For passengers, those passengers who also drive reported higher motivation to wear seatbelts. There was also a Level 3 slope effect for Blacks, showing that ethnic differences are more important in schools with a higher percentage of students on free lunch. There was also a significant association between intervention quality and passenger motivations to use seatbelts.

Barriers to Seatbelt Use. Barriers to regular seatbelt use included friends who don't wear them, wrinkling clothes, not cool, family doesn't use them, don't like people telling me what to do, takes too much time to put on, not comfortable, thinking they won't be in an accident, restricts movements, difficult to fasten, only traveling a short distance, forget to use them, and fear that they won't be able to get out of the car if they are in an accident (coefficient alpha = 0.92). Exhibit 5.6 presents the HLM results for barriers.

Barriers were higher in schools with larger African American populations. Drivers also reported more barriers than those who never drive. Intervention quality was not associated with barriers, but the cumulative intervention quality was positively associated with the slope for Blacks. The more a school is exposed to the seat belt intervention, the greater the

**Exhibit 5.6. HLM Analysis of Barriers
to Seatbelt Use in Drivers and Passengers**

| | Level 1 | Level 2 | | Level 3 | |
		Intervention	Cumulative Intervention	% Black	Free Lunch
Intercept	+++			++	
Age	0				
Male	0			++	0
Black	---		++	++	
Hispanic	0				
Other	0				
Driver	++				

Note: Negative association: $-p < 0.05$, $--p < 0.02$, $---p < 0.001$. Positive association: $+p < 0.05$, $++p < 0.01$, $+++p < 0.001$. Included but not significant: 0.

importance of Black ethnicity as a predictor of the number of barriers to seatbelt use reported.

Impact of Participation in Service-Learning Project on Student Participants: The Teen Service-Learning Survey

Next researchers looked at the characteristics of the service-learning experience, based on teacher reports (Postproject Teacher Report and K-12 Quality Assessment Survey) and data from the postproject Teen Service-Learning Survey. Four variables assessing the service-learning experience were considered: *Quality* is defined as service that students found interesting and important. This corresponds to Service-Learning Quality Standard # 1 (Meaningful Service) and Quality Standard # 5 (Youth Voice). *Reflection-discussion* is defined as frequent teacher and/or student led discussions about the meaning of service activities. *Reflection-writing* is defined as multiple student writing assignments related to project activities (Quality Standard # 3). *Engagement* is defined as the time devoted to the project (Quality Standard # 8). Results are shown in Exhibits 7 and 8.

These data were analyzed using linear regression. Exhibit 5.7 shows that student perceptions of the overall quality of their service-learning experience (Quality Standards # 1, 5) were strongly associated with the development of self-confidence, interpersonal and communication skills, respect for the views of others, and critical thinking. Frequent classroom

Exhibit 5.7. Association of Characteristics of Service-Learning on Personal Development Outcomes (*N* = 97 Participants Completing the Teen Service-Learning Survey)

	Self-Confidence	Interpersonal Skill	Communication Skill	Respect for Views	Think/Problem Solving
Quality of service experience	.259**	.312***	.457***	.138*	.203**
Reflection-discussion	.292**	.435***	.348***	.368***	.512***
Reflection-writing	.197**	.080	.028	.099	.103
Level of s-l involvement	.032	.099	.150*	.168**	.026

Note: Beta's from linear regression analysis ***$p < .01$; **$p < .05$; *$p < .10$. Results from single-tail tests for all variables.

discussions of service activities are positively associated with the same variables. Written reflection is positively associated with the development of self-confidence. A possible explanation for the lack of association with the other four variables may be that teachers reported using written reflection far less frequently than classroom discussions. The level of involvement (Quality Standard # 8) is positively associated with the development of respect for the views of others and critical thinking.

Exhibit 5.8 shows the association of the characteristics of service-learning participation and community engagement outcomes. Student perceptions of the overall quality of their service-learning experience were strongly associated with their sense that they made a difference in their community (school and/or wider community), an increased commitment to improve their community, and increased awareness of resources available to support their efforts. Frequent classroom discussions were strongly associated with the same three outcomes, while written reflection was not. As mentioned previously this is probably due to the fact that teachers reported using it far less often. The level of student involvement (duration and intensity) was positively associated with increased commitment to improve their community and awareness of resources.

Exhibit 5.9 shows the association of the characteristics of service-learning participation and school engagement outcomes. Student perceptions of the overall quality of their service-learning experience were strongly associated with feeling that they had increased opportunities to work closely with their teacher(s), increased involvement in their school and motivation to work harder. Frequent classroom discussions were strongly associated with all three outcomes, while written reflection is associated with only one—opportunities to work closely with their teachers. The

Exhibit 5.8.   Association of Characteristics of Service-Learning Participation and Community Engagement Outcomes (N = 97 Participants Completing the Teen Service-Learning Survey)

	Efficacy—Make Difference in Community	Commitment to Improve Community	Aware of Resources in Community
Quality of s-l	.446***	.256***	.079
Reflection – discussion	.386***	.367***	.524***
Reflection – writing	−.005	.037	.073
Level of s-l project involvement	.096	.155**	.157**

Note: Beta's from linear regression analysis ***$p < .01$; **$p < .05$; *$p < .10$.
Results from single tail tests for all variables.

Exhibit 5.9.   Impact of Characteristics of Service-Learning Participation on School Engagement Outcomes (N = 97 Participants Completing the Teen Service-Learning Survey)

	Opportunity to Work Closely With Faculty Member	Feel More Involved in School	Motivated to Work Harder in School
Quality of s-l	.172**	.456***	.304***
Reflection – discussion	.243**	.258***	.453***
Reflection – writing	.177**	−.048	.050
Level of s-l project involvement	.160**	.175**	.105*

Note: Beta's from linear regression analysis ***$p < .01$; **$p < .05$; *$p < .10$.
Results from single tail tests for all variables.

Exhibit 5.10.   Impact of Service-learning Characteristics on Automobile Safety-Related Outcomes (N = 97 Participants Completing the Teen Service-Learning Survey)

	Know More About Auto Safety	Tried to Influence Policymakers	Take More Responsibility for Own Safety	More Likely to Encourage Others to Use Seat Belts
Quality of service experience	.356***	.017	.229**	.260***
Reflection – discussion	.386***	.272***	.375***	.453**
Reflection – writing	.026	.264**	.134*	.083
Level of s-l project involvement	.036	.045	.160**	−.005

Note: Beta's from linear regression analysis ***$p < .01$; **$p < .05$; *$p < .10$.
Results from single tail tests for all variables.

level of student involvement was also associated with more opportunities to work with their teachers and feeling more involved in their school. This is consistent with previous service-learning findings which indicate that student involvement in quality service-learning changes their relationship with their teacher and improves their connections with and motivations to do well in school.

Exhibit 5.10 shows the association of the characteristics of service-learning participation and automobile safety-related outcomes. Student perceptions of the overall quality of their service-learning experience were strongly associated with three of four outcomes—knowing more about auto safety, taking more responsibility for one's own safety, and encouraging others to use their seatbelts regularly. This finding is probably due to the fact that all of the projects involved student research into injuries and deaths resulting from seatbelt use and nonuse. Having collected this information themselves, students reported that they took it far more seriously than if it had simply been given to them by their teachers. Frequent reflection through classroom discussions was strongly associated with all four outcomes; written reflection with only two. The level of student involvement was associated with only one outcome—taking more personal responsibility for personal safety. It may be that, while students engaged in the projects had increased information about the importance of regular seatbelt use, they still found it difficult to persuade their friends to wear theirs.

Qualitative Analysis of Teacher Reports

Teacher comments on the Postproject Teacher Report are consistent with data from the Teen Service-Learning Survey on the impacts of participating in the service-learning projects. These include the following:

- **Self-esteem and self-discipline**: Teachers reported that students involved in seatbelt safety service-learning projects became more actively involved in school, came to see themselves as leaders, and gained confidence about their roles in their school and community.
- **Interpersonal and leadership skills**: Teachers reported that their students took initiative and responsibility, collaborated, and developed patience and respect.
- **Acceptance of responsibility for the community**: Teachers reported that their students became more aware of the importance of serving the community and showed a broader sense of their responsibility to the community.
- **Desire to make a difference**: Teachers also noted that students took responsibility for communicating the importance of using seat belts to their peers, established themselves as leaders in their schools, and were more involved in other community service projects.
- **Improved knowledge and skills**: Teachers saw improved skills in Math (data gathering and analysis, graphing). Language Arts (oral and written communication, improved critical thinking skills, read-

ing), Science (physics of auto crashes, research on seat belt design and safety), and Health Occupations (anatomy and physiology).

- **Attitudes about school, learning, and self as a learner**: Teachers noted that students directly involved in service-learning project were able to make connections between the school-world and the real-world, became more dependable and trustworthy, and showed improvements in attendance and decreases in discipline referrals.
- **Value of the subject**: Teachers noted that students internalized the value of teamwork, dedication, commitment and came to value life (their own and others) more.

DISCUSSION AND LIMITATIONS

In considering the results of this study, there are a number of issues that may limit its findings. One of the issues common to many service-learning studies has been how to link student outcomes with student service-learning experiences. The difficulty relates to varying definitions of service-learning and service-learning quality. With the release of the "K-12 Service-Learning Standards for Quality Practice," researchers now have a common definition that should, in theory at least, define what quality service-learning practice looks like.

The question still remains, however, as to the most effective way to assess service-learning quality. Findings in this study, particularly for Year Four, rely primarily on teacher self-assessments followed up by interviews conducted by researchers. This approach mirrors a strategy that has been used for many years in the field of character education. However, because of the subjective nature of an approach utilizing self-assessment, questions remain about the validity of the results. While teachers involved in the Teen Service-Learning Project received a "Teacher Toolkit" that contained information about the "K-12 Service-Learning Quality Standards," some teachers had more experience with service-learning than others and were, therefore, better able to apply this information to projects in which they and their students were involved. These teachers tended to rate themselves lower than the researchers might have, probably because they were more familiar with what quality practice looked like and were overly critically of their efforts. At the same time, in at least one case, an inexperienced teacher rated himself higher than the researcher would have, probably because he didn't have a good understanding of what quality practice would look like.

In moving forward with this research and similar service-learning research, the question must be asked: is the K-12 Service-Learning Quality Assessment Survey a valid instrument for assessing quality? Or, are there other strategies researchers could use to assess quality that might be more effective? If so, what are they? A more robust design would remove teachers from doing these postproject assessments entirely and have researchers doing them, based on their knowledge of activities at each site. While this might result in a somewhat less subjective assessment of service-learning implementation quality at each site, it would also require many more site visits than available grant funds would support. By combining teacher self-reports with follow-up conversations with teachers—either in person or by phone—we have attempted to address some of subjectivity in our ratings of service-learning quality.

A second issue has to do with strategies used to measure outcomes of the service-learning experience. The Teen Service-Learning Project relies heavily on pre-/postobservations of seatbelt use by teens before and after school, as they enter and leave the schools' parking lots or drop-off/pick-up areas. Three questions need to be addressed. First, does the presence of the observation team influence seatbelt use, particularly for the post-project observations? Do students buckle up simply because they see the team standing there collecting data? Second, in our conversations with teachers and students, we have discovered that many seniors have "early release," meaning that they have already left by the time the observation team begins its after-school observations. This means that we are missing some of the very students we want to reach. Third, in what ways are the observed outcomes (seatbelt use and changes in student attitudes about and awareness of the importance of seatbelt use) related to variables such as personal development and school and community engagement? We have reported findings on each of these variables, based on data from students in the service-learning group (the "Teen Service-Learning Survey"). However, this survey, unlike the "Teen Seatbelt Usage Survey" also reported above, reflects postonly self-reports. Are there other ways we could measure the desired behavioral outcomes connected with this project? Many studies of students involved in service-learning address this by administering some type of survey about attitudes toward service, school and community engagement both pre- and postproject. We tried this during the Pilot year of the project but stopped doing so for two reasons: (1) comparison of pre-/poststudent responses showed very little change and (2) teachers said that administering surveys was taking up too much class time. However, now that we have a measure of service-learning quality, it may be time to try pre-/postadministration of the "Teen Service-Learning Survey" once more.

A third issue has to do with the unique challenges of implementing service-learning in urban settings. In most cases, reaching the population we are targeting (African Americans and other ethnic minorities), has meant focusing our interventions within urban high schools. In doing so, we face a number of challenges. First, the pressures of high-stakes testing and limited financial resources combine to limit student course options and learning opportunities to those administrators deem most critical for improving academic performance. This often results in a lack of time for things that are not part of the core curriculum and a focus on test preparation at the expense of other approaches to teaching, such as service-learning, which might be more conducive to student learning. This has made it difficult to find teachers who both understand service-learning and are willing to commit time to work with us. Second, with few exceptions, the number of students who actually drive to/from school is low. Some urban high schools do not even have student parking areas, meaning that students who do drive have to find parking on side streets near their school. This poses a challenge to our observation teams. Do they focus on drop-off/pick-up areas or try to find alternate observation sites "off-campus" or some combination of both?

A fourth issue may be that many urban students are already disconnected from the learning process. They are simply putting in "seat time." This disconnect may be due to the fact that many students in these schools do not learn the way most teachers teach—lecture and note-taking followed by testing. These students may also have difficulty connecting what they are being taught in the classroom with the world in which they live. "Relevance" is critical to them—hence the oft heard question, "Why do I have to know this?"

This leads to a fifth issue—finding a balance between meaningful service, curriculum links and youth voice for this project. On the surface, coming into a school with the theme (seatbelt safety) already set seems to violate the indicators connected with meaningful service and youth voice. How can students, many of whom do not use their seatbelts regularly, be motivated to see this theme as "meaningful" to them? At some of our participating schools this was an easy transition because students involved in the project knew of someone—perhaps a student at their school or a family member—who was killed or critically injured in an auto crash while not wearing a seatbelt. In at least one high school, students involved in the project dedicated it to the memory of two nonbelted classmates who died in auto crashes. At other schools the connection between the project theme, relevancy, and youth voice emerges when students begin researching and comparing statistics on auto injuries and deaths when drivers and passengers were and were not buckled up. Once they see the numbers for themselves many become very passionate about the issue and are excited about finding their own unique ways to convey the message about the importance of regular seatbelt use to their peers. In many cases, this has also led students to "personalize" seatbelt safety messages with messages about the dangers of texting while driving or other risky teen driving behaviors.

With respect to curriculum links, the ongoing challenge has been to help teachers find natural connections between what they teach and the project theme. In some ways, this is no different from the challenge any teacher faces in connecting the ideas students generate with the topic of instruction. If curriculum links are important, then quality service-learning projects, by definition, need to find a "home" in the curriculum – one that addresses academic standards while also honoring student voice in shaping project activities. Quality service-learning should enrich, enhance and reinforce what teachers are going to teach anyway by providing students with meaningful opportunities to apply what they are learning in the classroom to real-world issues. Finding the right balance between the teacher "picking" the project and giving students "free rein" to choose whatever project they want (regardless of possible connections to the curriculum) can be a challenge.

A conceptual model (Goldzweig & Bradley, 2010) for finding this balance might look something like this:

(1) → Evidence-based or curriculum-linked information as foundation for project ideas	(2) → Teacher interest in and expertise/familiarity with quality service-learning	(3) → Youth Voice – students brainstorm project ideas and select one or more for implementation	→ Teacher connects project activities to curriculum	→ Students become invested in and develop ownership of project through implementation and reflection

The Teen Service-Learning Project begins with evidence-based information (seatbelts save lives and teens are at greater risk for unintentional injury and death due to lower rates of seatbelt use) and then encourages youth to study the issues, challenges and barriers to teen seat belt use themselves. Based on this, they develop their projects and ways to use their voices to impact the safety behaviors of their peers.

One of our teachers accomplished this in her public speaking class by first having her students learn the fundamentals of defining a topic, researching information, and then preparing and delivering short (3 minutes or less) speeches on topics they chose. Once they had the basics, she repeated the assignment, this time using seatbelt safety as the theme. After researching relevant statistics for themselves, students developed public service announcements, posters, and a seatbelt DVD, and made numerous presentations to peers in other classes about the importance of regular seatbelt use. These activities, coupled with ongoing reflection about what they were doing, helped students develop ownership for the issue of seatbelt safety.

Is quality service-learning a viable strategy for reaching urban students? Research on the key elements that help students to reconnect and stay in school suggests that service-learning is one of a number of different approaches, including reducing class and school size and/or personalizing the school environment, linking the curriculum to students' lives and interests, and giving students real leadership and responsibility, that could be used (Bradley, 2003). The hands-on approach of service-learning addresses these issues and offers students opportunities to personalize their learning and make it relevant through real leadership and responsibility. Postproject interviews with students suggest that many find the Teen Service-Learning Project relevant because they know someone who was killed or seriously injured in a motor vehicle crash because of not wearing a seatbelt. Students also tell us that the project gave them an opportunity to develop a more personal relationship with their teachers and that they were able to develop and demonstrate leadership among their peers. Teacher observations also validate these outcomes.

In their postproject observations of student behaviors, teachers also noted that some of their most "problematic" students showed improved classroom performance and decreased discipline problems through their involvement in the seatbelt safety project. The next step in validating these results would be to link overall academic performance and discipline referrals of service-learning students to official school records.

A sixth issue relates to the challenge of getting teachers to change the way they teach. Research on teacher change suggests that many are reluctant to change unless they know it is safe for them to try something new (that might not result in immediate improvements in student grades or behaviors). Creating an environment that supports experimentation is extremely difficult in many of today's test-driven urban schools. Challenges include the following: *Relevancy*—If we want teachers to try service-learning in their classrooms we need to be able to show them how it helps them address an issue they are currently facing with their students. *Preferred teaching style*—Many older, and presumably more experienced teachers, utilize teaching methods that have worked reasonably well for them over the years and may be reluctant to try anything different. Newer teachers may be familiar with service-learning pedagogies from undergraduate training, but find themselves teaching in schools where there is very little support from administrators or colleagues for anything but the "tried and true." For many teachers, who may be evaluated on the basis of student test scores, academic outcomes are far more important than the perceived "feel good" outcomes typically associated with service-learning. This needs to be addressed in future research. *Probability of success*—While there is a growing body of research supporting positive academic outcomes resulting from quality service-learning, researchers and service-learning educators need to be cautious about making claims about "quick fixes." As with any other new pedagogy, service-learning requires a long-term commitment.

Overall, we have demonstrated a measure of success in this project but there is room for improvement as we move forward.

- Careful consideration needs to given to when we conduct observations—perhaps three times per day—before school, early release and normal release times. This will enable us to obtain a more complete picture of student seatbelt use at each site.

- More attention to matching of pre-/poststudent surveys—currently each student creates his/her own identification code based on first letter of their first, the first letter of their middle name and the last letter of their last name, plus the month and day of their birth. Despite efforts to emphasize the importance of entering this information accurately each time a student completes a survey, it has been very difficult to match pre-/postsurveys. Whenever possible, a member of the Meharry-State Farm Alliance research team needs to be present when surveys are administered. We have also created a scripted set of instructions for teachers to read when we cannot be present.

- More attention to teacher training—prior to the beginning of Year Five we revised Teacher Toolkit to more closely follow the "K-12 Service-Learning Standards for Quality Practice." We are also conducting in-person orientations for teachers whenever possible.

In Conclusion

This study identified groups of urban high school students at risk for preventable injury and death due to motor vehicle crashes. Results show that student-designed service-learning, peer-to-peer interventions have great potential for improving the health and safety of young people in urban high schools by influencing them to change risky behaviors. Results also show that the quality of service-learning intervention matters. Additionally, unlike most studies which rely on student self reports alone, this study uses observations of actual safety behavior. The findings that members of the school community are more likely to actually buckle up in schools after student developed seatbelt projects are conducted and that there is a cumulative effect in schools that implement programs over several years should be strong encouragement for using service-learning to address other high risk behaviors.

We believe that the model developed for this project can be generalized to other health-related issues affecting teens. Using evidence-based and/or curriculum-linked information on specific issues such as substance abuse, obesity, pregnancy prevention, risky sexual behaviors, and a broader range of issues such as the environment and global water use, students and their teachers could brainstorm possible projects and choose the one(s) about which they are most passionate. Following a pre-survey of students' knowledge and attitudes towards and behaviors related to the specific issue, students would then design and implement curriculum-based service-learning interventions. Teachers would ensure that projects and interventions are linked to the curriculum in appropriate ways. At the conclusion of the project, postproject surveys would be administered to assess changes in knowledge, attitudes and behaviors. Ongoing reflection throughout the project would help students develop ownership for this issue.

Second, the study shows that the quality of the service-learning interventions also influences the attitudes, knowledge and behavioral intentions of students in the wider student body and that this also has cumulative effects in schools with several projects over time. Student-led programs can change the way students think about seatbelt use, increasing motivations to use seatbelts as passengers and drivers and also reducing the number of barriers to using seatbelts perceived by African American students.

In addition, the study shows that the students who deliver the peer-to-peer intervention benefit in very important ways in development of their own personal commitments and leadership skills and in their engagement in school and community. These changes are also related to the quality of the service-learning experience.

This phase of the TSLP studies has also contributed a new measure of quality of service-learning for high school programs that has been associated with behavioral outcomes. This is a tool based on recent research and practitioner wisdom in the field that other researchers may find useful.

Student-designed safety projects can influence the behavior of their peers and the quality of the service-learning experience of those students makes a difference in the quality of the programs they produce for the school community. This is a potentially powerful tool for reducing other risky behaviors among urban high school students.

REFERENCES

Ammon, M., Furco, A., Chi, B., & Middaugh, E. (2002). *Service-learning in California: A profile of the CalServe service-learning partnerships, 1997-2000.* Berkeley,

CA: University of California, Service-Learning Research and Development Center.

Benson, P. (1993). *The troubled journey: A portrait of 6th-12th grade youth*. Minneapolis, MN: The Search Institute.

Berkas, T. (1997). *Strategic review of the W. K. Kellogg Foundation's service-learning projects, 1990-1996*. Battle Creek, MI: W. K. Kellogg Foundation.

Billig, S. H. (2002). *W. K. Kellogg Foundation retrospective of K-12 service-learning projects, 1990-2000*. Denver, CO: RMC Research Corporation.

Billig, S. H., & Brodersen, R. (2007). *Case studies of effective practices in the partnership in character education project: Evaluation for the School District of Philadelphia*. Denver. CO: RMC Research Corporation.

Billig, S. H., Root, S., & Jesse, D. (2005). The relationship between the quality indicators of service-learning and student outcomes: Testing professional wisdom. In S. Root, J. Callahan, & S. H. Billig (Eds.), *Improving service-learning practice: Research on models to enhance impact* (pp. 97-115). Greenwich, CT: Information Age Publishing.

Billig, S. H., & Weah, W. (2008). *K-12 Service-Learning Standards for Quality Practice*. Retrieved from http://www.nylc.org/objects/publications/G2G2008 _StdArticle.pdf

Bradley, R. (2003). *Building connectedness with school*. Columbus, OH: The John Glenn Institute at The Ohio State University,

Bradley, R., Eyler, J., Goldzweig, J., Juarez, P., Schlundt, D., & Tolliver, D. (2007). Evaluating the impact of peer-to-peer service-learning projects on seat belt use among high school students. In S. Gelmon & S. H. Billig (Eds.), *From passion to objectivity: International and cross-disciplinary perspectives on service-learning research* (pp. 89-110). Charlotte, NC: Information Age Publishing.

Briggs, N., Schlundt, D., Levine, R., Goldzweig, I., Stinson, N., & Warren, R. (2006). Seat belt law enforcement and racial disparities in seat belt use. *Journal of Preventative Medicine, 31(2)*, 135-141.

Conrad, D., & Hedin, D. (1982). Youth participation and experiential education. *Children and Youth Series. 4*(3 & 4).

Conrad, D., & Hedin, D. (1987). *Youth service: A guidebook for developing and operating effective programs*. Washington, DC: Independent Sector.

Conrad, D., & Hedin, D. (1989). *High school community service: A review of research and programs*. Madison, WI: National Center for Effective Schools, University of Wisconsin.

Conrad, D., & Hedin, D. (1991). School-based community service: What we know from research and theory. *Phi Delta Kappan*, June, 743-749.

Cuddy, M. M., Swanson, D. B., Dillon, G. F., Holtman, M. C., & Clauser B. E. (2006). A multilevel analysis of the relationships between selected examinee characteristics and United States Medical Licensing Examination Step 2 Clinical Knowledge performance: Revisiting old findings and asking new questions. *Academic Medicine, 81*(10), 103-7.

Duckenfield, M., & Swanson, M. (1992). *Service-learning: Meeting the needs of youth at risk* Clemson, SC: National Dropout Prevention Center.

Eyler, J., & Giles, D. E., Jr. (1999). *Where's the learning in service-learning?* San Francisco, CA: Jossey-Bass.

Fergus, S., & Zimmerman, M.A. (2005). Adolescent resilience: A framework for understanding healthy development in the face of risk. *Annual Review of Public Health, 26*, 399-419.

Follman. J. (August, 1998). *Florida Learn and Serve: 1996-97 outcomes and correlations with 1994-95 and 1995-96.* Tallahassee, FL: Florida State University, Center for Civic Education and Service.

Fredericks, Kaplan, E., & Zeisler, J. (2001). *Integrating youth voice into service-learning* Denver, CO: Education Commission of the States.

Furco, A. (2002). Is service-learning really better than community service? A study of high school service program outcomes. In A. Furco & S. H. Billig (Eds.), *Service-learning: The essence of the pedagogy* (pp. 23-50). Greenwich, Ct: Information Age Publishing.

Goldzweig, I., & Bradley, L. R. (2010). *A conceptual model for linking evidence-based information and/or curriculum with service-learning activities in order to enhance student voice.* Unpublished manuscript.

Hofmann, D. A. (1997). An overview of the logic and rationale of hierarchical linear models. *Journal of Management,23*(6), 723-744.

Juarez, P., Schlundt, D., Goldzweig, I., & Stinson, N. (2006). A conceptual framework for reducing risky teen driving behaviors among minority youth. *Injury Prevention, 12* (1), 49-55.

Kirkham, M. (2001). *Sustaining service-learning in Wisconsin: What principals, teachers, and students say about service-learning, 2000-2001.* Madison: Wisconsin Department of Public Instruction.

Lee, V. E. (2000). Using hierarchical linear modeling to study social contexts: The case of school effects. *Educational Psychologist 35*(2), 125-141.

Marzano, R., Pickering, D., & Pollock, J. (2001). *Classroom instruction that works: Research-based strategies for increasing student achievement.* Alexandria, VA: Association for Supervision and Curriculum Development.

Meharry Medical College (MMC) (1999). *Achieving a credible health and safety approach to increasing seat belts among African Americans.* Nashville, TN: Meharry Medical College.

Melchior, A. (1999). *Summary report: National evaluation of Learn and Serve America.* Waltham, MA: Center for Human Resources, Brandeis University.

Melchior, A., & Bailis, L. (2002). Impact of service-learning on civic attitudes and behavior of middle and high school youth: Findings from three national evaluations. In Furco & S. H. Billig (Eds.). *Service-learning: The essence of the pedagogy* (pp. 201-222). Greenwich, CT: Information Age.

Meyer. S., & Billig, S. H. (2003). *Evaluation of Need in Deed.* Denver, CO: RMC Research Corporation.

Meyer, S., Billig S. H., & Hofshire, L. (2004). *Wai'anae High School Hawaiian studies program.* Denver, CO: RMC Research Corporation.

Morgan, W., & Streb, M. (2003). First do no harm: The importance of student ownership in service-learning. *Metropolitan State Universities, 14*(3), 36-52.

Raudenbush, S. W., & Bryk, A.S. (2002). *Hierarchical linear models.* Thousand Oaks, CA: Sage.

Safer, N., & Fleischman, S. (2005). Research matters: How student progress monitoring improves instruction. *Educational Leadership, 62*(4), 81-83.

Schlundt, D., Easley, S., & Goldzweig, I. (2005, December). *Racial disparities in seat belt use: An observational study in four communities.* Paper presented at the 2005 American Public Health Association Conference, Philadelphia, PA.

Seal, H. L. (1967). Studies in the history of probability and statistics. XV The historical development of the Gauss linear model. *Biometrika,54*(1-2),1-24.

Singer, J. D. (1998). Using SAS PROC MIXED to fit multilevel models, hierarchical models, and individual growth models. *Journal of Educational and Behavioral Statistics, 23*(4), 323-355.

Spring, K., Dietz, N., & Grimm, R. (2005). *Youth helping America: Service-learning, school-based service and youth civic engagement.* Washington, DC: Corporation for National and Community Service.

Spring, K., Dietz, N., & Grimm, R. (2007). *Leveling the path to participation: Volunteering and civic engagement among youth from disadvantaged circumstances.* Washington, DC: Corporation for National and Community Service.

Verbeke, G., & Molenberghs, G. (2000). *Linear mixed models for longitudinal data.* New York, Springer-Verlag.

Ware, J. H. (1985). Linear models for the analysis of longitudinal studies. *The American Statistician, 39*(2), 95-101.

Weah, W., Simmons, V., & McClellan, M. (2000). Service-learning and multicultural/multiethnic perspectives: From diversity to equity. *Phi Delta Kappan, 81*(9), 673-675.

Weiler, D., LaGoy, A., Crane, E., & Rovner, A. (1998). *An evaluation of K-12 service-learning in California: Phase II Final Report.* Emeryville, CA: RPP International with the Search Institute.

Wells, J., & Williams, A. (2002). Seat belt use among African Americans, Hispanics, and Whites. *Accident Analysis & Prevention, 34*(4), 523-529.

PART III

SERVICE-LEARNING IN HIGHER EDUCATION

CHAPTER 6

SERVICE-LEARNING AND PREINTERNSHIP TEACHER SENSE OF EFFICACY

A Comparison of Two Designs

Trae Stewart, Kay W. Allen, and Haiyan Bai

This study aimed to determine if preinternship teacher education students' participation in service-learning activities in K-12 classrooms would significantly affect their sense of teacher efficacy. A secondary question was whether 1 type of service-learning activity (e.g., whole class instruction) would impact teacher efficacy more than another (e.g., small group tutoring). We found that preinternship service-learners in both types of service-learning activity increased significantly in teacher efficacy. However, neither type of service-learning activity was superior to the other. The discussion focuses on the factors shared between the two service-learning designs that might mediate a positive mastery experience.

Twenty-five percent of teachers in the United States are said to leave the profession within the first 2 years of teaching, and 40% leave within 5 years because they perceive that they are underprepared for the daily classroom

Research for What? Making Engaged Scholarship Matter
pp. 121–145
Copyright © 2010 by Information Age Publishing
All rights of reproduction in any form reserved.

and lack confidence to address their internalized shortcomings (Grant & Gillett, 2006). Based on these percentages, it becomes strikingly apparent that if we want new teachers to address the tremendous diversity in the classroom, appropriately challenge students and facilitate high achievement, and commit to the teaching profession, the schools, and their students, they must enter the teaching profession with a strong sense of teacher efficacy.

Teacher efficacy has been linked to myriad variables associated with teaching and student learning (Bandura, 1993; Goddard, Hoy, & Woolfolk-Hoy, 2000; Midgley, Feldlaufer, & Eccles, 1989; Soodak & Podell, 1993). Teacher efficacy, or teacher sense of efficacy, is defined as a teacher's perception of his/her perceived competence to facilitate positive educational outcomes for learners (Tschannen-Moran & Woolfolk-Hoy, 2001). In fact, Bailey (1999) found that teachers who choose to stay in the classroom have higher levels of self-efficacy than those who leave.

Teacher educators are naïve to expect significant gains in preservice teachers' efficacy if students in teacher education are required to engage in only a single authentic, complex teaching experience during their university education (Nelson, Tice, & Theriot, 2008). Butcher, Hogan, Surrey, and Ryan (2004) contend that the traditional approaches to teacher education are inadequate. They propose instead that preservice teacher education include more reciprocal commitment to school partners through civic engagement. Unfortunately, field-based experiences are most often limited to internship/student teaching experiences. Internships follow a sequence of required courses in a field of study and are commonly completed during the student's last semester prior to graduation. The aim of internships is to enhance students' academic learning and/or vocational development through student-interns' acquisition of skills and knowledge (Furco, 1996). Interns shadow and mirror authentic duties of the mentor, approximating the role of a teacher.

In contrast, preinternship students are still completing the requisite courses in their program of study. They retain the support of their instructors and fellow students, are able to reflect on their experiences simultaneously with the delivery of course content, and have several semesters in which to scaffold new academic content and experiences on one another. The current study investigates whether preinternship students' service-learning experiences in K-12 classrooms can enhance their sense of teacher efficacy.

Social Cognitive Theory and Self-Efficacy

Social cognitive theory posits that individuals learn usefulness, appropriateness, and consequences of behaviors through the "triadic reciprocality" among behavioral, environmental, and personal factors (Bandura, 1982a, 1986, 2001). Each factor operates as an interlocking determinant of, and bidirectionally influences, the other (Bandura, 1977a). Learners regulate their own actions and behaviors in part on the basis of comparisons between a performance and the personal standard against which it is measured. These self-evaluative reactions result in learners' beliefs about their capabilities, which Bandura and others have termed "self-efficacy."

Self-efficacy refers to an individual's beliefs about his/her capabilities to learn, organize, implement, and perform actions or behaviors in particular situations and at designated levels (Bandura, 1977a, 1977b, 1982b, 1986, 1993, 1997). Self-efficacy is future-oriented (Pajares, 1997) and is thus a strong predictor of initiation and persistence of behavior (Bandura, 1997). Self-efficacy affects an individual's choice of, effort toward, and persistence in tasks/activities (Bandura, 1982a, 2000; Bandura & Cervone, 1983, 1986; Schunk, 1991, 1995, 2001; Schunk & Pajares, 2002, 2004).

Information about self-efficacy expectations is derived from four sources. First, the most powerful source of information about efficacy is mastery experiences, or previous performances that are interpreted by the individual as successful (Pajares, 2002): "Enactive mastery experiences are the most influential source of efficacy information because they provide the most authentic evidence of whether one can muster whatever it takes to succeed" (Bandura, 1997, p. 80). Individuals with low self-efficacy may avoid attempting future tasks that are similar to those at which they previously failed or performed under their initial assumed capabilities. Their more efficacious peers, in contrast, will exert effort even when the task is accompanied with great difficulty. When we succeed, our efficacy beliefs will raise; failure may result in lowered self-efficacy.

Second, individuals observe others and learn from them. While not as powerful as mastery experiences, vicarious experiences (i.e., the influence of observing others and learning from them) can be a significant influence on the observer's efficacy. Vicarious experiences allow learners to assess their own capabilities through someone else's accomplishments or failures. In his early work, Bandura identified observational learning and modeling as significant components of learning. One important aspect of observational learning is the degree to which the observer identifies with the model. The stronger the observer's identification with the model, the more self-efficacy will be affected.

Third, self-efficacy is affected by social persuasion. Social persuasion refers to the feedback received during a performance of a task. Although positive feedback has not been shown to create enduring increases in self-efficacy (Bandura, 1982a), it can offset moments of self-doubt and interrupted persistence (Woolfolk, 2008). The impact of social persuasion on self-efficacy is correlated with the recipient's view of the persuader. A credible and trustworthy source is more potently influential than one for which the learner holds little admiration and respect (Bandura, 1997).

Lastly, physiological and emotional states (e.g., heart rate, sweating) or levels of arousal, affect self-efficacy, depending on how the condition is interpreted. Stressful, anxious, or troubling activities lower efficacy, while more exciting tasks tend to increase efficacy (Bandura, 1997; Pintrich & Schunk, 2002).

One's sense of self-efficacy is not determined by a single source, rather it is cognitively appraised by learners inferentially weighing the contributions of behavioral, environmental, and personal factors against their ability, expectations, efforts, difficulties, assistance received, and related successes and failures (Bandura, 1980, 1982b, 1993, 1997). Self-efficacy is also influenced by individual readiness and mindset, as well as the characteristics of the social milieu and task itself (Schunk, 2008).

Teacher Efficacy

Efficacy differs from self-concept in that self-concept is a global concept that is generalized to all aspects of one's life. The construct of self-efficacy appears to be domain-specific, specific to a set of capabilities or particular situations, showing little generalization across areas (Pajares, 1996; Smith & Fouad, 1999). Our concern in the present study was with efficacy in teaching. Teacher efficacy, or teacher sense of efficacy (TSE), refers to a teacher's judgment of his or her competence and ability to bring about meaningful and significant educational outcomes for students (Armor et al., 1976; Bandura, 1977b; Tschannen-Moran & Woolfolk-Hoy, 2001; Tschannen-Moran, Woolfolk-Hoy, & Hoy, 1998).

Researchers have concluded that teachers with high TSE are more enthusiastic about teaching (Guskey, 1984; Woolfolk, 2008), are less likely to interact negatively with students (Soodak & Podell, 1993), less likely to experience burn-out (Burley, Hall, Villeme, & Brockmeier, 1991), and more likely to remain in the teacher profession (Coladarci, 1992; Ebmeier, 2003; Evans & Tribble, 1986). Openness to instructional innovations and greater levels of planning and organization have also been found to be related to high TSE (Allinder, 1994; Ghaith & Yaghi, 1997; Guskey, 1984; Stein & Wang, 1988). Teachers with high teacher efficacy have reported a stronger commitment to the profession of teaching and to their schools (Coladarci, 1992; Ebmeier, 2003; Evans & Tribble, 1986). In fact, the collective efficacy of a faculty can be a stronger predictor of student achievement than the socioeconomic level of the students (Bandura, 1993; Goddard et al., 2000).

Because teachers with a high sense of teacher efficacy tend to believe in both themselves and their students, they tend to be more enthusiastic about and persistent in efforts to bring about positive student outcomes (Ashton, 1984; Woolfolk, 2008). Ashton and Webb (1986) found that such teachers are less critical of errors and mistakes made by students. Evidence is mounting that teacher efficacy has an impact on numerous desirable educational outcomes, including student achievement (Anderson, Greene, & Loewen, 1998; Ashton & Webb, 1986; Ross, 1992; Shahid & Thompson, 2001; Woolfolk-Hoy & Davis, 2006), student motivation (Midgley et al., 1989; Tschannen-Moran et al. 1998), and the students' own sense of efficacy (Tschannen-Moran & Woolfolk-Hoy, 2001).

Self-Efficacy and Service-Learning

Research investigating the impact on self-efficacy from participating in community service and service-learning activities has been somewhat inconclusive. A number of investigators have reported that service-learning participation increases general self-efficacy (Billig, 2000; Furco, 2003; Ikeda, 1999; McMahon, 1998; Morgan & Streb, 1999; Shaffer, 1993). Findings have been corroborated across diverse student groups: Students with emotional and behavioral disorders (Frey, 2003), high school students (Crosman, 1989; Marks, 1994), Catholic undergraduates (Bernacki & Jaeger, 2008), undergraduate sociology students (Kendrick, 1996), Bonners Scholars (Keen & Keen, 1998), youth enrolled in afterschool programs (Eccles & Gootman, 2002), graduate social work students (Williams, King, & Koob, 2002), and racially and socioeconomically diverse groups of middle school students (Scales, Blyth, Berkas, & Kielsmeier, 2000) have all reported increased senses of self-efficacy after participating in service-learning. Most of this documentation reports on the connection between increased self-efficacy and volunteering during the undergraduate years (Astin, Sax, & Avalos, 1999; Schmidt, 2000; Takahashi, 1991; Taylor & Trepanier-Street, 2007; Teranishi, 2007).

On the other hand, there are also a number of studies that do not show positive effects of service-learning participation on general self-efficacy. Miller (1997) found that undergraduate students who participated in a service-learning course with different service options showed no increase in their efficacy. In the same vein, special education students demonstrated no significant change in self-efficacy after participating in service-learning (Healy, 2000). Stewart (2008) found that first-year honor undergraduates' community service self-efficacy decreased significantly after volunteering in underserved schools. Furthermore, a major national study concluded that undergraduates who had participated in service-learning did not report significant changes in self-efficacy unless they were simultaneously participating in generic community service (Vogelgesang & Astin, 2000). In other words, generic community service was found to be a mediating variable for service-learning's effect on self-efficacy (Yee, Ikeda, Vogelgesang, & Astin, 2000). Thus, research concerning the impact of service-learning experiences on general self-efficacy is inconclusive. Presumably, there are as yet unspecified factors (e.g., student characteristics or experiences or components of the service-learning experience) that need to be considered in determining outcomes.

Teacher Efficacy and Service-Learning

Published studies examining teacher sense of efficacy and service-learning are few. Outcomes from those available are inconclusive about the relationship between the experiential pedagogy and the teacher sense of efficacy construct, and, in certain cases, have mistakenly extrapolated results from generalized self-efficacy to infer an impact on the more domain-specific teacher efficacy. For example, several studies have shown that preservice teachers increase in their commitment to teaching, community participation, self-esteem and self-efficacy, and feelings of compassion and concern (Flippo, Hetzel, Gribonski, & Armstrong, 1993; Green, Dalton, & Wilson, 1994; Wade, 1995). However, Root, Callahan, and Sepanski (2002) did not find significant effects for service-learning on teaching efficacy and commitment to teaching in 442 preservice teacher participants in nine teacher education programs that were members of the National Service-learning in Teacher Education Partnership (NSLTP).

In a more recent study of service-learning and teacher efficacy, Nelson et al. (2008) asked if preservice teachers' participation in service-learning increased their personal and teacher efficacy over levels shown by a control group of preservice teachers enrolled in a non-service-learning course. They found no significant change in either group over time. Although the students came from two courses taught by the same instructor, no information is given about how distinct these courses were in content or instructional methods. Further, the study does not situate the findings in social cognitive theory and literature on efficacy, thus limiting our interpretation. Through an analysis of oral and written reflections, the authors do identify themes to which teacher efficacy may be connected. These themes hint at four sources of self-efficacy: Authenticity of learning, required planning and preparation, collaboration and networking, and rewards gained from the teaching experience.

Research Questions

Service-learning shows promise in increasing perceived self-efficacy. However, findings remain inconclusive about the direct role that service-learning may have independent of simultaneous volunteer activities. In addition, there are few studies examining the impact of service-learning on preservice teachers' sense of teacher efficacy and even less work with preinternship students. With this in mind, the current study examined the impact of participation in service-learning in K-12 classrooms on preinternship teachers' sense of teacher efficacy and also asked whether the type of service project plays a role in these outcomes. Three questions guided the study:

1. Are there any significant changes in preinternship teachers' sense of teacher efficacy after participating in whole class K-12 service-learning projects?
2. Are there any significant changes in preinternship teachers' sense of teacher efficacy after participating in individual student and/or small group tutoring service-learning projects?
3. Are there any significant differences in preinternship teachers' sense of teacher efficacy between the two service-learning designs?

METHOD

Design

A two-group, pretest-posttest, quasi-experimental research design was used to study changes in self-efficacy expressed by undergraduate preinternship teachers. The study aimed to determine changes in the sense of efficacy expressed by these prospective teachers before and after participating in one of two junior-level education courses, each involving a K-12 service-learning experience appropriate to the content of the course.

Research Participants

The participants in this study were junior level undergraduate education majors at a large research-intensive metropolitan university in the southeast United States. The participants were enrolled in a service-learning course, Course 1 or Course 2, but not in both, during the spring, summer, or fall semester in 2008. As shown in Exhibit 6.1, the final sample was composed of 169 Caucasian, five African American, eight Hispanic, and two Asian participants. There were 163 female and 25 male students. All students were over 18 years of age. The 188 participants constitute

Exhibit 6.1.   Gender and Ethnic Representation in each Course

	Course 1		Course 2	
	Number (n = 101)	Percent	Number (n = 87)	Percent
Gender				
Male	15	14.9	10	11.5
Female	86	85.1	77	88.5
Ethnicity				
Black/African American	3	3.0	2	2.3
Latino/Hispanic	4	4.0	4	4.6
Caucasian/White	92	91.1	77	88.5
Asian	1	1.0	1	1.1
Middle Eastern/Arab	0	0	1	1.1
Other	1	1.0	2	2.3

80% of the students enrolled in the classes during the semesters in which data were collected.

Courses and Service-Learning Assignments

The service-learning courses used in this research were among the first courses that students take after matriculating into the College of Education. All course offerings were taught by the same instructor.

Course 1: Methods and Classroom Management

In Course 1, students were exposed to various instructional delivery techniques and organizational and management skills that promote the development of a classroom community. Students wrote and taught lessons, and then reflected on the process. Students were required to complete 15 hours of service-learning with a certified teacher in a K-12 classroom during normal school hours. They were to assist the teacher in any way s/he needed, deliver a lesson and get feedback from the teacher using an observation form provided by their college instructor, and complete one analytic assignment on classroom management.

In addition to weekly reflections via discussion prompts in the online portion of the course, two summative reflective assignments were required to address the teaching methods and classroom management foci of the course. Students were to write a lesson plan for an upcoming lesson in their service-learning classroom. Students decided on the topic of their lesson in consultation with their supervising teacher. The completed lesson plan was shared with the supervising teacher at least two days prior to the lesson. Supervising teachers used the lesson plan and their observation of the service-learners conducting the lesson to complete an observation form provided by the college instructor. The feedback was used by the student to reflect on the lesson and its delivery so that s/he could make the necessary changes before submitting the lesson plan for a grade.

To reflect on classroom management, students completed a meta-reflective PowerPoint presentation that joined together their in-class academic topics with their service-learning experiences. Students were provided with a PowerPoint template comprised of 15 slides. Each of the slides had detailed instructions about the information that should be provided, including an introduction to the site (e.g., site, teacher, and student demographics), engagement activities, and an analysis of classroom arrangement, rules, procedures, and management problem areas.

Course 2: Educational Psychology and Assessment

The focus of Course 2 is to examine principles of learning as applied to classroom teaching situations, with emphasis on behavior, cognition, motivation, and assessment. Course 2 students were required to complete 15 hours of service-learning with a certified teacher in a K-12 classroom during normal school hours. In contrast to Course 1 students, Course 2 service-learning hours were to be spent tutoring individual students or small groups of students, working with the same students over the 15 hours. These students had been identified by the host teacher as needing assistance. In contrast to Course 1, no work with the whole K-12 class was required, only individual tutoring or small group work.

In addition to weekly reflections via online discussion prompts, two assignments were required for Course 2: First, students were to maintain a human development journal. In this journal they summarized their service-learning activities and processes, tied their observations to a theorist and development stage discussed in the course, and explained how this new knowledge would inform their future teaching. The second assignment continued to develop students' understanding of developmental stages and theories of learning, while enabling them to employ their new knowledge of assessment. In a critical thinking curriculum evaluation project, students analyzed a textbook lesson to determine if it was developmentally appropriate for students and if it promoted students' critical thinking about the topic. Then, they were to design a series of new lessons, activities, and assessments to ensure that their students would be engaged in higher-order thinking about the specific topic.

Service-Learning Preparation and Procedures

Students in both courses completed an online module on the philosophical foundations of experiential education that included an article on the difference between service-learning and other experiential pedagogies. Focused discussion by the college instructor highlighted the importance of the preinternship students' service-learning activities toward addressing an actual need in today's classrooms and supporting their achievement of course goals. Students were provided with a log on which to have host teachers verify their attendance and activity participation, an evaluation form for host teachers to complete at the end of the service-learning experience, and a letter of introduction to present to the host school administration and teacher. Students were required to register with the county's volunteer program, which then conducted background checks.

Research Instrument

The Teacher Sense of Efficacy Scale (*TSE*-long form; Tschannen-Moran & Woolfolk-Hoy, 2001) was used to measure teacher sense of efficacy. The Teacher Sense of Efficacy Scale is a 24-item scale that measures teachers' beliefs about their own personal and task competence. Analyses (Tschannen-Moran & Woolfolk-Hoy, 2001) have identified three teacher efficacy factors: Efficacy in instructional strategies, classroom management, and student engagement.

The *instructional strategies* efficacy factor includes questions such as, "To what extent can you provide an alternative explanation or example when students are confused?" Factor 2, *efficacy for classroom management*, includes questions such as, "How much can you do to control disruptive behavior in the classroom? The last factor includes questions related to the efficacy of *student engagement*. A sample question is, "How much can you do to get students to believe they can do well in schoolwork?" Responses are measured on a 9-point Likert-type scale with the notations 1 (Nothing), 3 (Very little), 5 (Some influence), 7 (Quite a bit), and 9 (A great deal). High scores are indicative of a high self-perception of teaching competence.

Various studies (Brown, 2005; Tschannen-Moran & Woolfolk-Hoy, 2001; Tsigilis, Grammatikopoulos, & Koustelios, 2007) have found that the TSE has sound psychometric properties. The internal consistency of the scale was reported to be .94 (Tschannen-Moran & Woolfolk-Hoy, 2001) and .97 (Tsigilis et al., 2007). The validity of the instrument has been cross-validated through different studies using independent samples (e.g. Tschannen-Moran & Woolfolk-Hoy, 2001; Tsigilis et al., 2007). Tschannen-Moran and Woolfolk-Hoy (2001) concluded that the TSE-long form "should prove to be a useful tool for researchers interested in exploring the construct of teacher efficacy" (p. 801).

We further examined the reliability and validity of the TSE using the sample for the current study. We first conducted exploratory factor analysis (EFA) to assess the factor structure of the scale for this sample, and found a clear three-factor structure, consistent with the three constructs previously identified: Teacher efficacy for instructional strategies, teacher efficacy for classroom management, and teacher efficacy for student engagement. All items loaded significantly on the appropriate factor, with loadings ranging from .56 to .82, and 71.24% total variance explained by the three factors. The number of common factors to be retained was also consistent with the methodological recommended criteria for determining the number of factors in an exploratory analysis. Horn's Parallel Analysis (HPA; Horn, 1965), conducted using the Statistical Analysis System (SAS), also revealed three factors. The first three actual eigen values (13.98, 1.99, and 1.13) were greater than those generated by HPA using both the average and the 95th percentile criteria. The Cronbach's alpha coefficient assessing the internal consistency of the 24-item TSE was .97, indicating the high internal consistency of the instrument.

Procedure

During the second class meeting, before they engaged in any of the service-learning activities designed for their courses, students were asked to complete an informed consent form that had been approved by the university's Institutional Review Board. Those willing to participate in the research were asked to complete, by the third week of class, the Teacher Sense of Efficacy Scale, presented as a password-protected web survey. At the end of the course, students were asked to complete the web survey a second time. These postsurveys were not available to students until the penultimate week of the course, to ensure that required service-learning hours and accompanying assignments were completed by the time of the survey. Pre- and postresponses were matched by the last four digits of a student personal identification number (i.e., not social security number). Incomplete surveys and surveys without a pre- or postmatch (less than 5% of the total number of participants) were removed from the sample.

RESULTS

Descriptive Analysis

Exhibit 6.2 shows the descriptive statistics for each course. In general, we can see that Course 2, when compared to Course 1, started with somewhat higher scores on Instructional Strategies and Student Engagement,

**Exhibit 6.2.   Mean Pre- and Posttest Scores
on TSE Scales for Students From Two Courses**

Time	TSE Subscales	Course	M	SD	N
Pretest scores	Instructional strategies	1	57.41	10.148	101
		2	57.51	10.318	87
	Classroom management	1	58.12	9.109	101
		2	57.67	10.220	87
	Student engagement	1	59.89	8.829	101
		2	61.24	9.206	87
Posttest scores	Instructional strategies	1	61.59	7.887	101
		2	63.17	7.505	87
	Classroom management	1	61.69	8.185	101
		2	63.31	7.784	87
	Student engagement	1	61.11	8.667	101
		2	62.43	8.189	87

Note: 1 = Course 1; 2 = Course 2.

but slightly lower scores on Classroom Management than the participants in Course 1. After the treatment period, students in both courses showed increases in teacher efficacy, as measured by the three subscales of TSE. Participants in Course 2 had systematically higher scores than their peers in Course 1 on the posttest. In order to determine whether there were statistically significant differences as a function of course or over the treatment period, we conducted the analyses of participants' TSE scores, as described below.

Multivariate Analysis

We used a multivariate repeated measures analysis of variance to address the three research questions. First, Box's test was conducted to test the homogeneity of the multivariate data. Box's M value of $F(21, 121442) = .96$ ($p > .52$) revealed that the assumption for the homogeneity of the multivariate data was met for conducting multivariate analysis. An initial analysis showed that neither gender nor ethnicity interacted with group or time of test in determining scores on the three dependent variables, so these demographic variables were not included in the final analysis.

To assess changes in aspects of teacher efficacy after the treatment period, a repeated-measures MANOVA was conducted on the scores for teachers' efficacy for instructional strategies, efficacy for classroom management, and efficacy for student engagement. A Condition (Course 1 vs. Course 2) × Time (Pretest-Posttest) × Measure (TSE scale) factorial analysis of variance with repeated measures on the latter two variables was conducted.

Exhibit 6.3.   Repeated-Measures MANOVA Assessing Differences as a Function of Course, Time of Test, and TSE Scales

Effect	Wilks' Lambda Value	F	Hypothesis df	Error df	p	η^2
Time	.883	24.558[a]	1	186	<.001	.117
Time * Courses	.996	.658[a]	1	186	.418	.004
TSE	.927	7.273[a]	2	185	<.001	.073
TSE * Courses	.995	.511[a]	2	185	.601	.005
Time * TSE	.803	22.754[a]	2	185	<.001	.197
Time * TSE * Courses	.982	1.666[a]	2	185	.192	.018

Note: [a]Exact statistic. [b]Computed using alpha = .05. [c]Design: Intercept + Course Within Subjects Design: Time + TSE + Time * TSE

The results confirmed a statistically significant interaction effect between Measures and Time, with Wilks' λ = .80, multivariate $F(2, 185)$ = 22.75 (p < .001), and η^2 = .197, which qualifies overall effects of Time and TSE, as shown in Exhibit 6.3. Each of three outcome measures changed significantly over the treatment period (see Exhibit 6.4), although there were differences in the extent and nature of change shown. There were no significant differences between the participants in the two courses on any of the self-efficacy measures.

DISCUSSION

Preinternship service-learners in both types of service-learning activities increased significantly in their sense of teacher efficacy. However, neither type of service-learning activity was superior to the other. It appears, therefore, that the number of K-12 students with whom the preinternship student is interacting during service-learning is not a significant factor, nor is the nature of the academic course in which they are participating. One might conclude, rather, that the dynamics created by the service-learning experience result in increased teacher sense of efficacy for the preinternship students.

For an experience to be categorized as a mastery experience, the individual must perceive the outcome to be one of having demonstrated the cognitive and behavioral capabilities for executing appropriate courses of action (Bandura, 1995). Based on the highly significant increases in

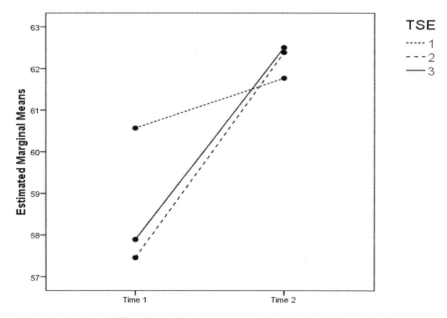

Note: 1 = Teachers' efficacy for student engagement. 2 = Teachers' efficacy for classroom management. 3 = Teachers' efficacy for instructional strategies.

Exhibit 6.4.   Changes over the treatment period on each of the three TSE scales (Courses 1 and 2 Combined).

teacher sense of efficacy resulting from the service-learning experience in the current study, we believe that the preinternship students' perception was that they had, in fact, demonstrated the necessary cognitive and behavioral capabilities in the areas of classroom management, student engagement, and instructional strategies.

With this in mind, the discussion will focus on the factors shared between the two service-learning designs that might mediate a positive mastery experience. The potential role of these factors on teacher efficacy will be discussed in line with social cognitive theory, the construct of efficacy, and service-learning.

Preparation

As advocated in service-learning best practices, preinternship teacher education students in both courses were appropriately prepared in their college courses prior to beginning their service-learning activities. Specifically, service-learners were required to complete a module on the philosophical foundations of experiential education which included an article on the difference between service-learning and other experiential pedagogies. Purposive attention was placed on having the preinternship students understand that they would be helping to meet an actual need and that these volunteer activities were, in fact, supporting their achievement of course goals. The anticipation of contributing may aid in formulating the experience in a positive light. Students might be excited for their possible impact, approach the tasks with greater confidence and earnestness, and take greater pride than in their typical course assignments. Service-learners who were challenged to develop their own projects or to take responsible roles in and control over meaningful activities have reported an increased sense of efficacy (Billig, Root, & Jesse, 2005; Furco, 2002).

The seriousness and professionalism of the service-learning activities were reinforced by the structure provided to the students by their college instructor. Service-learners were provided with time lines, clear expectations on focused assignments, forms and logistical support, and were advised to meet with the host teacher prior to engaging in their documented service hours. The process of preparation may, therefore, create a more positive, comfortable, and motivating effect on the preinternship students' physiological and emotional states. Through the lenses of social cognitive theory and teacher efficacy, experiencing less stress from the demands of academic tasks can be associated with feeling more efficacious and more likely to master a task (Schunk, 2008). With this said, results can be attributed to a variety of complex external factors (e.g., a motivating instructor) and causal claims should not drawn strictly from the service-learning intervention alone.

Having the Teacher in K-12 Classrooms

Modeled behavior is a fundamental part of observational learning. Completing service-learning activities in the K-12 classrooms alongside a K-12 teacher potentially provided opportunities for preinternship students to watch their host teachers throughout their visits. As a mentor and reflection of who the service-learners were to become, the host teacher was most likely accepted as a credible model and an incredible source of persuasion.

Service-learners were able to glean practices, approaches, and techniques that experienced teachers utilize and that work. By seeing these approaches in action, and the outcomes that they cause, preinternship students can feel more confident in utilizing the same approaches later, even if they simply replicate what the host teacher has modeled. On the other hand, preinternship service-learners may also notice their host teacher using a instructional strategy, classroom management approach, or student engagement technique that failed, or was in contrast to the best practices that they had learned in their college coursework. In the latter case, these future educators might feel more confident in their abilities knowing that they should avoid certain approaches that would negatively impact student learning or classroom ambiance.

Authentic Teacher Tasks

Becoming a teacher is a process that involves the development of a new identity. With regard to their professional development, the preinternship student's identity arguably has been primarily that of a "student." Going into the classroom and becoming the "teacher" allowed the preinternship student to step temporarily into the identity of a teacher while retaining his/her student identity and, thus, the support of the K-12 teacher and the college instructor. The dual identity (e.g., student/teacher) can serve to decrease service-learners' performance anxiety by sanctioning the preinternship student's "I don't have to know it all" mindset.

For example, Course 1 service-learners were required to work alongside a K-12 teacher and ultimately teach a lesson to their host class. Before the lesson, service-learners were required to provide a copy of their lesson plans and observational rubrics on which their host teachers would provide the service-learner feedback in a one-on-one meeting. Teaching the lesson allowed the preinternship students to practice instructional strategies, to engage students, and to manage classroom discipline. The observation by the host teacher mimicked an administrator's assessment of the classroom teacher's performance. Knowing that they were to submit the completed form and lesson plan to their college instructor afterwards further evidenced the authenticity and seriousness of their tasks.

A second assignment for Course 1 was to examine the classroom management practices, rules, and procedures in the host classroom. Although a more structured approach, this activity is common practice for classroom teachers, who must constantly rethink the layout of the classroom, the approach to dealing with disciplinary issues, and how to minimize distractions through the creation of routines through which K-12 students become almost self-guiding.

Course 2 preinternship service-learners also had opportunities to work in authentic teaching roles. Being trusted to work independently with students needing assistance, and even design the tutoring lessons and activities themselves, parallel the lesson planning and implementation of their

Course 1 peers. As individuals, Course 2 service-learners had to attend to behavior issues and to motivate students in their small group to engage. In addition, the small group service-learning design provided the opportunity for the preinternship student to see how their efforts directly resulted in K-12 student change and achievement. Per social cognitive theory, the perceived impact, or lack of impact, that they made on these young learners would certainly color the internalization of their experiences. The reactions that were expressed by the K-12 students could have served as a viable persuader. The K-12 students would have been a credible and trustworthy source because they tend to be open and honest, and because they represent the audience with which preinternship students aim to work. Because the K-12 students were receiving individual attention, they most likely demonstrated a high level of engagement and management of disciplinary issues may have been minimized. If K-12 students in either situation showed excitement, high levels of engagement, good behavior, and appreciation, coupled with increased academic achievement, the preinternship teacher would arguably exit the experience more efficacious.

Course 2 service-learners also had college course assignments that echoed actual K-12 teacher tasks. First, students were required to examine a textbook lesson and assess its potential for developing K-12 students' critical thinking. This activity provided preinternship students with perhaps their first access to teacher materials and teacher editions of a textbook and demonstrated to students that they cannot take information in publisher supplied materials for granted. They must be conscientious about choosing their materials and lessons if they aim to provide opportunities for their future students to think critically. Charting, through journaling, the development of one of their tutees is another significant assignment completed by the preinternship students. At the end of the semester, they analyzed their findings using one of the developmental theories presented in their educational psychology course. Although K-12 teachers may not, as routine practice, follow the specifics of this assignment, there is no doubt that the practice of assessing the human development of a learner so as to best meet his/her needs educationally is paramount.

Direct Interaction With Support Mechanisms

According to Eyler and Giles (1999), "Students need considerable ... support when they work in settings that are new to them" (p. 185). In both service-learning designs, the preinternship students would have experienced the on-going support of the college instructor, the availability of the K-12 teacher to address questions and concerns, and the interactions of their fellow students who were engaged in a similar service-learning activity. In essence, these service-learning course designs created a triple safety net to lessen the stress factors that might hinder efficacy development. Arguably, the more comfortable one is in a situation, the more likely efficacy is to increase.

As highlighted above, the K-12 teacher was always available to assist, provide direction as needed, and to step in if there was a problem. The college instructor and preinternship classmates also could have served as sources of vicarious learning and social persuasion. The college instructor was available for the student to discuss the experience as the student reflected on the process. While these sources were probable social persuasion influences, it should also be noted that the encouragement received from the college instructor was likely perceived as an emotionally positive influence for the preinternship students. Knowing that they are not alone in their experiences and hearing supportive comments by an educator that they may respect can reinforce their beliefs in their ability to perform teaching tasks in their host K-12 classrooms and in the future independently. In short, the preinternship student would have the feeling that "I can do this—I can teach."

Through these service-learning designs and in line with best practices in service-learning vis-à-vis reflection, preinternship students were able to learn vicariously from the experiences of their classmates and future colleagues. Students engaged in ongoing, formative reflections of their service-learning experiences. In these reflective discussions, the course instructor and other students were able to share experiences, react to situations, and provide information or ideas to others in the class. Although each student might not have had a certain experience or opportunity to practice a strategy themselves, hearing the steps, successes/failures, and lessons learned from their classmates, and advice from the instructor could have served as a vicarious learning experience and could have even been practiced during the service-learning experience. These possibilities parallel previous research which shows that teacher efficacy increases when participants collaborate with colleagues, including observing one another and offering feedback and guidance (Henson, 2001; Roberts, Henson, Tharp, & Moreno, 2001). Progress monitoring has similarly been linked to student efficacy (Billig et al., 2005).

Lastly, persuasive reinforcements must not all be external to the learner. Social cognitive theory embraces the role of self-reinforcement which echoes the role of reflection and introspection advocated for and central to service-learning. Service-learners might have been reinforced internally through the required course and nonrequired personal reflections which aided them in processing their experiences.

Opportunities for Future Research

Based on the findings from the current study, several opportunities for future research are possible.

1. Additional courses should be added to future studies to replicate and extend the present findings. The inclusion of control groups would allow for more definitive conclusions about the impact of service-learning engagement on teacher efficacy. Alternative comparison groups might be constituted by asking preinternship teachers to spend time simply observing in K-12 classrooms or engaging with young learners in nonschool settings.

2. This study utilized quantitative methods and was framed by previous literature and theory. A mixed methods approach would be an informative extension of this work. Specifically, analyzing student written reflections and transcripts of class reflections would deepen our understanding of the efficacy increases found here.

3. Future research should include demographic questions that paint a picture of service-learners' previous experiences. For example, it would be helpful to know if participants had engaged in service-learning, tutoring, substitute teaching, leading a Scout troop, or had had any other experience that would make them more or less comfortable and confident with their role as a "teacher."

4. Future studies should also aim to find more diverse samples. In particular, having more male students and students of color might affect outcomes in a white, female dominated profession.

CONCLUSION

In this study, we found that having preinternship teachers engage in service-learning activities that are in line with their level of knowledge and skills increases teacher efficacy. During the preprofessional period, a major aspect of the preinternship student's development is associated with identity formation. The primary identity of the preinternship student is that of a student. Preinternship service-learning opportunities in K-12 settings allow participants to begin their professional development from student to student/teacher well before their internship. As students move from student to student/teacher to teacher/student and eventually to teacher, the mastery experiences along the way facilitate an incremental increase in overall teacher efficacy.

Initially exposing preinternship students to a somewhat less traditional teaching situation permits them to focus and more appropriately process the experience. In reference to the sources of efficacy beliefs (Bandura, 1986, 1995), an incremental and progressive approach would very likely contribute to the perception of having achieved a mastery experiences at each stage. In short, matching ability to task allows students to engage in challenging, yet not overwhelming, tasks and the perception of the experience will more likely result in higher teacher efficacy.

In conclusion, we agree with Root et al. (2002) that teacher educators need to conscientiously consider service projects and course goals when designing service-learning activities, especially if increasing preinternship teachers' sense of teacher efficacy is a goal. Findings from this study should aid in teacher educators' considerations of program designs and expectations.

REFERENCES

Allinder, R. M. (1994). The relationship between efficacy and the instructional practices of special education teachers and consultants. *Teacher Education and Special Education, 17*, 86-95.

Anderson, R., Greene, M., & Loewen, P. (1998). Relationships among teachers' and students' thinking skills, sense of efficacy, and student achievement. *Alberta Journal of Educational Research, 34*(2), 148-156.

Armor, D., Conroy-Oseguera, P., Cox, M., King, N., McDonnell, L., Pascal, A., Pauly, E., & Zellman, G. (1976). *Analysis of the school preferred reading programs in selected Los Angeles minority schools* (Report No. R-2007-LAUSD). Santa Monica, CA: Rand Corporation. (ERIC Document Reproduction Service No. 130 243).

Ashton, P. (1984). Teacher efficacy: A motivational paradigm for effective teacher education. *Journal of Teacher Education, 35*(5), 28-32.

Ashton, P. T., & Webb, R. B. (1986). *Making a difference: Teachers' sense of efficacy and student achievement.* New York, NY: Longman.

Astin, A. W., Sax, L. J., & Avalos, J. (1999). Long term effects of volunteerism during the undergraduate years. *Review of Higher Education, 22*(2), 187-202.

Bailey, J. (1999). Academics' motivation and self-efficacy for teaching and research. *Higher Education Research & Development, 18*(3), 343-359.

Bandura, A. (1977a). Self-efficacy: Toward a unifying theory of behavioral change. *Psychological Review, 84*(2), 191-215.

Bandura, A. (1977b). *Social learning theory.* Englewood Cliffs, NJ: Prentice-Hall

Bandura, A. (1980). Self referent thought: A developmental analysis of self-efficacy. *Gestalt Theory—An International Multidisciplinary Journal, 2*(3/4), 147-174.

Bandura, A. (1982a). Self-efficacy mechanism in human agency. *American Psychologist, 37*(2), 122-147.

Bandura, A. (1982b). The assessment and predictive generality of self-percepts of efficacy. *Journal of Behavior Therapy and Experimental Psychiatry, 13*(3), 195-199

Bandura, A. (1986). *Social foundations of thought and action: A social cognitive theory.* Englewood Cliffs, NJ: Prentice Hall.

Bandura, A. (1993). Perceived self-efficacy in cognitive development and functioning. *Educational Psychologist, 28*(2), 117-148.

Bandura, A. (Ed.). (1995). Exercise of personal and collective efficacy in changing societies. In *Self-Efficacy in changing societies* (pp. 1-45). Cambridge, England: Cambridge University Press.

Bandura, A. (1997). *Self-efficacy: The exercise of control.* New York, NY: Freeman

Bandura, A. (2000). Self-efficacy: The foundation of agency. In W. J. Perrig & A. Grob (Eds.), *Control of human behaviour, mental processes and consciousness* (pp. 17-33) Mahwah, NJ: Erlbaum

Bandura, A. (2001). *Guide for constructing self-efficacy scales.* Unpublished manuscript.

Bandura, A. (2006). Adolescent development from an agentic perspective. In F. Pajares & T. Urdan (Eds.), *Self-efficacy beliefs of adolescents* (pp. 1-43). Greenwich, CT: Information Age

Bandura, A., & Cervone, D. (1983). Self-evaluative and self-efficacy mechanisms governing the motivational effects of goal systems. *Journal of Personality and Social Psychology, 45*(5), 1017-1028.

Bandura, A., & Cervone, D. (1986). Differential engagement of self-reactive influences in cognitive motivation. *Organizational Behavior and Human Decision Processes, 38*(1), 92-113.

Bernacki, M. L., & Jaeger, E. (2008). Exploring the impact of service-learning on moral development and moral orientation. *Michigan Journal of Community Service-learning, 14*(2), 5-15.

Billig, S. H. (2000, May). Research on K–12 school-based service-learning: The evidence builds. *Phi Delta Kappan, 81*(9), 658–664.

Billig, S. H., Root, S., & Jesse, D. (2005). The relationship between quality indicators of service-learning and student outcomes: Testing professional wisdom. In S. Root, J. Callahan, & S. H. Billig (Eds.), *Improving service-learning practice: Research on models to enhance impacts* (pp. 97–115). Greenwich, CT: Information Age.

Brown, E. (2005) The influence of teachers' efficacy and beliefs on mathematics instruction in the early childhood classroom. *Journal of Early Childhood Teacher Education, 26*, 239-257.

Burley, W. W., Hall, B. W., Villeme, M. G., & Brockmeier, L.L. (1991, April). *A path analysis of the mediating role of efficacy in first-year teachers' experiences, reactions, and plans.* Paper presented at the annual meeting of the American Educational Research Association, Chicago, IL.

Butcher, J., Hogan, G., Surrey, M., & Ryan, M. (2004). *Whose focus? The case for new forms of partnerships which enhance community and university capacity.* Paper presented at the Australian Universities Community Engagement Alliance National Conference, Charles Sturt University, Bathurst Australia.

Coladarci, T. (1992). Teachers' sense of efficacy and commitment to teaching. *Journal of Experimental Education, 60*, 323–337.

Crosman, M. D. (1989). *Effects of required community service on the development of self esteem, personal and social responsibility of high school students in a Friends School.* Unpublished doctoral dissertation, Lancaster Theological Seminary, Lancaster PA.

Ebmeier, H. (2003). How supervision influences teacher efficacy and commitment: An investigation of a path model. *Journal of Curriculum & Supervision, 18*(2), 110.

Eccles, J., & Gootman, J. (2002). *Community programs to promote youth development.* Washington, DC: National Academies Press.

Evans, E. D., & Tribble, M. (1986). Perceived teaching problems, self-efficacy and commitment to teaching among preservice teachers. *Journal of Educational Research, 80,* 81-85.

Eyler, J., & Giles, D. E., Jr. (1999). *Where's the learning in service-learning?* San Francisco, CA: Jossey-Bass.

Flippo, R. F., Hetzel, C., Gribonski, D., & Armstrong, L. A. (1993). *Literacy, multicultural, sociocultural considerations: Student literacy corps and the community.* Paper presented at the Annual Meeting of the International Reading Association, San Antonio, TX.

Frey, L. M. (2003). Abundant beautification: An effective service-learning project for students with emotional or behavioral disorders. *Teaching Exceptional Children, 35*(5), 66-75.

Furco, A. (1996). Service-learning: A balanced approach to experiential education. In Corporation for National Service (Ed.), *Expanding boundaries: Serving and learning* (pp. 2-6). Washington, DC: Corporation for National Service.

Furco, A. (2002). Is service-learning really better than community service? A study of high school service program outcomes. In A. Furco & S. H. Billig (Eds.), *Advances in service-learning research: Vol. 1. Service-learning: The essence of the pedagogy* (pp. 23–50). Greenwich, CT: Information Age.

Furco, A. (2003). Issues of definition and program diversity in the study of service-learning. In S.H. Billig & A. S. Waterman (Eds.), *Studying service-learning: Innovations in education research methodology* (pp. 13-34). Mahwah, NJ: Erlbaum.

Ghaith, G., & Yaghi, H. (1997). Relationships among experience, teacher efficacy, and attitudes toward the implication of instructional innovation. *Teaching and Teacher Education, 13*(4), 451-458.

Goddard, R. D., Hoy, W. K., & Woolfolk-Hoy, A. (2000). Collective teacher efficacy: Its meaning, measure, and impact on student achievement. *American Educational Research Journal, 37*(2), 479-507.

Grant, C., & Gillett, M. (2006). A candid talk to teacher educators about effectively preparing teachers who teach everyone's children. *Journal of Teacher Education, 57*(3), 292-299.

Green, J., Dalton, R., & Wilson, B. (1994). *Implementation and evaluation of TEACH: A service-learning program for teacher education.* Paper presented at the annual meeting of the Association of Teacher Educators, Atlanta, GA.

Guskey, T. R. (1984). The influence of change in instructional effectiveness upon the affective characteristics of teachers, *American Educational Research Journal, 21*(2), 245- 259.

Guskey, T. R. (1988). Teacher efficacy, self-concept, and attitudes toward the implementation of instructional innovation. *Teaching and Teacher Education, 4*, 63-69.

Healy, D. P. (2000). *Jordan-Evers Mentor & Service (JEMS) Project: A look at the effect of service-learning and peer mentorship on self-esteem, school social skills, and self-efficacy.* Unpublished doctoral dissertation, Our Lady of the Lake University, San Antonio.

Henson, R. K. (2001). The effects of participation in teacher research on teacher efficacy. *Teaching and Teacher Education, 17,* 819-836.

Horn, J. L. (1965). A rationale and test for the number of factors in factor analysis. *Psychometrika, 30,* 179-185.

Ikeda, E. K. (1999). *How does service enhance learning? Toward an understanding of the process.* Unpublished doctoral dissertation, University of California, Los Angeles.

Keen, C., & Keen, J. (1998). *Bonner Student Impact Survey.* Princeton, NJ: Bonner Foundation.

Kendrick, J. R. (1996). Outcomes of service-learning in an introduction to sociology course. *Michigan Journal of Community Service-learning, 3,* 72-81.

Marks, H. M. (1994). *Effect of participation in school sponsored community service programs on student attitudes toward social responsibility.* Unpublished doctoral dissertation, University of Michigan, Ann Arbor.

McMahon, R. (1998). *Service-learning: Perceptions of pre-service teachers.* Paper presented at the 27th annual meeting of the Mid-South Educational Research Association, New Orleans, LA.

Midgley, C., Feldlaufer, H., & Eccles, J. (1989). Changes in teacher efficacy and student self- and task-related beliefs in mathematics during the transition to junior high school. *Journal of Educational Psychology, 81*(2), 247-258.

Miller, J. (1997). The impact of service-learning experiences on students' sense of power. *Michigan Journal of Community Service-learning, 4,* 16-21.

Morgan, W., & Streb, M. (1999). *How quality service-learning develops civic values.* Bloomington, IN: Indiana University.

Nelson, L. P., Tice, K., & Theriot, S. (2008). Impact of service-learning on teachers' efficacy. *Academic Exchange Quarterly, 12*(3), 102-106.

Pajares, F. (1996). Self-efficacy beliefs in achievement settings. *Review of Educational Research, 66*(4), 543-578

Pajares, F. (1997). Current directions in self-efficacy research. In M. Maehr & P.R. Pintrich (Eds.), *Advances in motivation and achievement* (Vol. 10, pp. 1-49). Greenwich, CT: JAI Press.

Pajares, F. (2002). *Overview of social cognitive theory and of self-efficacy.* Retrieved from http://www.emory.edu/EDUCATION/mfp/eff.html.

Pintrich, P. R., & Schunk, D. H. (2002). *Motivation in education: Theory, research, and applications* (2nd ed.). Upper Saddle River, NJ: Merrill/Prentice Hall

Roberts, J. K., Henson, R. K., Tharp, B. Z., & Moreno, N. (2001). An examination of change in teacher self efficacy beliefs in science education based on duration of inservice education. *Journal of Science Teacher Education, 12,* 199-213.

Root, S., Callahan, J., & Sepanski, J. (2002). Building teaching dispositions and service-learning practice: A multi-site study. *Michigan Journal of Community Service-Learning, 8*(2), 50-60.

Ross, J. A. (1992). Teacher efficacy and the effect of coaching on student achievement. *Canadian Journal of Education, 95*, 534-562.

Scales, P. C., Blyth, D. A., Berkas, T. H., & Kielsmeier, J. C. (2000). Effects of service-learning on middle school students' social responsibility and academic success. *Journal of Early Adolescence, 20*(3), 332-358.

Schmidt, B. C. (2000). *Service sojourn: Conceptualizing the college student volunteer experience.* Unpublished doctoral dissertation, University of Utah, Salt Lake City.

Schunk, D. (1991). Self-efficacy and academic motivation. *Educational Psychologist, 26*, 207-231.

Schunk, D. H. (1995). Self-efficacy and education and instruction. In J. E. Maddux (Ed.), *Self-efficacy, adaptation, and adjustment: Theory, research, and application* (pp. 281-303). New York, NY: Plenum Press.

Schunk, D. H. (2001). Social cognitive theory and self-regulated learning. In B. J. Zimmerman & D. H. Schunk (Eds.), *Self-regulated learning and academic achievement: Theoretical perspectives* (2nd ed.) (pp. 125-151). Mahwah, NJ: Erlbaum.

Schunk, D. H. (2008). *Learning theories: An educational* perspective (5th ed.). Upper Saddle River, NJ: Pearson.

Schunk, D. H., & Pajares, F. (2002). The development of academic self-efficacy. In A. Wigfield & J. S. Eccles (Eds.), *Development of achievement motivation* (pp. 15-31). San Diego, CA: Academic Press.

Schunk, D. H., & Pajares, F. (2004).Self-efficacy in education revisited: Empirical and applied evidence. In D. M. Mcinerney & S. Van Etten (Eds.), *Big theories revisited* (pp. 115-138). Greenwich, CT: Information Age.

Shaffer, B. (1993). *Service-learning: An academic methodology.* Stanford, CA: Stanford University Department of Education.

Shahid, J., & Thompson, D. (2001, April). *Teacher efficacy: A research synthesis.* Paper presented at the annual meeting of the American Educational Research Association. Seattle, WA.

Smith, P. L., & Fouad, N. A. (1999). Subject-matter specificity of self-efficacy, outcome expectancies, interests, and goals: Implications for the social-cognitive model. *Journal of Counseling Psychology, 46*(4), 461-471.

Soodak, L., & Podell, D. (1993). Teacher efficacy and student problem as factors in special education referral. *Journal of Special Education, 27*(1), 66-81.

Stein, M. K., & Wang, M. C. (1988). Teacher development and school improvement: The process of teacher change. *Teaching and Teacher Education, 4*, 171-187.

Stewart, T. (2008). Community service self-efficacy and first-year undergraduate honors service-learning. In M. Bowdon, B. Holland, & S. Billig, (Eds.), *Scholarship for sustaining service-learning and civic engagement: Research and the K-20 continuum* (pp. 29-53). Charlotte, NC: Information Age.

Takahashi, J. S. (1991). *Minority student retention and academic achievement.* Unpublished doctoral dissertation, University of California, Los Angeles.

Taylor, J. A., & Trepanier-Street, M. (2007). Civic education in multicultural contexts: New findings from a national study. *Social Studies, 98*(1), 14-18.

Teranishi, C. S. (2007). Impact of experiential learning on Latino college students' identity, relationships, and connectedness to community. *Journal of Hispanic Higher Education, 6*(1), 52-72.

Tschannen-Moran, M., & Woolfolk-Hoy, A. (2001). Teacher efficacy: Capturing an elusive construct. *Teaching and Teacher Education 17*(7), 783–805.

Tschannen-Moran, M., Woolfolk-Hoy, A, & Hoy, W. K. (1998). Teacher efficacy: Its meaning and measure. *Review of Educational Research, 68*(2), 202-28.

Tsigilis, N., Grammatikopoulos, V., & Koustelios, A. (2007). Applicability of the Teachers' Sense of Efficacy Scale to educators teaching innovative programs. *International Journal of Educational Management, 21*, 634-642.

Vogelgesang, L. J., & Astin, A. W. (2000). Comparing the effects of community service and service-learning. *Michigan Journal of Community Service-learning, 7*, 25-34.

Williams, N. R., King, M., & Koob, J. J. (2002). Social work students go to camp: The effects of service-learning on perceived self-efficacy. *Teaching in Social Work, 22*(3/4), 55-70.

Wade, R. (1995). Community service-learning in the elementary teacher education program at the University of Iowa. In B. Gomez (Ed.), *Integrating service-learning into teacher education: Why and how?* (pp. 42-54). Washington, DC: Council of Chief State School Officers.

Woolfolk, A. (2008). *Educational psychology. Active learning edition* (2nd ed.). Boston, MA: Allyn & Bacon.

Woolfolk-Hoy, A., & Davis, H. (2006). Teacher self-efficacy and its influence on the achievement of adolescents. In F. Pajares & T. Urdan (Eds.), *Self-efficacy beliefs of adolescents* (117-138), Charlotte, NC: Information Age.

Yee, J. A., Ikeda, E. K., Vogelgesang, L. J., & Astin, A. W. (2000). *How service-learning affects students*. Retrieved from http://www.gseis.ucla.edu/heri/PDFs/HSLAS/HSLAS.PDF

CHAPTER 7

SERVICE-LEARNING IN SINGAPORE

Preparing Teachers for the Future

Robert Shumer, Kim Chuan Goh, and Vilma D'Rozario

The key to expansion of service-learning at the K-12 level is the development of education programs that effectively prepare teachers in the pedagogy and practice of service and civic engagement. While many countries around the world are experimenting with various approaches, Singapore has initiated a program that mandates service-learning as an integral part of their preparation of teachers' values, skills, and knowledge. Using a variety of approaches and courses, especially a required class in *group endeavors in service-learning*, preservice teachers spend up to 9 months developing and implementing a service-learning project with schools and community organizations. Quantitative and qualitative studies reveal that the effort is having a positive effect with preservice teachers, enriching their civic attitudes and ability to carry out group service learning projects.

One of the most important factors in expanding the use of service-learning around the world is strengthening the role of service-learning in teacher education. With more elementary and secondary students learn-

Research for What? Making Engaged Scholarship Matter
pp. 147–170
Copyright © 2010 by Information Age Publishing
All rights of reproduction in any form reserved.

ing the value and process of service learning and community engagement, there is a greater likelihood that students in higher education will demand such programs and be more efficient and more effective in participating in community connected learning. One challenge for the last decade has been how to expand service-learning in teacher education to accommodate the growth in the K-12 sector and how to ensure quality experiences in such programs. Part of this expansion requires an answer to the question: What is the purpose of preservice education?

Singapore has taken the challenge of expanding the number of teachers prepared in service-learning by initiating programs that focus on developing quality experiences for all teachers. The overarching purpose for inclusion of service-learning in teacher preparation is to fulfill Singapore's vision for the essential constructs that undergird all teacher preparation: values, skills, and knowledge (VSK). Articulated in the National Institute of Education (NIE) *Foundation Programme Report* (2004), each component has its own set of attributes. They are:

Values
- Belief that all pupils can learn
- Care and concern for all pupils
- Respect for diversity
- Commitment and dedication to the profession
- Collaboration, sharing, and team spirit
- Desire for continuous learning, excellence, and innovation

Knowledge
- Knowledge of educational context
- Knowledge of content
- Knowledge of curriculum
- Knowledge of pupils
- Knowledge of pedagogy
- Knowledge of self

Skills
- Pedagogical skills
- Interpersonal skills
- Reflective skills
- Personal skills
- Administrative and management skills

Service-learning is viewed as one of several approaches designed to fulfill this mission and to provide the kind of experiences necessary to ensure that new teachers understand the three components in the context of schools and communities.

Background Information

Singapore, officially the Republic of Singapore, is an island off the southern tip of the Malay Peninsula, south of the Malaysian state of Johor and north of Indonesia's Riau Islands. It is a highly urbanized country of almost 5 million people, with a key role in international trade and finance. The country is the world's third leading financial center, behind New York and London.

The Singaporean economy is often ranked amongst the world's top 10 on a variety of dimensions. The population is made up of Chinese, Malays, Indians, Asians, and Caucasians of different origins, and Eurasians. Forty-two percent of the population is made up of foreigners and approximately 50% work in the service sector. It is considered one of the wealthiest countries in the world. It has one of the busiest ports and is considered a logistics hub for commerce. Its economy is focused on industry, education, and urban planning.

Singapore's educational system is managed by the Ministry of Education, which sets programming from elementary education through to junior college (ages 17 and 18). Students take a series of exams that direct their progress through the educational system. Unlike the United States, student choices for advanced educational opportunities are highly dependent on their test scores in elementary and secondary school education programs. While there are more than 13,500 school districts in the United States, Singapore's educational system is run by a central agency that controls the curriculum and programming in all schools throughout the country. In other words, education in Singapore is highly centralized.

The NIE is the teacher training organization for the country. It is responsible for preparing and maintaining the teaching system for Singapore's 30,000 teachers. Unlike in the United States and many other countries where a multitude of colleges and universities offer teacher preparation programs with varied curricula and requirements, in Singapore all of the courses designed to prepare teachers for instructional activities, including service-learning and civic engagement, are sponsored by NIE faculty and programs. Like the schools, teacher preparation is highly centralized and unified in its organization and application.

What is distinctive about the *Group Endeavors in Service Learning* (GESL) in NIE is that first, it is a response to the Singapore government's initiatives to encourage the young to be involved in community service and to learn and develop soft skills in the process and, second, it is central to the NIE's program emphasis on *values* as core and foundational to its initial teacher preparation programs. With regard to the former, the National Youth Council, Ministry of Community Development, Youth and Sports has been active in promoting and facilitating service learning (SL) and providing funds for youth to be involved in SL within and outside the country over the past 10 years. In line with this national policy, the Ministry of Education has also introduced the Community Involvement Program (CIP) in all schools.

For many years, the thrust of SL in all this was very much the experience of volunteerism and community service with little deliberate learning being targeted. However, GESL at NIE has incorporated some aspects of learning through reflections at different stages of the projects, and sharing at project completion, and some assessment of this learning.

What is unique about NIE's GESL is the campuswide implementation since 2005, using a model that does not correspond to those used in institutions abroad, where very often SL is pegged to a particular course. In the United States and other countries, SL is an "intentional effort made to utilize the community based learning on behalf of academic learning, and to utilize academic learning to inform community service" (Markus, Howard, & King, 1993, p. 411) To have done it through a module or course to achieve the above quoted objective would not be logistically possible in NIE when 2,400 students are involved each year. Thus, out of necessity, the model adopted has had to be different.

Theoretical Foundation of Teacher Education in Singapore

Service-learning is but one of many approaches to developing the values, skills, and knowledge of teachers. The program is based on the solid foundation of a few theories and principles of learning. They include learning by doing, constructivist learning, and laws of learning transfer.

Teacher education in Singapore is based on several foundations of learning. First, learning is a process that involves important experiential components. Experiences need to be carefully constructed so they allow students exposure to realistic environments and they need to allow students to build upon their preexisting knowledge base and background. According to American philosopher John Dewey (1938), experiences must be provided that allow for individual growth through continuity and integration. Learning begins with an impulse to learn, and then grows as the student acquires knowledge and skills. This means students need to have continuously connected experiences that allow them to integrate cognitive principles and constructs with affective states. Thus, the goal for Singapore in developing a preservice program that focuses on values, skills, and knowledge is to ensure that students learn values as an integrated experience with their teacher practice.

This theoretical framework is buttressed by constructivist theories of learning that suggest that learning is based on previous experience and must build on foundational concepts already acquired by the learner. Bruner (1966) describes the actions as one of movement, where the outcome itself is a process. He discusses teaching and instruction in the following terms:

> to instruct someone … is not a matter of getting him to commit results to mind. Rather, it is to teach him to participate in the process that makes possible the establishment of knowledge. We teach a subject not to produce little living libraries on that subject, but rather to get a student to think mathematically for himself, to take part in knowledge getting. Knowing is a process, not a product. (p. 62)

Instruction and teaching involve students in "knowledge getting," making an effort to discover information and skills by themselves as they participate in the process. For Bruner, learning is about using experience to construct meaning and understanding as the ultimate goal for instruction—thus active engagement of the student in the determination of knowledge is the key to understanding.

This philosophy is supported by Vygotsky (1978) and Lave and Wenger (1991), who suggest that learning is a social process. Learners engage by interacting with others as they watch and model behavior and performance. In their book on "situated learning," Lave and Wenger claim that knowledge gathering is coconstructed and situated in a specific context. Knowledge is based upon the active engagement of learners in an environment where they work in a community of practice, and where application is connected to abstract ideas. Learning, as described by the constructivist theorists, is a group process, where individuals interact with one another to acquire knowledge about a particular topic or skill activity.

Csikszentmihalyi and Csikszentmihalyi (1992) further define the "optimal learning experience" as one of a continuous process of mediated challenge, where the learner takes on learning adventures that are filled with achievable challenges. This means that there is a balance between skill and knowledge, with the person only taking on tasks that are neither too boring nor too anxiety-producing and that are perceived to be possible to achieve. The learner negotiates this process through a system of clear and unambiguous feedback from the environment and the direct actions of learning. It is the feedback that provides a self-correcting force, constantly telling the learner whether or not they are progressing in a reasonable and effective manner. When the motivational state is right and the "flow" process is occurring in these optimal learning experiences, the learner loses track of time and of self, becoming absorbed in the action. Thus, the learning becomes "autotelic" or self reinforcing (Csikszentmihalyi, 1990). It, in Deci's (Deci & Ryan, 1985) terms, becomes intrinsically motivating and is done for the sheer joy of doing it. For educational systems, that is the ultimate goal of learning programs: To have them become an integral part of the learner's motivational schedule, so that the activities called for in the educational system becomes one with the desires of the learner to engage.

Lastly, Thorndike (1913) reminds us that learning takes place in a context. The more the learning environment models the actual implementation environment, the more likely there will be a transfer of learning. Thorndike's theory (1932) consists of three primary laws: (1) law of effect - responses to a situation which are followed by a rewarding state of affairs become strengthened and habitual responses to that situation; (2) law of readiness—a series of responses can be chained together to satisfy some goal which will result in annoyance if blocked; and (3) law of exercise—connections become strengthened with practice and weakened when practice is discontinued. This theory suggests that transfer of learning depends upon the presence of identical elements in the original and new learning situations. Therefore, it is important to construct learning environments that closely model application settings, and real world education and application are the ideal settings for conducting any training and education

One finds models of teacher preparation in Singapore that demonstrate understanding of these theoretical principles of learning and instruction. Students must be in environments that allow them to build on their own knowledge, construct learning challenges that are within their skill and knowledge repertoire, provide clear feedback, closely model settings where they will ultimately be earning a living, and are constructed in a way to ensure learning outcomes that parallel education goals and intent.

A good example of application of these theoretical principles is found in the Group Endeavors in Service-Learning course. It has as its core learning outcome that students learn and work in group environments. Here they have a chance to model leadership, develop values of engagement, create curriculum through a group endeavor, develop activities that are meaningful to them and to the context of the experience, provide for social learning and personal learning simultaneously, and contribute to society.

Research on Service-Learning and Teacher Education Is Foundational to Teacher Preparation

There is much research on service-learning and teacher education that provides a foundation for the construction of the Singaporean model of teacher preparation. Remembering that the overall philosophy of the NIE is to promote values, skills, and knowledge, the supporting research suggests that the development of the various components, including the GESL, are consistent with previous efforts in teacher education.

One of the goals of the GESL course is to promote active engagement in the service-learning process through a group experience in the context of service-learning. Research suggests that such involvement helps preservice teachers develop the professional attitudes and values needed for effective teaching (Root, Howard, & Daniels, 2004). Other outcomes occurring through community service/service-learning internships are the increased success of preservice teachers in planning ability, communicating with parents, and interpersonal skills in dealing with students (Sullivan, 1991). There are gains connected to attitudes about community participation and improvement in self-esteem and self-efficacy (Wade, 1995). Such experiences also lead to a higher level of analysis regarding the social problems of young people (Root & Batchelder, 1994). Other outcomes associated with involvement of preservice teachers in service-learning experiences during their educational program include deeper insights into personal, professional, academic, and career functioning (Swick & Rowls, 2000). Further, having students actually conduct studies and reflections about their service-learning experience through GESL activities exposes preservice teachers to the process of research and helps them gain a better understanding of the some of the critical issues.

Perhaps most importantly, the foundations of the teacher preparation program and activities in the NIE model conform to the ten essential elements found in research that lead to good service-learning practice (Root & Furco, 2001). From (1) preparing to use service-learning as a pedagogy by participating in service-learning experiences, as well as in-class study of good service-learning practice, through (10) the teacher education program, institution, and the community should support service-learning by providing the resources and structural elements necessary for continued success—the elements contained in the preservice program in Singapore cover all the important components and foster a strong commitment to the implementation of service-learning in schools. While not existent in a majority of educational programs in the United States, the NIE commitment to mandatory courses and programs places the Singapore teacher preparation program near the top of the heap in worldwide efforts to engage preservice teachers in meaningful experiences with communities and schools through service-learning practice.

The Teacher Education Model

At the NIE, service-learning is promoted through four programs: Individual voluntary projects with welfare experiences, a campus club that promotes service-learning among college students, youth expedition projects (where students do service projects in developing countries), and a GESL program where all student teachers engage in a group experience with community agencies actually performing service-learning (Ch'ng, D'Rozario, Goh & Cheah, 2009). The purpose of the GESL program is to inculcate values of service (care, respect for diversity, spirit of collaboration, and concern for the wider community) and to expose future teachers to the process of service-learning.

Some of the students engage in voluntary projects to learn how to work with community agencies and to have a personal experience doing service. The purpose of this activity is to help students gain a healthy attitude toward volunteerism and community service. Students also learn about community needs and fulfill the desire to contribute to the welfare of individuals and organizations that serve local communities.

The campus club is supported by NIE and an umbrella Trainee Teachers Club and is intended to provide students with opportunities to organize community projects within the framework of voluntary organizations. One of the expected outcomes of this experience is for teachers to discover the challenges and benefits of service-learning and to learn how to manage various community projects.

The Youth Expedition Projects engage students in activities in developing nations to learn about the challenges of service initiatives in countries and communities with far greater needs than those typically found in Singapore. Here students manage the projects from beginning to end. The leaders of each expedition project are participants of a previous project and they are provided with some leadership training before leading a group abroad. Each group often has to raise the funds to operate the programs and is exposed to other components of international work that broadens their understanding of world-wide community needs.

Group Endeavors in Service-Learning

Perhaps the most comprehensive program designed to acquaint preservice teachers to service-learning is the GESL. This component of the teacher preparation program has been required of all students since 2005. Students participate in a nine-month program where they organize, plan, and execute a service-learning initiative in a school and/or community agency. Much of the early activity is focused on learning about how diverse groups plan and manage school/community programs. The groups are intentionally diverse, with composition created with attention to including different ages, races and genders, as well as subject areas. Students go through a service-learning experience where they attempt to identify community needs, develop service efforts that address those needs, and then reflect on the outcomes of the projects.

Research on GESL (Goh, Lim, Ch'ng, D'Rozario, & Cheah, 2009; Teo & Lim, 2009) has examined growth in self knowledge (in terms of creativity, academic, social and emotional intelligence, and enhancing leadership talent). One study, based on pre/post survey data, found that participants' self-knowledge and prosocial behaviors were significantly increased as a result of completing the GESL project. Students liked the service-learning experience and achieved personal satisfaction from the service activities. Interview data revealed student teachers reported learning more about themselves and developed improved personal relationships and problem solving skills (Teo & Lim, 2009).

Another study of GESL demonstrated that student teacher attitudes toward social behavior were positively affected. Areas such as student attitudes about working towards equal opportunity for all Singaporean citizens and desires to give to charity were significantly changed. Students wanted to become involved in programs to improve the community, wanted to volunteer their time to help others, and wanted to make a difference in the world (Goh et al., 2009). More recent research involving document reviews, focus groups, and interviews probed some of the impacts of the program and its processes on student learning and value development (Shumer, 2009). Results of this research indicate that GESL is meeting many of its intended goals and providing opportunities for preservice teachers to gain unique perspectives on service and group work.

GROUP ENDEAVORS IN SERVICE-LEARNING (A QUALITATIVE STUDY)

GESL was piloted in 2004 and the first cohort was started in 2005. The program was designed to equip teachers with experiences in service-learning and to promote the knowledge, skills, and values articulated by NIE for all beginning teachers (Foundations Programme Report, 2004). The specific areas of focus included the VSK outcomes mentioned at the beginning of this article. The explicit purpose and goals of GESL are mostly related to learning about several of the NIE goals: the pedagogy and practice of service-learning, learning about self-knowledge and care and concern for others, respecting diversity, and learning about collaboration, sharing, team spirit, and administrative management skills.

The GESL experience typically lasts from January through October for the postgraduate student cohort group (PGDE) (the largest cohort group) and from July through May for the diploma in education and BA/BSc undergraduate students. GESL participants go through five phases during the year. During Phase 1 the focus is on team building and group norming. Here students begin to learn about the various roles they will play in the experience. NIE and peer facilitators help the groups to get organized to begin the next level. In Phase 2 they are involved in exploration of the project and project planning. They do background work and feasibility studies to determine a specific plan. The plan includes an area of focus, an action plan, a timeline, and an allocation of tasks for group members. In Phase 3 they implement the plan, gathering appropriate material and making the arrangements for involvement with youth and the community. They spend almost two months on this part of the program. In Phase 4 the students terminate the GESL program by completing evaluation forms that ask for reflections on how they and their group did and what they learned from the experience. In Phase 5 GESL students share their experiences and reflections with others at a *Show and Tell* session arranged by the NIE staff.

As far as logistics, GESL students meet with their NIE or peer facilitator for two hours per week throughout the program period. Sometimes the meetings are held on campus; other times students arrange to meet in community settings. During these formal class sessions students and facilitators discuss the challenges of group work, planning, and implementation of service projects.

NIE facilitators receive training in service-learning and facilitation skills from staff at the Raffles Institute for Experiential Learning (RIEL). They initially receive two full days of training on service-learning and facilitation skills; more recently, however, that training has been reduced to a half-day experience. Some facilitators, because of time conflicts and other reasons, do not receive any formal training in facilitation. NIE facilitators receive an information handbook during the training that covers topics such as basic principles of service-learning, experiential learning, and community engagement. They also receive instruction in the facilitation process and in working with service-learning programs.

Student peer facilitators are selected for each group and also receive training from RIEL staff. Their training lasts for 2 days (usually two successive Saturdays). On the first day they cover foundations of service-learning, experiential learning, and basic facilitation skills, facilitation practice, and project management. On the second day they cover more on facilitation practices, delineating learning objectives, connecting social emotional learning and service-learning, managing conflict, service-learning design, and conclude with feedback and evaluation of the training. Sessions cover several important topics related to service-learning, such as addressing the "messiah" complex, high quality service-learning, and how to use the experiential learning cycle as a framework for facilitating group meetings.

Research/Evaluation Design

The purpose of this most recent research/evaluation was to gain an understanding of the GESL program, and based on that knowledge, to make recommendations for changes that would lead to increased efficiency and improved learning. In order to accomplish this, information was gathered from a variety of sources, including documents and professional article review, interviews, and focus groups with all stakeholders (students facilitators, trainers, community agencies, NIE facilitators, student peer facilitators, and others involved in related programs, such as the Youth Expedition Project (YEP), which is an international service-learning initiative of the Singapore National Youth Council).

Data were collected from March 5 through to March 18, 2009. Articles and documents were reviewed prior to a visit to Singapore. Onsite work was conducted from March 11 to 18. Data collection activities included the following: an interview with the two NIE program directors (Drs. Goh and D'Rozario); an interview with the director of the RIEL training program (Cheng Chye Chua); an informal discussion with RIEL staff; a focus group discussion with three members of a community organization that works with GESL students (Students Care Services); an interview with National Youth Council staff connected with the YEP effort (Kenneth Tan and Dawn Soh); a focus group meeting with eight NIE GESL facilitators; a focus group meeting with nine Service Learning Club members from NIE; a focus group meeting with nine GESL student facilitators and one NIE facilitator; and informal interviews with GESL students and observations of student projects at the Character Education/Service-Learning conference sponsored by NIE on March 17 and 18. Overall, more than 40 individuals who collectively represented all phases of the program and levels of student involvement (PGDE, Diploma in Education, and BA/BSc programs) contributed to this study.

Specific document review occurred during the on-site visit. Fifteen program CDs for projects conducted between January and September 2008 were reviewed, along with hard copies of reports for five programs. In addition, more than 100 student assessment forms were analyzed.

FINDINGS

Greatest Impact: Group Learning

Without doubt the greatest impact of GESL is in the project itself. Every group experience culminated in a one, two, or three day event, characterized by symposia, all day events, and group camps. Data from every focus group discussion and interview included information about the power of the experience and how meaningful it was to participants. Even where individual group members had not been very actively engaged in the planning or carrying out of preparatory tasks, they showed up at the culminating event and found the experience to be moving and powerful.

The greatest learning experience found in the data referred to the group experience. Every focus group participant and almost every GESL participant reflection reviewed indicated that the power of learning in GESL relates to learning how to function in a group. While not every group functioned as effectively as it might, learning about group skills, from managing time, to setting goals, and working toward a common agenda and purpose, proved to be the most frequently mentioned outcome of the GESL experience. Reflections from some participants indicated the range and scope of this learning:

> Student D: I have learned that cooperation and teamwork were important in making this project a success. I learned how to barbeque ... [a] very big quantity of food ... This barbeque skill, I can use it for my future in other school camps. I have learned that time management and planning were very important factors from this project. I will be using these skills and knowledge in my everyday life during my teaching. I will use this skill by making sure that sufficient time was planned for any class activities during my teaching.

> Student Q: I have gained insights into how a project of such scale should be planned and carried out. Also, I have learnt that planning an excursion for students is not as easy as it seems and a lot of thought and planning work have to be put in place before a successful excursion can occur. Working in a huge group is not easy and through this project, our group has learnt to accommodate and tolerate each other to make this project a successful one. I have also learnt the ways of organization and planning a project of such nature. I think GESL is a meaningful project because as trainee teachers, we are given the opportunity to organize an event and we learnt the skills

required. This will be helpful when we become full-fledged teachers and have to organize events on our own.

Student Y: For the first time, I have experienced the great amount of time and effort it takes to organize such a relatively large-scale project.

Clearly, honing of group skills was a significant outcome from the GESL activity. Students identified numerous learning components such as how to manage a group, resolving group conflict, enhancing interpersonal skills, and managing all aspects of a project (execution, details of financial planning, allocation of tasks and responsibilities, and motivating team members).

While there were many successful initiatives, among the most exemplary was the Group 7 project (January 2008), entitled *Chek Mates*, an environmental walk developed with a school and community agency. A summary of the final report on the project is as follows:

This project was in conjunction with the NIE PGDE module called "Group Endeavors in Service Learning," which focuses on providing teachers with valuable experience in working as a team to produce a project which benefits society as a whole. Support from nature groups was essential since this project required specialized training and commitment which was provided by a GESL team member who belonged to a prominent external environmental group called "Naked Hermit Crabs."

The team collaborated with Zhenghua Primary School on raising awareness on the plight of the natural habitats in Chek Jawa, especially its coastal areas. After much discussions and visits to Chek Jawa, the group came to be affectionately known as "Chek-Mates."

"Chek-mates" had a total of 18 members, and was divided into 3 separate teams: Prewalk, Walk and Post walk. The Prewalk team was in charge of the initial proposals as well as the liaison with the target school. The Walk team took charge of the event itself, and the Postwalk team reflected on the experience and extended the awareness through the internet. The workload was reflected by the number of people attached to each team: Walk (8 members) Prewalk (6 members) and Postwalk (4 members).

For efficiency of information sharing, "Chek-mates" were also divided into Publicity, Finance and Logistics teams. Each member had two responsibilities to allow a more efficient way of handling the time constraints and workload. Nearing the day of the event, the team members inevitably took on other roles and even crossed over to other teams, while maintaining their own tasks. This was because of the timing of each team's deadlines as well as their own PGDE training schedule in NIE.

Prewalk section of the project was executed on 25th April, Friday. The 45-minute Presentation to Primary 6 students was conducted at 10.55 am to 12.25 pm. This was followed by the Mini Workshop for science teachers of Zhenghua Primary School. The 45-minute presentation consisted of a short activity and game section followed by the PowerPoint presentation on Chek Jawa. Students were given an overview of Chek Jawa and its history. They were also introduced to the different types of wildlife that could be found in Chek Jawa. Dangers to this natural area and its wildlife were also brought to the students' attention. This was to bring environmental awareness to these students about Singapore's biodiversity. A mini workshop for teachers provided information for the walk and to supplement their lesson plan.

The Chek Jawa Nature Walk was conducted whereby 80 to 90 students, parent volunteers and teachers were divided into 10 groups of 12 members. All the participants and the group facilitators gathered at Zheng Hua Primary School at approximately 7:15am. The journey to Changi Village took about an hour. Thereafter it took another 45 minutes for the teams to travel to Pulau Ubin by means of a bumboat and then they were ferried to Chek Jawa via taxis. By 10 am the teams had all gathered at Chek Jawa, been introduced to their guides and were also given a briefing on some basic safety procedures and regulations. As the walk progressed, the guides directed the participants' attention to interesting sights and provided information. Participants were also provided with a walk booklet put together by the GESL team that had quizzes to reinforce their learning. The Postwalk team created a website consisting of photos taken during the walk, reflections by Chek-Mates and links to other environmental sites (see: http://chek-mates.edublogs.org/). The Chek-Mates also had to come up with a learning package reflecting the primary school's syllabus and other materials that complemented the excursion to Chek Jawa.

With the coincidental celebration of the International Year of the Reef launched on National Day 2008, the Chek-Mates team has been successful in trying to promote the message of saving the sea shores from the dangers of further deterioration.

Here we learn of the details of the project, working from initial planning stages to actual implementation of the program with the school, and finally the reflective activities afterward that led to the development of more curriculum and future goals. This report demonstrates the kind of activities that go into a well designed service-learning program and how it unfolds through a course such as Group Endeavors in Service Learning.

Personal Growth

Another outcome highlighted was the personal growth of the GESL participants. Areas of growth revealed through focus groups and written documents suggested that personal ability to work within a group structure (interpersonal skills and interactive reflection) and personal skills involved with planning, time management, and assessment were all major outcomes. The ability to be more patient, to resolve interpersonal conflicts, and to learn how to manage and execute plans were also cited as important outcomes of the GESL experience. These personal growth outcomes seemed to be related to the age of the participants, with younger members citing the sheer excitement of being involved in a large project and learning how to participate in such a challenging adventure, while more mature individuals in the postgraduate program discussed their growth in leadership skills, conflict resolution, and ability to work with community agencies in a collaborative manner. Much of the personal growth was focused on the group experience and how GESL students managed to learn to personally interact with others, including students and members of community agencies. In summing up the benefits, one GESL student commented:

> Student A: On the event proper, what this project needed from me was understanding, insight, socialization skills, discipline, and teamwork. These concepts were not only involved in the performance of leadership tasks or facilitation, but also in establishing rapport with the campers. As some of the students were adamant to speak up or participate in the activities, it required a certain level of discernment and "putting oneself in the other's shoes" in order to gauge what they were feeling and where they were coming from, thus knowing how to rationalize their behavior or to approach a situation appropriately.

The project required this participant to grow in areas of understanding, insight, socialization and teamwork. S/he also learned about empathy, "putting oneself in other's shoes", in order to properly assess their feelings and their perspective. This was necessary to then move to address the behavior appropriately. In a similar fashion, another student reflected that:

> Student G: I have learnt to coordinate with people from different backgrounds. It was a good experience to facilitate the discussions and to solicit ideas from them. Furthermore, I have learnt a great deal in the methods to handle different students in difficult situations.

Learning coordination skills with people from different backgrounds, facilitating discussion, and handling different students in different situations all relate to learning in contextual settings. This growth, as does the information shared from Student A, demonstrates the importance of the GESL experience in helping students to learn to function in contextual environments that require immediate judgments and analysis in order to offer appropriate instruction and advice. These two descriptions clearly show mastery of the NIE goals of learning in context, learning interpersonal skills, learning to believe in student's ability to learn, and demonstrating care and concern for student success.

Awareness of Community and Student Issues

By engaging in the project process, GESL students indicated that they learned to appreciate the problems faced by students, by communities and by society. Most felt the project activity, whether it was a camp or one day event, helped raise levels of awareness for both the youth being served and the GESL students themselves. Said other program participants:

> Student Z: I learnt more about bio-diversity in Singapore. Because of this project I made a total of 3 trips to Chek Jawa (which is a place I would not go myself without this project), and I saw for myself how devoted environmentalists are to their cause: fighting to preserve Chek Jawa.

> Student A: Through this project, I had the opportunity to know more about other local agencies who are supporting the green movement. This project also created awareness within me that Singapore still has much room for improvement in its green initiatives.

Many GESL students commented about learning how to appreciate, understand, and address student issues, especially when students had behavioral or learning challenges. Typical comments included:

> Student S: I have gained a deeper insight into the world of the intellectually challenged individuals.

> Student D: I have gained the realization that the line between "normalcy and abnormalcy" is a very fine one and that it is an unfortunate practice of society. It has highlighted the reality of "branding" in our society. It [the experience] has given me the insight that the routine habits of special needs kids.

GESL participants developed greater awareness of the particular challenges of special needs students. Interaction with students during the preparation activities and the actual project events encouraged new levels of understanding on how students of different backgrounds functioned and responded to various teaching and interaction strategies, skills that are critical for success in the teaching profession.

Issues for GESL

Despite its successes, several participants identified areas for improvement for the GESL program, though there was no definitive consensus on how to address these issues.

Mandatory Versus Voluntary Program

Almost half those who participated in the focus group discussions raised issues about the mandatory nature of GESL. Some suggested the program should be offered as a voluntary option for Nanyang Technical University/NIE students. They claimed there were members of their group who did not buy in to the whole process of project-based service-learning and were reluctant participants in the discussion sessions and in the actual projects. They suggested that by making the program voluntary only those who truly believed in service and service-learning would participate and be more committed to building quality, reciprocal and sustainable partnerships between students, schools and community groups.

An opposite viewpoint was presented, suggesting that eliminating the required component of the program would remove the incentive for most students to become involved. They cited the extremely busy schedules of NIE students in their educational programs: By eliminating the mandatory nature, they would help lose those who felt it took too much time to become engaged in a community-connected educational program. If the mandatory requirement was eliminated, many felt there would be few enrolled in GESL and this would greatly reduce its influence, and perhaps even threaten its existence.

Diverse Versus Homogeneous Grouping

GESL has, as one of its important goals to develop an appreciation for diversity, one of NIE's key knowledge and value outcomes. Each GESL is organized around diverse populations, with the group composition, so far as possible, including people of different ethnic groups, age, gender, and disciplinary backgrounds.

Much of the discussion suggested that the heterogeneous groupings were working well. Participants liked the diversity and said they had an opportunity to learn from one-another and to better experience and come to understand different perspectives. Others, though a minority, said their groups did not work very well. There were some conflicts because people had different backgrounds and even different reasons/expectations for the GESL program. In some cases diverse groups actually reconstituted themselves into homogenous subgroups and worked in isolation on their projects. For instance, one discussant said her GESL experience involved subgroups re-dividing by gender.

To complicate this discussion, many individuals suggested the success of the diversity goal of the GESL program was primarily the responsibility of the group facilitators. Both the NIE and student peer facilitators were the ones who seemed to have the most control over how the groups worked, especially with regard to getting people of different backgrounds to cooperate. Thus, the problem of effective diversity may be more an issue of facilitator training than actually changing the mixture of the groups.

Offer GESL in the First Year or Second Year?

Discussions in three of the focus groups included comments on the timing of the GESL program. Several individuals, including many who had experienced GESL and YEP, thought students were too overwhelmed during the first year and that the amount of work from other courses/modules put too much pressure on them and compromised motivation to do well in GESL, especially since results were graded on the basis of "approaching expectations," "meeting expectations," and "exceeding expectations," which made satisfactory results comparatively easy to obtain. There was a belief that offering the program during the second year would attract participants with more maturity, who had had opportunities to acclimate to college life. Some participants indicated that a few community agencies were concerned about the maturity level of students and that there was a perception that first-year students might not be prepared to do community/youth work. This obviously was of most concern for the undergraduate Diploma in Education and BA/BSc program (although it should be noted that schools have introduced CIP, and many junior college and polytechnic students actually have some SL experience or voluntary work before they enroll in NIE).

One-Time Training Versus Continuous Training

Two focus groups discussed the possibility of extending the training offered at the beginning of the program for NIE staff and student peer facilitators to a period extending throughout the GESL program. They cited examples of times during the year where they experienced a few serious conflicts between GESL members and would have benefitted from additional support in resolving the issues. They also encountered GESL students whose motivation was not as strong as it should have been to actively participate in all the planning and assessment processes. Evaluation/assessment activities were especially problematic after the event had taken place, when some students seemed to think most of the program was over and thus did not invest time to actively reflect on the experience.

Group Size: Large Group Versus Small Group

One constant theme that emerged throughout the focus groups was the issue of group size. Typically, GESL groups ranged from 20 to 24 participants. Most believed a group of this size presented challenges for management and engagement. For some, however, group size did not present a problem; they worked effectively together and things went smoothly. More generally, however, challenges presented by large groups included getting people from various backgrounds and experiences to bond around a common project and agenda; getting people to all work with the same level of effort instead of having a few do most of the work; resolving conflict between a few members when the bulk of the group worked together effectively; and getting the group to participate in postevent activities because of other commitments.

One suggestion raised in two focus groups was to rearrange the groups by theme. While groups could still maintain their size and diversity of background, at least they would have a preestablished purpose for the service work. It was felt this would help the group, even one as large as 24, work more smoothly and more effectively.

Efforts to reduce the size of the cohort groups present several challenges, both financial and logistics. Clearly more facilitators would have to be supported from both NIE and student peer participants. The existence of smaller groups would produce an increased demand for more community partners, which could complicate logistics. If, for example, the groups were reduced to 12 instead of 24, there would be more than 200 different operations to monitor and supervise, which would also increase demands on training.

DISCUSSION AND RECOMMENDATIONS

Before we discuss the results of the research and make recommendations, it is important to acknowledge the nature and scope of the GESL effort. The fact is that few, if any, nations around the world are developing teacher education programs that require all their students to engage in service-learning preparation. This is an undertaking of massive scope and size. Engaging thousands of student teachers in a program that requires more than six months of engagement is to be commended and admired.

GESL and Knowledge, Skills, and Values

Realizing that GESL is a teacher preparation program of substantial size and duration, it is important to discuss the study in those terms: size and scope as it relates to quality, sustainability, and attainment of teacher training objectives. Clearly NIE's framework of VSK needs to be the driving force behind the program and its outcomes. Students engage in GESL not only to learn about service-learning, but more generalized values, skills, and knowledge that make up any educational program. Service-learning is one of many pedagogical approaches to teach students about all three elements and should be assessed as to how effective it is in achieving those goals.

Data collected from all the sources indicate that GESL is effective in helping student teachers gain knowledge in areas of educational context, pupils, pedagogy, and self. Every GESL program discussed in the focus groups or reviewed through documents existed in a specific context. Contexts ranged from thematic areas such as environmental, special schools, or camp settings. Similarly, every program exposed GESL students to some type of pupils encountered in an educational setting, from primary or secondary students, to special needs and linguistically different children. All programs required student teachers to examine the pedagogy of service-learning and focused specifically on learning by doing. And all programs required GESL students to examine some of their personal learning by commenting on the growth of their self knowledge. Students responded by indicating that they learned about their ability to interact with people from different backgrounds, their ability to learn patience and understanding by dealing with special students or students with behavioral issues. Clearly they reflected on their personal change in terms of how they functioned as members of an educational team.

Consistent with their knowledge gains, GESL students learned important teaching skills. They learned how to participate in the management of an educational project. They practiced interpersonal skills in their group meetings. They learned skills in planning and implementing a service-learning project, from arranging for transportation and supplying food and other necessities, to developing curriculum modules for playing games or going on nature walks. Reflective skills were acquired as GESL students assessed the impact of their projects on students and communities and the growth of self and group cohesion.

Values attained included learning to care about and be concerned for pupil success in service-learning projects. Each group wanted to help the children they worked with to be happy, to feel a sense of pride and accomplishment in their participation, and to feel confident in their ability to interact with the world. The group experience and the GESL project helped students to develop greater respect for diversity as they engaged in their group endeavor with children from different backgrounds. Many of the projects were designed to support children's learning in a fun and engaging context—and this supported their attitude toward a belief that all children could learn. The challenge of the service project and the contexts of many programs required groups and individuals to seek innovative approaches to their educational challenge and fostered a sense that service-learning programs required an ability to think beyond traditional classroom learning. And many of the projects sparked a desire to continue their acquisition of skills and knowledge they could use in their own classrooms when they became practicing teachers.

GESL and Service Learning

GESL was designed as an educational program to introduce prospective student teachers to the theory, pedagogy, and practice of service-learning. The question for this study concerned the effectiveness of the GESL in accomplishing this goal. A secondary question concerns what might be done to improve the GESL's efficiency.

The question is difficult to address, simply because of the variety of projects and processes undertaken in the more than 130 GESL initiatives that occur throughout the year. This research only touched the surface, reviewing only 15 projects in some detail and discussing the program with 40 or so individuals. Yet, the information acquired is sufficient to raise what appear to be the most important issues.

The GESL experience lasts for approximately 6-8 months. Students typically begin in January and end in September (with a break in June and July) or begin in July and complete in May of the following year. They meet formally for 2 hours each week throughout the academic year in preparation for their culminating event and then meet less frequently after the activity for another 2 months. Thus, they spend a total of 40 hours in preparation for the event, approximately 4 to 72 hours at the event and, after its completion, approximately 16 hours postevent doing reflections and final activities (such as developing curriculum for teachers to do follow up with their students).

It seems that a program with 40 hours devoted to preparation might be more effective in its introduction of service-learning if there was more direct contact with students and perhaps less sophisticated events produced. There are some programs that spend some of this preparation time meeting with students, teachers, or community members, often going through workshops and educational experiences that prepare the GESL students for their service-learning engagement. That seems to be an appropriate use of the time allocated. Others, though, seem to spend an undue amount of time in the planning stages at the expense of the opportunity to have direct contact with students in service-learning activities. It might be more effective if GESL students were to meet at least four to six different times with students to help them practice critical phases of the service-learning experience, such as developing a needs assessment directly with students, undertaking preparatory exercises so the GESL students could develop a better sense of client abilities and behaviors, engage students more in the actual evaluation of the program, and lastly, engage students and their teachers/community members in developing plans to sustain some of the service-learning experiences.

CONCLUSIONS

Based on the description of teacher education programs in Singapore focused on service-learning and basic teacher preparation, it appears that when one asks: *service-learning in teacher preparation for what?* the answer is "for everything." The options mentioned, culminating in the GESL program which engages students for months in an intensive service-learning group experience, are designed to develop the values, knowledge, and skills necessary for any teacher to prepare for classroom instruction. In this case, the strong commitment made by the NIE to the values of service, and of working with students and communities for the betterment of both, is an important goal for preservice education. It is both visionary and necessary if participation by teachers and students in society to build social capital is a desired outcome.

The GESL program is indeed one that deserves further study and understanding. Preliminary studies indicate it has strong impact on preservice teachers in a variety of ways and has the potential to influence teacher preparation efforts around the globe. Not every country is as small as Singapore, nor does every country have such a centralized educational system, but Singapore offers a model of varied efforts designed to expose preservice teachers to service-learning and community service in a multitude of settings. And they do it through a vision that is much larger than just service-learning itself.

The National Institute of Education is the sole provider of teachers for Singapore schools and almost all teachers produced since 2006 would have had some experience in service learning through GESL, while some others would have had additional experience through personal volunteerism, expedition projects abroad or service learning club activities. The national education policy to expose all school pupils to community involvement has undoubtedly influenced in an opportune manner the incorporation of GESL into teacher education programs at NIE since 2005, thus ensuring that all teachers produced have the values, skills and knowledge to help their pupils in the schools' community involvement programs. Few countries involve all their student teachers in service-learning experiences. Singapore is leading the way in ensuring that teacher educators expand service and community engagement to all areas of society.

REFERENCES

Bruner, J. S. (1966) *Toward a theory of instruction*. Cambridge, MA: Belkapp Press.

Ch'ng, A., D'Rozario, V., Goh, K. C., & Cheah, H. M. (2009). Service-learning in teacher education at the National Institute of Education, Singapore. In K. C. Goh, V. D'Rozario, A. Ch'ng, & H. M. Cheah (Eds.), *Character development through service and experiential learning* (pp. 83-92). Singapore: Pearson Education.

Csikszentmihalyi, M. (1990). *Flow: The psychology of optimal experience*. New York, NY: Harper & Row.

Csikszentmihalyi, M., & Csikszentmihalyi, I. (1992). *Optimal experience: Psychological studies of flow in consciousness*. New York, NY: Cambridge University Press.

Deci, E., & Ryan, R. (1985). *Intrinsic motivation and self-determination in human behavior*. New York: Plenum.

Dewey, J. (1938). *Experience and education*. New York, NY: Macmillan.

Goh, K. C., Lim, K. M., Ch'ng, A., D'Rozario, V., & Cheah, H.M. (2009). An evaluation of student teachers' experience of group endeavors in service-learning (GESL) at the National Institute of Education, Singapore. In K. C. Goh, V. D'Rozario, A. Ch'ng, & H. M. Cheah (Eds.), *Character development through service and experiential learning*. Singapore: Pearson Education.

Lave, J., & Wenger, E. (1991). *Situated learning: Legitimate peripheral participation*. New York, NY: Cambridge University Press.

Markus, G., Howard, J., & King, D. (1993). Integrating community service and classroom instruction enhances learning: Results from an experiment. *Educational Evaluation and Policy Analysis, 15*(4), 410–419.

National Institute of Education. (2004). *Foundation Programme Report*. Singapore: National Institute of Education, Nanyang Technological University.

Root, S. C., & Batchelder, T. (1994, April). *The impact of service-learning on pre-service teachers' development*. Paper presented at the annual meeting of the American Educational Research Association, New Orleans.

Root, S. C., & Furco, A. (2001). A review of research on service-learning in pre-service teacher education. In J. Anderson, K. Swick, & J. Yff (Eds.). *Service learning in teacher education* (pp. 86-101). Thousand Oaks, CA: Sage.

Root, S. C., Howard, R., & Daniels, J. (2004). *The impact of a service-learning experience in teacher preparation on preservice teachers' prosocial moral development*. Paper presented at the annual conference of the Association for Moral Education, Dana Point, CA.

Shumer, R. (2009). *Group endeavors in service-learning: An evaluation submitted to the National Institute of Education*. Singapore: National Institute of Education.

Sullivan, R. (1991, February). *The role of service-learning in restructuring teacher education*. Paper presented at the annual meeting of the Association of Teacher Educators, New Orleans.

Swick, K., & Rowls, M. (2000). Voices of pre-service teachers on the meaning and value of their service-learning. *Education, 120*(3), 461-468.

Teo, C.T, & Lim, K.M. (2009). Character transformation through education on volition and service-learning. In K. C. Goh, V. D'Rozario, A. Ch'ng, & H. M. Cheah (Eds.), *Character development through service and experiential learning* (pp. 93-107). Singapore: Pearson Education.

Thorndike, E. (1913). *Educational psychology: The psychology of learning*. New York, NY: Teachers College Press.

Thorndike, E. (1932). *The fundamentals of learning*. New York, NY: Teachers College Press.

Vygotsky, L. (1978). *Mind and society: The development of higher mental processes*. Cambridge, MA: Harvard University Press.

Wade, R. (1995). Developing active citizens: Community service-learning in social studies teacher education. *Social Studies, 86*(3), 122-128.

CHAPTER 8

BENEFITS TO STUDENTS OF SERVICE-LEARNING THROUGH A FOOD SECURITY PARTNERSHIP MODEL

Connie Nelson and Mirella Stroink

This research adds to service-learning knowledge by positing student outcomes within the context of a themed universitywide approach to community service learning (CSL) and a unique partnership model. The 5 dimensions of the partnership model delineate features of a CSL program organized around a food security theme. Research questions concerned the impact of the food security CSL experience on students' attitudes and skills in academic and civic domains. We found that CSL participation enhanced the students' development beyond the acquisition of academic course knowledge: Over a semester in CSL courses, our sample of 231 students showed gains in academic skills, attitudes about aspects of civic responsibility, and knowledge of current events. Some gender and age group differences were identified, as well. The approach we have taken in organizing our CSL program around a food security theme challenges traditional university approaches to knowledge transmission.

Research for What? Making Engaged Scholarship Matter
pp. 171–199
Copyright © 2010 by Information Age Publishing
All rights of reproduction in any form reserved.

As universities strive to become engaged campuses, the need exists to expand our understanding of how different institutional approaches to service-learning affect students' learning outcomes. Prior to 2005, it is estimated that only six universities in Canada engaged their students in community service through academic courses (Charbonneau, 2009). Then, in 2005-2006, the J.W. McConnell Family Foundation instigated a Canada-wide commitment to service-learning as a pedagogical tool through its 5-year funding of 10 universities and a national office (Canadian Alliance for Community Service-Learning (CACSL), 2010). In contrast, in the United States, an extensive and deeply rooted history of CSL thrives, and many have suggested that it is embedded in the fabric of American society (Kraft, 1996; Parker-Gwin, 1996). This relatively late arrival of service-learning in Canadian universities affords an opportunity to study student learning outcomes in unique institutional settings. The research presented here adds to the existing knowledge base by positing student outcomes within the context of a themed universitywide approach to service-learning and a unique partnership model of community engagement. This theme approach and the community partnership model are first described, followed by a presentation of research methods, findings, and a discussion of student outcomes.

A Food Security Theme Approach to Community Service-learning

Community service-learning is distinguished from other community based experiences in that it is course-based and embedded in the requirements of the learning environment (Bringle & Hatcher, 1996; Vogelgesang & Astin, 2000). Lakehead University, located in Thunder Bay, Ontario, has embarked on an ambitious path to entrench CSL with a food security theme into its curriculum across all academic disciplines. The idea for a theme approach to CSL originated from one of the coprincipal investigators for the university's application to the J.W. McConnell Family Foundation. Nelson, the coinvestigator had been engaged for several years in teaching university credit courses with a CSL component focused on food security issues. Specifically, this coinvestigator had partnered with over 20 community groups to engage students in 2003-2004 in a face-to-face survey of 356 charitable food program users. In 2004-2005, the students carried out a qualitative phenomenological case study of charitable food program users asking the question: How is food security maintained? In 2005-2006, the students collected focus group data on how food security issues affect intake, assessment and treatment decision-making by social service agencies. In 2006-2007, students engaged in a qualitative evaluation of the Ogden-Simpson Veggie Project, in order to understand the dynamics of how the project was contributing to the community.

Early in the development of the grant application, the co-principal investigators invited faculty across all departments to attend a university-wide meeting to discuss potential interest in developing CSL around the theme of food security. Potential community partners were also contacted and invited to a meeting to obtain their feedback on a theme approach to CSL. There was early endorsement by faculty across a broad spectrum of disciplines and by potential community partners. With this support from both faculty and the community, the university administration gave their enthusiastic support to this application. Once the LOI (letter of intent) was approved, there was ongoing involvement of both the community and faculty in the development of the full proposal. (See the Food Security Research Network [FSRN], 2009a, website for the full proposal and all annual reports.)

Once the grant was approved, all interested faculty and community members came together to begin to shape concrete CSL initiatives for university credit courses around the theme of food security. All faculty and community organizations were welcome to participate. The grant parameters placed emphasis on the sustainability of CSL beyond the 5-year grant period across a broad spectrum of disciplines. Hence the emphasis was not on quantity of courses, but on the breadth of disciplines engaged in CSL and the encouragement of interdisciplinary CSL approaches to meeting the food security interests of the community, from food production, marketing, distribution, policy and management practices in forestry and mining, to health issues and charitable food challenges.

The grant contained $5,000 funding for each of 15 new courses that could be used to acquire resources for the CSL component that would sustain the courses past the term of the grant, and also could be used for student research assistants and interns. The grant also included a community capacity building fund of $10,000 each year to be used as matching money to leverage additional grants to assist in building CSL partnerships. The university is committed to sustaining CSL after the grant, and has been putting in a larger portion of the funding each subsequent year. No emphasis has been placed on creating specialized CSL staff positions. Rather, this funding has been a catalyst for building the resources that will allow the courses to continue through departmental commitments to include the CSL courses as part of the regular teaching load.

The FSRN (2009a, 2009b) facilitates this theme approach to service-learning across the university. It embraces all aspects of building a just and sustainable local food system that is inclusive of alternative farming systems and the reclaiming of the boreal forest as a resilient food source. Food security is a theme approach to CSL that has universal roots that can be adapted to specific time and place.

Food security is a complex issue that necessitates coordinated networks across a broad span of academic programs, as well as cooperation among community service providers, governments and the private sector. Food security theme CSL courses have been offered in 17 academic disciplines, spanning six university faculties, with a total of 53 CSL courses completed to date. Participation has included 964 undergraduate students, as well as food security community-based research for both undergraduate and graduate students. FSRN began with 14 community partners that signed on to the original grant application, and now has increased to over 60 active local and regional community partners as well as food-focused provincial and national networks.

Selecting a food security theme for CSL encourages interdisciplinary approaches and the incorporation of CSL into an expansive range of academic disciplines. Tapping into a variety of disciplines assists in expanding the partnership base in a very natural and meaningful way. This ability to engage so many community partners through a food security theme has allowed us to avoid the issue of CSL being a burden on the time and resources of community partners (Stoecker, 2009). Thus, this inclusive theme reduces fatigue on community partners (Zlotkowski, 1995). Exhibit 8.1 shows examples of CSL courses that have been developed around the food security theme.

Additionally, food security has a human dimension that touches all regardless of socio-economic classification. Our community partnerships may be more inclusive than those focused on a charity/poverty reduction model of civic engagement which has been found to limit rather than facilitate civic engagement (Barber & Battistoni, 1993; Boyle-Baise et al., 2006). When charity rather than social change becomes the focus, CSL students often become involved with vulnerable individuals and groups and disavow concern with larger policy issues (Markus, Howard, & King, 1993; Serow, 1991).

Community Engagement Partnership Model

We chose to implement the food security theme in service-learning using the contextual fluidity (CF) partnership model (Nelson & McPherson, 2003, 2004; Nelson, Stadey, & Lyons, 2005). This model's strength rests in the ability to embrace the complex dynamics behind service-learning. Holland (2001) identifies these complex dynamics as the collaborative work of students, faculty, their institutional context, and their

**Exhibit 8.1.   Service Learning Course Examples
and Community Partners**

• Biology Plant Propagation Course • Partners: local commercial growers and home-based gardeners	Students engage with the community to gain the community's knowledge of local native food sources. The students learn how to apply propagation techniques to these local food sources; thus enhancing the possibility of saving and reproducing local food sources.
• Forestry Soils Course • Partners: community gardens (city, churches, civic organization supporters of local gardens, and agencies dealing with food security issues.	Never before has food security been so vital to building healthy and sustainable communities. At the root of food security is stable, productive soil. Students will work closely with community members to collect, analyze and interpret soil samples from local gardens and/or farms.
• Forestry: Fish and Wildlife Practice • Partner: Northwestern Ontario Sportsmen's Alliance (NOSA)	The students conduct a survey to better understand why the people of Northwestern Ontario hunt. We are interested in the amount of time people spend hunting and angling, and whether or not these activities make a significant impact on enhancing food security by consuming fresh and preserving the meats for winter use.
• Forestry: Aboriginal Forest Management • Partners: Matawa First Nations	The students engage with First Nation communities to understand how current management practices affect food security from boreal forest food sources.
• Sociology: Research Policy Course • Partners: First Nation communities, Treaty governance staff, sports fisher people, sportswriters, CBC radio staff, ministry personnel, local restaurants	Students are given topics like "Why is milk 5 times more expensive in Thunder Bay than in Attawapiskat?", "Why is bannock not sold at McDonald's?", and "What are the food security implications of declaring sturgeon to be a species at risk?" Different and divergent stakeholders' perspectives are explored. The outcome is a roundtable presentation of various stakeholders' positions on the issue. Debating and discussing different positions aids the community partners and the students to being more sensitive to the complexity of food system issues and the challenges to resolving them.
• Psychology: Environmental Psychology • Partners: EcoSuperior, Earthwise, Lakehead University Community Garden, Lakehead University Student Union, City of Thunder Bay -Active Transportation	Students work with community partners to link academic material on the social-psychological, cultural, and structural factors underlying sustainable behavior with community knowledge and experience in building sustainability. This exchange of knowledge feeds students' development of a research proposal and community presentation that demonstrate the potential for community-based research to contribute to the development of resilience and sustainability in the food system and wider community.

(Table continues on next page)

Exhibit 8.1.   (Continued)

• Master of Public Health: Directed Studies • Partners: First Nation communities	Students engage with First Nations communities in developing a place-based program manual for use in programs that promote food security and holistic health. The emphasis is on establishing guidelines where communities are encouraged to connect with their cultural teachings, food knowledge and existing resources.
• English: Food, Writing and Community • Partners: Local farm marketing operations, local farm production organizations, networks that deal with food security	Students will work in groups with an interested community partner to offer writing support: first auditing existing discourse (advertising, promotions, mission statement, web, public relations, and advocacy) and then working with the partner to create and implement a communications/writing plan. As part of the course, students will get hands-on training in a variety modes and genres of writing.
• Social Work: Theory Course • Partners: The Ogden-Simpson Veggie Garden Project and their networks of city planners, corrections farm, local churches, neighbors	The Community Service Learning (CSL) component of this course focuses on students assisting the Ogden-Simpson Veggie Garden Project in building city block- based community capacity in the activity of using gardening to enhance food security and simultaneously to build relationship between neighbors 'over the backyard fence'. The long term vision is to effect sustainable changes in how we relate as human beings towards each other, our environment and our own wellbeing while enhancing local food security so that all can put food on their own tables with dignity.

community partners. This model has proven beneficial for our food security theme service-learning program, as it endorses a reciprocal and mutually benefiting triangular partnership between the academy, students and community partners. The five dimensions of the CF community partnership model are represented by the schematic in Exhibit 8.2 and are described below. In practice, the five dimensions are simultaneously occurring within our service-learning program. All faculty members, their students in CSL courses, and their community partners are all simultaneously considered in a theme approach to CSL where the vision is to enhance and support a resilient local food system. All points of the theme CSL network approach (community, students and faculty) are centres and provide input in moving forward on food security issues. A successful CSL network organized around a theme has similarities to a good jazz composition that flows from everyone's contribution (centre) achieved by simultaneously listening to all other participants (centres). In other words, a theme approach to CSL thrives on a dense and active network approach rather than treating each individual CSL course and partners as individual silos. Contextual fluidity, the model we have chose to

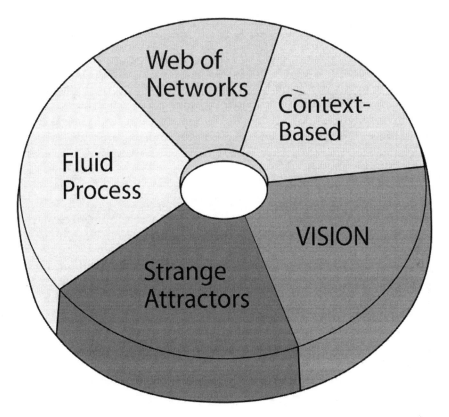

Exhibit 8.2.   The five dimensions of the contextual fluidity partnership model.

support and to nourish this approach to CSL, exhibits the following characteristics:

Context-Based

When the planning and implementation of service-learning are context-based, partners' needs and goals, instructors' teaching objectives and students' learning requirements are all considered. The context-base dimension facilitates the blending of both community service and learning goals in a way that nurtures and enriches both. This context base in the academic-community partnership ensures that service-learning is not just an added course requirement, unrelated to either community needs or learning goals. For example, a CSL seminar course in sociology that explores food in contemporary cultural and political contexts becomes relevant to the community partners by regionalizing the specific topic to an examination of why milk costs five times more in a northern community than in the city while alcohol and cigarettes are price-neutral across the region. In another example, an English course in food and writing expands and diversifies the rhetorical skills of students and trains them to participate in discourse communities outside the academy. Students begin by studying particular discourses relating to food, as found in areas of natural history, agricultural science, and commodity histories, to cookery and cookbooks, restaurant reviewing, cultural studies, and food security. Then, through focused assignments, they enter those conversations themselves. The method begins with choosing a problem/topic/initiative, then moves to identifying a community partner and entering the discourse in a way that seeks to contribute to or advance a given conversation. At the same time that students learn how to produce knowledge about food security, they will also be learning how to turn that awareness into direct and critically informed social action/service. A strong focus on written reflection activities makes it possible to combine knowledge transfer, critical thinking, and social service in one.

A context focus to service-learning planning and implementation promotes dialogue and place-based opportunities to know how academia and community organizations function and communicate both inside each organization and with their external environments. In other words, the various factors that can challenge community-university partnerships, such as differences in organizational cultures, power imbalances and communication styles are more easily minimized within context. Context can assist in overcoming difference. A strong signal that the partnership functions from a context-based approach is when the community and the academy both use 'our students' as the frame of reference. Moreover, a focus on context facilitates the development of service-learning experiences that build on local and place-based existing community initiatives. The decision to create a theme approach to CSL around food security has amplified the high level of enthusiasm throughout the community to partner with the university in enhancing regional locally based and sustainable food security initiatives.

Vision

The CF partnership model endorses vision as the "glue" for keeping an organization on course. CF is designed for the complexities of a context-based approach where the ordering of specific activities is inconsequential as long as the ultimate vision is the guiding framework for actions. In our case, the vision of building a local sustainable and resilient food system can be achieved by a multitude of approaches to service-learning. In the words of a few of the community partners, the following examples demonstrate our shared community-academic vision. These examples have been incorporated into service-learning experiences that offer students opportunities for community engagement in food security.

Food security is an issue for our members. One area we would like to see researched is the impact of high food costs in remote First Nations.

A challenge for the Lodge has always been to provide the clients with "traditional" food. Hence, the Lodge's Meal Plan has, with the assistance of the TBRHSC dieticians, recently introduced fish and wild rice into the menu. If possible the Lodge would, if allowed, purchase "wild" meat such as moose, caribou, deer and fowl such as ducks and geese.

We have had some great partnerships already with students from the School of Social Work working with mainly the Regional Food Distribution Association. It is wonderful for students to get involved with real community projects and for them to be able to provide time and expertise in both research and community capacity building. We are always expanding our programming in the area of food security and students in all faculties of the university could be helpful with the Food Action Network objectives outlined in the strategic plan. Some examples include:

- Business and economics students can explore the possibilities for growth in the food production and processing industry—what is the market like, who are the consumers, what is our capacity to grow our own, what are the economic benefits?
- Social work students can work with the various food action projects including gleaning, the Good Food Box and community gardens to do research or direct work on community capacity building.
- Geography students can help us by using GIS software to define the barriers to accessing food and how to improve access to various individuals or neighborhoods.
- History students can explore the relationship to food that different ethnic groups continue to have that originally settled in this area; they can look at heritage seeds and the farming community and get a picture of what was grown here in the recent past.
- Students in health professions such as the MPH, nursing, and medical school can look at the health implications of food insecurity or the benefits of various eating patterns.
- Other projects might include looking at the environmental impacts of where food is grown vs. eaten.

Fluidity

CF endorses the dimension of fluidity as essential when working from the other dimensions of context-based and vision. The service-learning activities that support our vision are constantly changing depending on context, and thus remain fluid. Engaging in situational responsive activities keeps the "ship's course" toward a clear vision despite changing circumstances.

Bringle and Hatcher (1996) offer the terminology of "keep to the course" for vision and acknowledge the constantly changing nature of the CSL activities. This fluidity characteristic can be exemplified by examining the constantly changing nature of our CSL activities to enhance local food production. For several years, CSL students worked with local farmers, household consumers, bakeries and restaurants to determine the demand to increase wheat production for the milling of local flour. When this goal was successfully met, feedback from our community requested that we provide similar assistance in enhancing local beef production. Hence, our model provides us with the guidance to achieve our vision by adapting our specific CSL activities to address relevant food security issues with our community partners. This CF approach avoids community partner fatigue, as well, in that it supports CSL responsiveness to new challenges and opportunities for addressing community food security needs.

Web of Networks

The CF model suggests that complex issues whose solutions demand coordination and cooperation across organizational jurisdictions are more effectively handled when organizations join together in network configurations to tackle these issues (Kickert, Klijm, & Koppenjan, 1997). As discussed earlier, the development of local food systems is a complex system as its reorganization involves governance and policy issues of food production, processing, transportation, marketing, diversity of agriculture education training and connections between agriculture and health. In developing service-learning around this theme of building a sustainable and resilient local food system, we need webs of collaboration across academic disciplines and among community partners. Network interactions receive, relay and interpret information through both formal and informal linkages, within dynamic and ever-changing webs of networks that have no designated centre. Instead, these interactions are grounded within the context of each activity.

Our FSRN network has become a web of networks that can be viewed as a constellation comprised of a very dense network that nurtures many sub-networks. For example, in our CSL activities we have students doing thesis and undergraduate research with our community garden partners. Each of these community garden projects are comprised of many additional community partners. For example, in the Field of Greens community garden project, partners include the Salvation Army, local Rotarians, and many local construction and landscaping businesses, architects, and horticulturalists. In working with our First Nations' partners, we have many sub-networks at an individual community level comprised of elders, band councilors, health workers, economic development staff and interested community families. We also have the network that connects First

Nation communities interested in reviving their once-thriving local food systems with our local nonnative farming community. These webs of networks enrich our CSL activities and eliminate community burnout.

Strange Attractors

The fifth dimension of CF offers insights into how components of complex systems can exhibit energy that can draw in and hold other components. This phenomenon is called a "strange attractor" as the energy or force can be observed even when it is difficult to identify (Gleick, 1987). A vision can act as a strange attractor, as can individuals or organizations that are drawn into a web of networks. The CF model endorses the strange attractors of formal and informal, planned and unplanned, and conscious and unconscious interactions in distinct, and at times distant, components of the partnership that are drawn into the web of networks.

Receptiveness to strange attractors provides a mechanism for potential community partners to self-identify their interest in participating as a community partner. Individuals and organizations previously unknown to the FSRN become part of the constellation of networks that enhance CSL initiatives. For instance, a local environmental film network contacted us because of their interest in telling the story of why our area is unique in the world for being virus-free for honey bees. This has led to new contacts with 80 beekeepers in the area that are assisting us in developing a CSL course-based experience that will create educational tools to enhance awareness of how we maintain our virus-free status. Another example is a CSL partnership that began when our FSRN network was contacted by an Economic Development Officer from a regional community in need a feasibility plan for a blueberry-drying facility. This CSL initiative is being developed in the Faculty of Forestry through an economic marketing course aiming to facilitate diversification of forest products including food uses. A further example is the success we have had in CSL with two First Nations: Strengthening the connections between health and local food has lead to further initiatives with First Nations in rebuilding local agriculture food systems that were shattered during the era of residential schools. New partnerships that emerge out of strange attractors can strengthen relationships between academia and community, enhance the density of webs of networks and enhance shared norms.

Impacts of the Five Dimensions

The five dimensions of the community engagement partnership model create some unique features of our delivery mechanism for a food security theme approach to service-learning. First, because we are grounded in context, the instructors remain autonomous in developing their own particular relationships with the community and in facilitating creative ways for their students to engage with the community. This contextual approach offers opportunities for the students' reflections to be incorporated into the classroom learning goals. Without the genuine faculty involvement, student reflection may happen in a vacuum, negatively influencing CSL outcomes (Kraft, 1996; Noddings, 1992).

Second, this contextual approach heightens the potential sustainability of community knowledge in subsequent offerings of the same course. Being context-based, the instructor is intimately involved in the 'messiness' of community engagement and is better able to bring community knowledge back into the classroom. In other words, a faculty member interacts with the community, learns from the community, brings this knowledge back into the classroom and ensures this community knowledge base continues on when the course is offered again for a new group of students. Faculty can engage more deeply with community and recognize community as coeducators (Sandy & Holland, 2006). Using Exhibit 8.1 as examples, the instructor in the plant propagation course can take the knowledge gained from the community about local viable food sources and build this knowledge into subsequent offerings of the course. By having students each year adding new gardens to their soil analysis, the instructor in the soils course builds over time a base of local soil characteristics that can augment information provided in soil textbooks. The instructor in the sociology policy seminar course uses the policy example of species at risk as part of his lecture material in future courses. The English instructor's courses can assist organizations in retooling for a more localized food system on the basis of a repertoire of students' discourse with community partners built up in previous courses. This potential for the community knowledge to be sustainable as a valuable pedagogical tool applies to all of our food security service-learning courses. The instructor engages with the community, so the integration of the community's knowledge organically embeds itself into future offerings of each course.

Thirdly, a contextual and fluid approach makes certain that the community partners are engaged as full participants (Illich, 1990). The inclusion of the partner's voice in the development of the CSL experience makes it possible for the service to be meaningful and useful to the community (Stoecker & Tyron, 2009). Moreover, students may gain more when community partners are involved as coeducators; and community partners may benefit from being more actively involved in the relationship with the university (Miron & Moely, 2006). Butin (2010) proposes that an engaged institution of higher education draws from the peculiarities of community, institutions and faculty so that the transformative power of service-learning arises out of the details of faculty and community interactions viewed as normal day to day practice.

Fourth, this partnership model makes possible the potential for long-term community- based projects and community-based research (Stoecker & Tyron, 2009). As CSL emerges from context, driven by a shared vision and has density in the web of networks, it creates more opportunity to ensure that CSL is reciprocal and mutual in meeting all participants' needs (Furco, Moely, & Reed, 2007; Geertz, 1973; Morton, 1995).

In summary, this partnership model assists in the CSL process by providing a supportive infrastructure for CSL that is facilitative, not prescriptive, flexible, inclusive, convergent, and generative. The food security theme implemented through use of this model encourages our students to be concerned with policies and to advocate for social change in developing local food systems. While some of our students may take on social justice issues of enhanced food distribution to those in need, in other service-learning experiences, students and professors explore with the community the cultural and political contexts of food. CSL courses may provide opportunities for our students to empower people to grow, harvest and store their own food. They may examine policy issues such as national seed-saving regulations or municipal pollination by-laws that can affect the development of local food systems. They may collaborate with First Nation communities to support the revitalization of local boreal forest food sources. CSL courses join forces with local farmers to enhance the marketing of local beef and CSA operations, or team up in the development of a local flour milling operation. Thus, the CSL food security theme promoting the local food system allows more diversity of courses for which CSL is appropriate, more partnering organizations appropriate for CSL, and a larger variety of CSL experiences for our students.

In the present study, we examine the impacts of a university-wide theme of food security in service-learning within our community engagement partnership model. There were two primary research questions: (1) What is the impact of the food security theme CSL experience on students' academic experience and skills? and (2) What is the impact of the CSL experience on students' civic engagement, responsibility, and awareness? We were also interested in examining the impacts on students' knowledge of current events and their sense of community belonging, as well as the barriers that they encounter in community involvement.

METHOD

Participants

The impact of service-learning on students has been tracked since the first food security theme service-learning courses were offered in the fall of 2006. The data included in this analysis spans through Winter Term

2009. The survey instrument was administered at the beginning of each course and again at the end of the course. Survey respondents included 750 individuals who completed the pretest and 394 individuals who completed the posttest. Of these, 231 completed both pre and post tests. To determine if the students who completed both surveys were representative of students in CSL courses, this group was compared with those who only completed one survey. Students who completed both surveys did not differ from the larger group in proportion of men and women or part-time/full-time status. However, they were significantly older and more likely to be beyond the first year of college than the larger group. These findings may have resulted from a problem in data collection: Two large first-year courses in 2007, a biology and a political science course, gave the pretest but failed to schedule the posttest. Otherwise, no systematic bias influencing student participation was identified.

The present study reports findings from students who completed both surveys ($N = 231$). Included in this group were 155 females and 74 males (2 did not report gender). With respect to age, 14.7% were under 20 years old, 59.7% were 20-24 years of age, 14.3% were 25 to 29 years of age, and 10.8% were age 30 years or older. For year in university, 4.8% were in first year, 22.9% were in second year, 28.6% were in third year, 37.2% were in fourth year, 3.9% were in fifth year or higher. Most participants (94.4%) were full time students.

Measures

Measures focused on (1) the students' academic experience and skill set, and (2) students' levels of civic engagement, responsibility, and awareness. In addition, we examined students' knowledge of current events and their felt sense of community belonging, as well as the barriers to community involvement they perceived. Scales and items addressing key constructs were drawn from published materials where possible, and all materials were reviewed with feedback by CSL course instructors. See the Appendix for all questionnaire items. Scales were included to assess each of the following:

Academic experience

Participants rated 5 items using a 5-point Likert scale of agreement. These items were drawn from the scale assessing academic experience in Furco's (2000) Higher Education Service-Learning Survey (HESLS). The HESLS has been used by Astin, Vogelgesang, Ikeda, and Yee (2000), Moely, Furco, and Reed (2008), and many others. One item was removed from this scale to improve reliability. Reliability of the remaining items was found to be alpha = .71 at Time 1 and alpha = .77 at Time 2.

Academic skills

Participants rated each of 14 skills in how they felt their own levels compared to others their own age on a 5-point Likert scale (1 = *below average*, 2 = *just below average*, 3 = *average*, 4 = *just above average*, and 5 = *above average*). Six of these items were drawn from the St. Francis Xavier University survey (St. Francis Xavier University, 2006) and these were supplemented with 8 items developed for the present study. Reliability of this scale at Time 1 was alpha = .85 and at Time 2, alpha = .88.

Civic Engagement

For each participant, the total number of 11 civic activities they indicated participating in (e.g., voting, signing petition) was calculated. These items were drawn from the General Social Survey of Canada (GSS, 2003).

Civic Responsibility.

Participants responded to 11 items regarding their felt sense of responsibility and concern toward their community, as well as their beliefs that people should contribute to their community and actions relating to community participation. Participants indicated their agreement with these items using a 5-point Likert scale of agreement. Nine of these items were drawn from Furco's (2000) HESLS and the remaining two from the Student Civic Engagement Survey used by the American Association of Community Colleges (AACC, 2006). Reliability of this scale was found to be alpha = .87 for Time 1 and alpha = .87 at Time 2.

Civic Awareness

Participants responded to 6 items asking them to rate their understanding relative to others their age on problems facing their community, social problems in Canada, as well as poverty and food security specifically. Two of these items were drawn from the survey used by Parker-Gwin and Mabry (1998), one from the AACC (2006), and three were developed for the purposes of this study with a focus on food security issues. Participants provided their ratings on a 5-point scale (1 = *below average*, 2 = *just below average*, 3 = *average*, 4 = *just above average*, and 5 = *above average*). Reliability was alpha = .85 at Time 1 and alpha = .86 at Time 2.

Knowledge of Current Events

Participants' self-rated knowledge of current events was assessed with the following item from the GSS (2003): "How frequently do you follow news and current affairs (e.g., international, national, regional, or local)?" Participants indicated their responses using the following scale options, "daily," "several times each week," "several times each month," or "rarely or never."

Community Belonging

This was assessed by asking participants' agreement, using a 5-point Likert scale, on the following item drawn from the Canadian Community Health Survey (2002), "I have a strong sense of community belonging."

Perceived Barriers

Participants' perceptions of the factors preventing them from engaging in community service were assessed with the question, "What prevents you from being more involved in your community?" This item is followed by a list of 6 potential barriers that participants could select.

Procedure

Instructors from courses in which a food security themed CSL component was offered were approached to invite their students to complete the survey. These courses represented a broad spectrum of disciplines including biology, business, history, outdoor recreation, psychology, social work and women's studies. Research participants came from 14 different courses, one at the first-year level, two at the second-year level, five at the third-year level, and six at the fourth-year level. The nature of the CSL component varied across these different courses, emerging out of unique interactions among the faculty member, community partner(s), and student(s). Some involved projects carried out by the whole class in partnership with a community group (e.g., a survey of market-goers to assess the viability of a local flour mill in a business class), others involved community service experiences initiated by individual students (e.g., alleviating food insecurity in low-income neighborhoods), all incorporated a food security component in one of its varied forms.

An administrative assistant attended each course early in the semester to administer the pretest survey and again near the end of the semester to administer the posttest survey. In each case, students took approximately 15 minutes of class time to complete the survey.

RESULTS

Each of the dependent variables described above was subjected to a repeated measures Analysis of Variance with age group and gender as between subjects' factors and time of test as the repeated measure. Means

Exhibit 8.3.   Student Responses on Selected Variables Showing Change Over Time

Variable	Time 1 M (SD)	Time 2 M (SD)
Academic skills[a]	3.61 (.03)	3.66 (.04)
Civic engagement[b]	7.16 (.15)	5.77 (.20)
Men[b]	7.23 (.25)	5.26 (.33)
Women[b]	7.10 (.18)	6.29 (.23)
Civic awareness	3.44 (.06)	3.51 (.06)
Under 20 years	3.27 (.12)	3.18 (.12)
20-24 years[b]	3.26 (.06)	3.51 (.06)
25-30 years	3.48 (.12)	3.48 (12)
30+ years	3.77 (.14)	3.89 (.14)
Knowledge of current events[b]	2.15 (.08)	2.91 (.08)
Under 20 years	2.82 (.16)	2.21 (.16)
20-24 years[b]	2.23 (.08)	2.90 (.08)
25-30 years[b]	1.84 (.16)	3.12 (.17)
30+ years[b]	1.72 (.18)	3.40 (.19)
Community belonging	3.26 (.06)	3.34 (.06)
Men	3.22 (.10)	3.23 (.10)
Women[a]	3.29 (.07)	3.46 (.07)
Item #9: Concern about community issues[b]	3.72 (.04)	3.84 (.05)
Item #11: Responsibility to serve community[a]	3.70 (.06)	3.81 (.05)

Note: [a]Significant at $p = <.05$; [b] Significant at $p = <.01$.

and standard deviations from Time 1 and Time 2 for dependent variables showing change over time (including gender and age group means, where appropriate) are shown in Exhibit 8.3.

The first research question concerned the impacts of the food security theme CSL experience on (a) students' self-reported academic experience and (b) their self-reported academic skills. No group differences or change over time was shown for academic experience. For the academic skills measure, a significant effect of time was observed, $F(1,226) = 4.50$, $p = .04$, along with a significant main effect of gender, $F(1,226) = 15.82$, $p < .001$. Academic skills increased from Time 1 to Time 2 and, overall, males scored higher on self-reported academic skills, $M = 53.3$, $SD = .75$, than females, $M = 49.7$, $SD = .52$.

The second research question concerned impact of the food security theme CSL experience on students' civic attitudes. In the analysis of civic responsibility scores, no significant main effects or interactions were found. For civic engagement, a significant main effect of time was observed, $F(1,225) = 44.18, p < .001$, which was qualified by a significant interaction with gender, $F(1,225) = 7.70, p = .006$. Simple effects analyses revealed that there was an overall *decline* in levels of civic engagement from time one to time two, but this decline, while significant in both groups, was slightly larger among male participants, $F(1,72) = 25.1, p < .001$, than female participants, $F(1,153) = 13.59, p < .001$. The analysis of the civic awareness scale showed a significant main effect of age group, $F(3,225) = 4.33, p = .005$, and a significant interaction between age group and time, $F(3,225) = 3.16, p = .026$. Simple effects analyses revealed that there was a significant effect of time on civic awareness only in participants aged 20 to 24, $F(1,137) = 20.34, p < .001$. Students younger than 20 and those 25 years and older did not show a significant effect of time on levels of civic awareness.

Also of interest in this study was the possible impact of the CSL experience on students' knowledge of current events and their sense of community belonging. For knowledge of current events, a repeated measures ANOVA yielded a significant main effect of time, $F(1,215) = 10.62, p = .001$, which was qualified by a significant interaction between age group and time, $F(3,215) = 8.71, p < .001$, as shown in Exhibit 8.3. For all age groups except the youngest, there were significant increases in knowledge of current events from Time 1 to Time 2: For ages 20-24, $F(1,135) = 22.12, p < .001$; ages 25-30, $F(1,30) = 18.34, p < .001$; ages 30+, $F(1,23) = 30.42, p < .001$.

Exhibit 8.4.   Student Perceptions of the Barriers Preventing Community Involvement

Barrier	Number Who Selected Barrier at Time 1	Number Who Selected Barrier at Time 2
Academic commitments	82%	80%
Work commitments	55%	55%
Income limitations	47%	48%
Family commitments	26%	27%
Lack of transportation	23%	27%
Lack of knowledge of how to get involved	11%	13%

Note: Participant were asked to select all that applied, so percentages do not add to 100.

To test for effects of time on sense of community belonging, a similar repeated measures ANOVA was conducted. A significant interaction between gender and time was found, $F(1,214) = 4.50$, $p = .04$. Simple effects analyses revealed that there was no significant effect of time for male participants but there was a significant increase in sense of community belonging from Time 1 to Time 2 in female participants, $F(1, 150) = 6.83$, $p = .01$.

Student perceptions of the barriers preventing them from being involved in their communities were also examined. At both Times 1 and 2, the most frequently cited barriers to community involvement were academic commitments, work commitments, and income limitations, in that order. See Exhibit 8.4 for percentages of students reporting each kind of barrier.

Exploratory Analyses

In order to further consider the impact of the CSL experience on students' conceptualizations, an exploratory analysis was made of items on the civic responsibility scale. As indicated above, no significant effects were obtained for this measure. However, given the range of qualities assessed with the civic responsibility scale, from behavioral to prescriptive to felt responsibility, the 11 items comprising the scale were further analyzed as single items. Responses on each item at Time 1 and Time 2 were compared using paired-samples t tests. We found that two items, specifically (#9) participants' levels of concern about community issues, $t(226) = -2.99$, $p = .003$, and (#11) their sense of responsibility to serve their community, $t(226) = -2.11$, $p = .04$, increased significantly from Time 1 to Time 2 (Exhibit 8.3). The remaining items, which focus on prescriptions for others' behavior and plans to engage in community work, did not change significantly over time.

DISCUSSION

This research was guided by two primary questions. The first dealt with the impact of the food security theme CSL experience on students' academic experience and skill. Results indicated no significant change over time in participants' self-reported academic experience. Thus, students participating in the CSL courses did not show an increase in the degree to which they found their courses to be intellectually stimulating and relevant to the real world. One possible explanation for this null finding is that the items in the academic experience scale refer to courses in general and not to the specific CSL course in question. Therefore, students may have been thinking about their overall university experience at both Times 1 and 2, as opposed to their experience in the CSL course relative to other courses, and this may have obscured any impact on this variable. There was a significant change over time in participants' self-reported academic skills. Participants rated themselves more highly at the end of their course on skills such as communication, leadership, facilitation, and community capacity building than they did at the beginning of the CSL course.

The second research question concerned the impact of the CSL experience on students' civic engagement, responsibility, and awareness. Contrary to our expectations, students' levels of civic engagement, measured as participation in political and social action, revealed a significant decrease from the beginning to the end of the CSL course. This effect was moderated by gender such that the decrease was more marked in males than in females, though significant in both groups. While this could suggest a negative impact of the CSL experience on civic engagement, this result is more likely an artifact of the student experience during the academic year in general. Most students reside in the university community only for the academic year, and thus are uprooted from their established networks of social and political action. Students may also be too busy with academic demands to engage in social action at the end of the semester, thus producing a decline in civic engagement scores. In future research on the effects of CSL, scales should be developed that include more pointed and subtle indicators of civic engagement.

While there were no significant effects of time on civic responsibility, exploratory analyses of particular items from the civic responsibility scale did suggest some impact on the more individually-focused items of this scale. Participants felt more personal responsibility to serve their community and more concern for their community at the end of the CSL experience than at the beginning. In future research, reliable scales tapping these direct and personal aspects of civic responsibility may reveal more significant changes over time.

Participants' levels of civic awareness, or their understanding of social and food security issues, were found to increase from the beginning to the end of the CSL experience, although only among students aged 20 to 24. These results are particularly interesting, as a key goal of CSL courses is to enhance students' understanding and awareness of community issues through direct, first-hand experience in the community (Kahne, Westheimer, & Rogers, 2000; Morton, 1995; Vogelgesang, 2009). While we did not have a control group of students in non-CSL courses against which to compare these results, they do provide some early evidence that the CSL experience may catalyze students' awareness of community issues to a more profound level of understanding. That this increase was only significant in the age group of 20 to 24 years may suggest a sensitive period in which exposure to a CSL experience brings maximum benefit. It is also possible that these slightly older students drew from smaller, more intensive CSL courses at the third and fourth year levels. Younger students in larger introductory courses may experience less impact from a CSL component that may be necessarily less intensive than that offered in smaller advanced-level classes. Findings for civic awareness parallel those obtained for the students' knowledge of current events, in that younger students showed less positive change over time. Interestingly, a significant overall increase over time in civic awareness was qualified by an interaction with age such that those in the youngest group (under 20) showed a slight decline in their self-rated knowledge of current events, while all other groups increased significantly.

There has been considerable positive feedback over the past few decades on the effects of CSL on student academic grades, attitudes and perspectives about engaging in civil society (Astin & Sax, 1998; Stoecker & Tyron, 2009). Service-learning is premised on assumptions that more active forms of pedagogy are more effective in teaching and learning than more passive approaches, and that experiential, hands-on teaching can enhance civic responsibilities and engagement (Jeavons, 1995). Connecting community service learning with academic courses is found to positively affect cognitive skills (Vogelgesang & Astin, 2000). Our results support assertions that service-learning is a form of engaged pedagogy that enhances skills such as leadership and critical thinking and has a positive impact on sense of social responsibility and commitment to activism (Astin, Vogelgesang, Ikeda, & Yee, 2000; Eyler & Giles, 1999). The significant effects on academic skills, civic awareness, knowledge of current events, and community belonging suggest that the CSL experience enhanced the students' development beyond the acquisition of conceptual knowledge. While we did not compare this approach with other forms of CSL, it is possible that embedding service-learning within a food security framework provides an overall ambience to CSL at the university and within the surrounding region. It reinforces community issues and a sense of responsibility, having more impact on students as they go about interacting with other students outside of their particular CSL course and in their daily interactions with the community, than a more singular and isolated approach to course based CSL and community engagement. Because of this central theme of food security, there is a cohesiveness and synergy created on campus among faculty and students across CSL courses in a diversity of disciplines and faculties of the academy. Positive effects of CSL have been shown to occur as students discuss experiences with each other and their instructors (Astin et. al., 2000). Likewise, students are embedded in a community where this theme approach appears to encourage enthusiastic networking and sharing among community groups with varied interests in the enhancement of a local food system. The synergistic complexity of the local food system web—students, faculty and community may effectively enhance the impact of service learning on some aspects of civic responsibility.

In addition, students' rating of their sense of community belonging was found to increase significantly from Time 1 to Time 2, suggesting that participation in this food security-themed CSL increased participants' sense of belonging within the community. Community belonging is a strong indicator of social capital, an essential component of active civic engagement (Eyler & Giles, 1999; Putnam, 2000). The food security theme may have aided in enhancing sense of community belonging in the students, since the theme crosses all social-economic dimensions, and perhaps helps students find personal relevance and a personal connection with the community through their CSL projects, in a way that a charitable or poverty-reduction model cannot. Kraft (1996) eloquently expresses his views that this is a new and more effective paradigm for service-learning: "no voice is silence, no role is invisible" (p. 140).

There have been a number of studies that provide evidence of a close association between CSL and improved academic performance (Cooks & Scharrer, 2006, p. 45-46). Perhaps the reason we find a lack of significance in academic experience is because the students perceive a separation between learning in academic courses and learning within the community. Cooks and Scharrer argue that the transformative aspect of CSL learning occurs in the social and contextual approach. This follows Dewey's (1922, 1938) historic positioning of learning as acting in experience. Further, learning outcomes may be meditated by the amount of time devoted to reflection, the degree of integration of CSL into the academic courses, and the match between student preferences for a charity or social change approach to CSL and their actual experiences (Astin et al., 2000; Eyler & Giles, 1999; Marley, 2008).

The examination of the perceived barriers to participation in CSL by students appears not to have been previously studied. Our findings that students perceive the top barriers to participation in CSL to be academic commitments, work commitments, and income limitations may reflect the high cost of attending a postsecondary institution where tuition rates have soared in the last two decades, combined with widespread job loss that has decreased the availability of parental support and decreased the opportunity for students to find high-paying full-time summer employment. From these results, students appear not to have the luxury of independently volunteering. CSL may be a needed window of opportunity for students to gain life-time skills in citizenry.

A commitment to service learning requires faculty time and expertise, coordination and planning, transportation, community time and expertise, student time and commitment and resources to fund supplies, materials and products (Holland, 2001). A university-wide themed approach to CSL within a contextual fluidity model that facilitates but is not prescriptive in directing faculty and student involvement with community partners appears from our results to have a positive impact on students' levels of civic engagement.

CONCLUSIONS

These results demonstrate that through implementation of a food security theme for CSL, using a CF partnership model, Lakehead University is becoming an engaged campus where the students are making significant gains in aspects of civic responsibility and community belonging. The students are connected in community through a process that seeks to transform the university through credit-bearing courses whereby students bring the knowledge of the community back into the university learning environment in respectful and trusting ways. Our findings do confirm that CSL makes a difference and that this difference challenges universities to explore the underlying epistemological assumptions about how we learn and know (Knowledge Commons Initiative, 2010; Liu, 1995). Knowledge appears to be profoundly learned within context and raises challenges to a more traditional positivistic university oriented approach to knowledge transmission.

APPENDIX: QUESTIONNAIRE ITEMS

Part 1: Academic Experience and Skills

Academic Experience:
Instructions. Please indicate your level of agreement with the following statements:

1. I find the content in school courses intellectually stimulating.
2. I enjoy learning in school when course materials pertain to real life.
3. I learn more when courses contain hands on activities.
4. The things I learn in school are useful in my life.
5. Courses in school make me think about real-life in new ways.

Alpha of scale = .71 (Time 1) and .77 (Time 2)

Academic Skills:
Instructions. Please rate your skills, as compared to someone your own age.

1. Written communication skills
2. Verbal communication skills
3. Leadership skills: Managing yourself
4. Leadership skills: Managing others
5. Leadership skills: Conflict management
6. Leadership skills: Risk taking
7. Facilitation skills
8. Patience
9. Problem solving skills
10. Research skills
11. Critical thinking skills
12. Cooperative action
13. Community capacity building
14. Project management

Alpha of scale = .85 (Time 1) and .88 (Time 2)

Part 2: Civic Engagement, Responsibility, and Awareness

Civic Engagement:
Instructions. In the past 12 months, have you done any of the following (yes or no):

1. Did you vote in the last federal election?
2. Did you vote in the last provincial election?
3. Did you vote in the last municipal election?
4. Searched for information on a political issue
5. Volunteered with a political party
6. Expressed your views on an issue by contacting a politician or newspaper
7. Signed a petition (paper or online)
8. Boycotted a product or chose a product for ethical reasons
9. Attended a public meeting

10. Spoken out at a public meeting
11. Participated in a demonstration or march

The number of items checked "yes" by each participant was summed.

Civic Responsibility:

Instructions. Please indicate your level of agreement with the following statements:

1. Being involved in a program to improve my community is important.
2. It is important that I work toward equal opportunity for all people.
3. It is not necessary to volunteer my time to help people in need. (reversed)
4. Giving some of my income to help those in need is something I should do.
5. It is important for me to find a career that directly benefits others.
6. I think that people should find time to contribute to their community.
7. I plan to participate in improving my neighborhood in the near future.
8. I feel that I can have a positive impact on local social problems.
9. I am concerned about local community issues.
10. If everyone works together, many of society's problems can be solved.
11. I have a responsibility to serve my community.

Alpha of scale = .87 (Time 1) and .87 (Time 2)

Civic Awareness:

Instructions. Please rate your skills, as compared to someone your own age:

1. Understanding the problems facing your community
2. Understanding social problems facing Canada
3. Understanding of poverty issues
4. Understanding of food security issues.

Instructions. Please indicate your level of agreement with the following statements:

5. I have a good understanding of the needs and problems facing the community in which I live.

6. I try to understand issues around homelessness.

Alpha of scale = .85 (Time 1) and .86 (Time 2)

Part 3: Single-Item Measures and Perceived Barriers

Knowledge of Current Events:

How frequently do you follow news and current affairs (e.g., international, national, regional, or local)? Check one:

__ Daily
__ Several times each week
__ Several times each month
__ Rarely or never)

Community Belonging:

Instructions. Please indicate your level of agreement with the following statement:

I have a strong sense of community belonging.

Perceived Barriers to Community Involvement:

Instructions. What prevents you from being more involved in your community (check all that apply)?

1. I am involved in my community
2. Lack knowledge of how to get involved
3. Family commitments
4. Work commitments
5. Academic commitments
6. Lack transportation
7. Income limitations

REFERENCES

American Association of Community Colleges. (2006). Resource centre. *Assessment. Student Pre-Survey*. Retrieved from http://www.aacc.nche.edu/Resources /aaccprograms/horizons/Documents/student_pre_survey.pdf

Astin, A. W., Vogelgesang, L., Ikeda, E., & Yee, J.(2000). *How service learning affects students*. Los Angeles, CA: UCLA Higher Education Research Institute.

Astin, A. W., & Sax, L. J. (1998). How undergraduates are affected by service participation. *Journal of College Student Development, 39*(3), 251-263.

Barber, B. R., & Battistoni, R. (1993). A season of service: Introducing service learning into the liberal arts curriculum. *Political Science and Politics, 26*(2), 235-240.

Boyle-Baise, M., Brown, R., Hsu, M., Jones, D., Prakash, A., Rausch, M., Vitols, S., & Wahlquist, Z. (2006). Learning service or service learning: Enabling the civic. *International Journal of Teaching and Learning in Higher Education, 18*(1), 17-26.

Bringle, R. C., & Hatcher, J.A. (1996). Implementing service learning in higher education. *The Journal of Higher Education, 67*(2), 221-239.

Butin, D. W. (2010). *Service-learning in theory and practice: The future of community engagement in higher education.* New York, NY: Palgrave MacMillan.

Canadian Alliance for Community Service-Learning. (2010). Retrieved from http://www.communityservicelearning.ca/en/

Charbonneau, L. (2009, October). Community connections. *University Affairs, 50*(8), 18-21.

Cooks, L., & Scharrer, E. (2006). Assessing learning in community service learning: A social approach. *Michigan Journal of Community Service Learning, 13*(1), 44-55.

Dewey, J. (1922). *Human nature and conduct.* New York, NY: Henry Holt.

Dewey, J. (1938). *Experience and education.* New York, NY: Collier.

Eyler, J., & Giles, D. E., Jr. (1999). *Where's the learning in service-learning?* San Francisco, CA: Jossey-Bass.

Food Security Research Network (2009a). *J.W. McConnell proposal.* Retrieved from http://www.foodsecurityresearch.ca/resources/Original_McConnell_Proposal.pdf

Food Security Research Network. (2009b). *Research student publications.* Retrieved from www.foodsecurityresearch.ca

Furco, A. (2000). The Higher Education Service-Learning Survey. Retrieved from http://www.servicelearning.org/filemanager/download/HEdSurveyRel.pdf

Furco, A., Moely, B., & Reed, J. (2007, July). *Formulating a model of effects of college students' service-learning experience.* Paper presented at the International Conference on Psychology, Athens Greece.

Geertz, C. (Ed.). (1973). Thick description: Toward an interpretive theory of culture. In *The interpretation of cultures* (pp. 3-32). New York, NY: Basic Books.

Gleick, J. (1987). *Chaos: Making of a new science.* New York, NY: Viking.

General Social Survey. (2003). *Social engagement, Cycle 17.* Retrieved from http://www.statcan.gc.ca/bsolc/olc-cel/olc-cel?catno=89-598-X&lang=eng

Holland, B. A. (2001). A comprehensive model for assessing service-learning and community-university partnerships. *New Directions for Higher Education, 114,* 51-60.

Illich, I. (1990). To hell with good intentions. In J. C. Kendall (Ed.), *Combining service and learning* (pp. 314-320). Raleigh, NC National Society for Internships an Experiential Education.

Jeavons, T. H. (1995). Service-learning and liberal learning: A marriage of convenience. *Michigan Journal of Community Service Learning, 2* (Fall), 134-140.

Kahne, J., Westheimer, J., & Rogers, B. (2000, Fall). Service-learning and citizenship: Directions for research [Special Issue]. *Michigan Journal of Community Service Learning*, 42-51.

Kickert, W. J. M., Klijm, E. -H., & Koppenjan, J. F. M. (Eds.). (1997) In *Managing complex networks: Strategies for the public sector* (pp. 1-13). Thousand Oaks, CA: Sage Publications Ltd.

Kraft, R.J. (1996). Service learning: An introduction to its theory, practice and effects. *Education and Urban Society, 28*(2), 131-159.

Knowledge Commons Initiative. (2010). *An invitation to explore the role of knowledge in society.* Retrieved from http://knowledgecommons.ning.com/

Liu, G. (1995). Knowledge, foundations, and discourse: Philosophical support for service learning. *Michigan Journal of Community Service Learning, 2,* 5-18.

Markus, G. B., Howard, J. P. F., & King, D.C. (1993). Integrating community service and classroom instruction enhances learning: Results from an experiment. *Educational Evaluation and Policy Analysis, 15*(4), 410-419.

Marley, E. K. (2008). *Food for Thought: Introducing organic food in Norwegian schools.* Unpublished Master's thesis, University of Oslo, Blindern, Norway.

Miron, D., & Moely, B. E. (2006). Community agency voice and benefit in service-learning. *Michigan Journal of Community Service Learning, 12*(2), 27-37.

Moely, B. E., Furco, A., & Reed, J. (2008) Charity and social change: The impact of individual preferences on service learning outcomes. *Michigan Journal of Community Service Learning, 15*(1), 37-48.

Morton, K. (1995). The irony of service: Charity, project and social change in service-learning. *Michigan Journal of Community Service Learning, 2,* 19-32.

Nelson, C. H., & McPherson, D. H. (2003). Cultural diversity in social work practice: where are we now and what are the challenges in addressing issues of injustice and oppression? In W. Shera (Ed.), *Emerging perspectives on anti-oppressive practice* (pp. 81-100). Toronto, Ontario, Canada: Canadian Scholars Press.

Nelson, C. H., & McPherson, D. H. (2004). Contextual fluidity: An emerging practice model for helping. *Rural Social Work, 9,* 199-209.

Nelson, C. H., Stadey, M., & Lyons, A. A. (2005). Community-academic research partnership: A key recipe for food security. In A. M. Kirbyson (Ed.), *Recipes for success: A celebration of food security work in Canada* (pp. 27-31). Winnipeg, Manitoba, Canada: Social Planning Council of Winnipeg.

Noddings, N. (1992). *The challenge to care in schools: An alternative approach to education.* New York, NY: Teachers College Press.

Parker-Gwin, R. (1996). Connecting service to learning: How students and communities matter. *Teaching Sociology, 24,* 97-101.

Parker-Gwin, R., & Mabry, J. B. (1998). Service learning as pedagogy and civic education: Comparing outcomes for three models. *Teaching Sociology, 26,* 276-291.

Putnam, R. (2000). *Bowling alone: The collapse and revival of American community.* New York, NY: Simon & Schuster.

Sandy, M., & Holland, B.A. (2006). Different worlds and common ground: Community partner perspectives on campus-community partnerships. *Michigan Journal of Community Service Learning, 13*(1), 30-43.

Serow, R. C. (1991). Students and voluntarism: Looking into the motives of community service participants. *American Educational Research Journal, 28*(3), 543-556.

Statistics Canada. (2003). *Canadian community health survey mental health and well-being.* Retrieved from http://www.statcan.ca/english/freepub/82-617-XIE/index.htm

St. Francis Xavier University. (2006). *Confidential Student Evaluation of Course Based Service Learning 2005-2006.* Retrieved from http://www.mystfx.ca/academic/servicelearning/

Stoecker, R. (2009) Are we talking the walk of community-based research? *Action Research, 7,* 385. Retrieved from http://arj.sagepub.com/cgi/reprint/7/4/385

Stoecker, R., & Tyron, E. A. (Eds.). (2009). *The unheard voices: Community organizations and service learning.* Philadelphia, PA: Temple University Press.

Vogelgesang, L. J. (2009). Civic engagement and service-learning: The challenge and promise of research. In B. E. Moely, S. H. Billig, & B. A. Holland (Eds.), *Creating our identities in service-learning and community engagement* (pp. 237-250). Charlotte, NC: Information Age.

Vogelgesang, L. J., & Astin, A. W. (2000). Comparing the effects of service-learning and community service. *Michigan Journal of Community Service Learning, 7,* 25-34.

Zlotkowski, E. (1995). Does service-learning have a future? *Michigan Journal of Community Service Learning, 2*(1), 123-33.

PART IV

CONCLUSION

CHAPTER 9

JOURNEY TO SERVICE-LEARNING RESEARCH

Agendas, Accomplishments, and Aspirations

Dwight E. Giles, Jr.

This chapter reviews the development of service-learning research in higher education in the United States over the past 2 decades. Drawing on the author's own involvement in the development of service-learning research and the evolution of the field, the journey to service-learning research moves from establishing research agendas, to key research milestones, and to a vision for future research.

"Service, combined with learning, adds value to each and transforms both."

—Honnett and Poulsen (1989)

The bold statement above was created collaboratively over 20 years ago and has often been considered the central claim of service-learning. It demands research to examine its operation in practice and to document the extent to which such outcomes really do accrue from service-learning.

Research for What? Making Engaged Scholarship Matter
pp. 203–221
Copyright © 2010 by Information Age Publishing

This claim is from the preamble of the Wingspread Special Report, *Principles of Good Practice for Combining Service and Leaning* which became one of the foundation documents of the field (Honnett & Poulsen, 1989). Ten principles were identified that were derived from an earlier statement developed in the United States by the National Society for Internships and Experiential Education (NSIEE)[1] and were circulated in draft form among 70 organizations related to education, human services and public policy as the nascent field of service-learning was seeking definition, creating standards of practice, and forging consensus about the work.

In May, 1989, a small group of representatives of the key sponsoring organizations met at the Johnson Foundation's Wingspread Conference Center in Racine, Wisconsin to finalize and prepare the principles document. The 2-decade journey to service-learning research presented here is based on the premise that the story of the evolution of service-learning research is one of examining, unfolding and giving empirical support and critique to the claim that it enriches both learning and service.

This chapter was originally given as the Distinguished Research Award Presentation at the 2009 Conference of the International Association for Research on Service-Learning and Community Engagement held in Ottawa, Ontario, Canada. I was asked to speak about my work in service-learning research that was the basis of the award. I have elected here, as I did in the presentation, to weave a story of the evolution of this field of service-learning research over the past 2 decades, moving between the evolution of the field and my own work. This work, along with that of a number of other dedicated pioneer researchers, illustrates the evolution of the cooperatively constructed agendas, the collaborative accomplishments, and the aspirations that I and others hold for the future of service learning.

Since this approach may seem unorthodox, it is useful to locate it in some methodological considerations. At a basic level it could be considered a participant observer design (Creswell, 2006), particularly if linked to more contemporary qualitative methods with interpretive approaches that include the observer's narrative as part of the larger phenomenon. This approach has parallels in autoethnography and personal narrative as well as interactive interpretations of a phenomenon (Maxwell, 2004). It is equally important to note what this chapter is not: It is not a literature review or a research bibliography; neither is it a history of service-learning research. Indeed the *journey* metaphor best captures the story of the sojourner, the fellow travelers, the waypoints, and—especially in retrospection—the routes and detours taken. Given this anchoring in a specific journey, the limitations are that it is only about service-learning research in the United States, it focuses mostly on higher education, and most importantly, it is limited by the scope of the author's work and the works that have been selected. The criteria for selection of studies will be clarified below in the Accomplishments section.

AGENDAS

In the 1980s, the emerging field of experiential education, as represented by the National Society for Internships and Experiential Education, became concerned with a research base for its arena of practice and its research committee began to work on research bibliographies and a research agenda. At the same time, Professor John Duley and his colleagues at Michigan State were writing about how to assess the *learning* in service-learning and other forms of experiential learning, forming a foundation for future research agendas (Yelon & Duley, 1978/1990). The agenda that the research committee developed became the basis for the first agenda and subsequent agendas in service-learning as it was emerging from a subfield of experiential education to a separate arena of practice. During this decade, several members of the NSIEE Research Committee were active in forming and running a special interest group (SIG) in the American Educational Research Association (AERA) and used it as a then rare venue to present research about service-learning as one type of field education at the AERA annual meetings. Today this SIG has evolved into "Service-Learning and Experiential Education."

A First Agenda: 1991

Like the first conceptual and practice document of service-learning, *The Principles of Good Practice* (Honnett & Poulsen, 1989), the first service-learning research agenda was also the product of a Wingspread Conference sponsored by the Johnson Foundation (Giles, Honnett, & Migliore, 1991) and organized by NSIEE. Forty-eight participants, including researchers, educators, service-learning practitioners, students, representatives from government agencies, foundations and national associations crafted the agenda that was designed primarily to "identify critical research questions that need further research" (Giles et al., 1991). Before specifying the detailed questions and areas of research, the conference participants developed two broad thematic questions:

1. What is the effect of service-learning on the intellectual, moral, and citizenship development of participants?
2. What is the effect of service-learning on the advancement of social institutions and democracy (Giles et al., 1991)?

The Forgotten Agenda: 1993

Two years after the original agenda, NSIEE and Campus Compact convened another research agenda conference, this time focusing mostly on service-learning researchers and practitioners, to review and update the original agenda. While minutes were taken and two of the co-conveners, Janet Eyler and Dwight Giles, prepared a draft report it was never circulated or published. It is this participant's recollection that there were few if any new areas of research or research questions, but mostly affirmation, elaboration and refinement of the original 1991 questions along with some progress reports on national studies that were taking shape.

More Than an Agenda: 1997

In November, 1997, Campus Compact, as part of its effort to create a research emphasis and focus, convened a conference comprised mainly of service-learning researchers, held at the Education Commission of the States office in Denver, Colorado. While the conference themes stated two objectives relating to the pursuit of research, most objectives were much more advocacy-oriented, using verbs and phrases like *advance, build, strengthen, further catapult,* and to *inform funders* (Howard, Gelmon, & Giles, 2000). A comparison of the relative simplicity of the 1991 agenda and the evolving complexity as evident in 1997 agenda is presented in Exhibit 9.1.

One of the outcomes of this Denver meeting was the agreement to produce a special issue of the *Michigan Journal of Community Service-Learning* focusing on what was needed in service-learning research. Journal editor Jeffrey Howard was joined by conference cofacilitators Sherril Gelmon and Dwight Giles to produce this special issue, with the initial idea that it would serve to inform about and to facilitate new, innovative, and important research directions. As the concept grew, the coeditors expanded the

Exhibit 9.1.   Comparison of the 1991 and 1997 Research Agendas

1991	*1997*
• Impact on students learning	• Student learning
• Impact on educational institutions	• Community impact
• Impact on community participants	• Community participation in Research
• Need for theory	• Testing concepts
• Program models	• Historical research
	• Faculty and institutional impacts
	• Effect on practice

focus and solicited invited articles from both conference participants and others in the field. During this period the editors presented the preliminary idea at a number of conferences to solicit input into the final volume, which grew substantially over the three-year period of its development (see Howard et al., 2000). The final product, entitled *Strategic Directions for Service-Learning Research*, presented a variety of topics in terms of what research existed and what was needed. The topics ranged from Areas of Study (such as students, community partnerships, faculty, diversity, disciplines, and institutional impacts) to Perspectives (such as in relation to practice, campus presidents' views, and methodological debates). What is distinctive about this volume was the interweaving of literature reviews, research questions, and strategic directions from key researchers and practitioners in the field. In short, it provided both questions and answers in regard to surveying and furthering research.

A Top 10 Unanswered Questions Agenda: 1998

This agenda was in draft form for the November 1997 Denver meeting and was published the next year (Giles & Eyler, 1998). Based on a review of current research, this agenda concluded that we knew quite a bit about student learning outcomes and community satisfaction with service-learning, but less about the motivation for faculty involvement in service-learning, institutional policies and effects, types of community partnerships and their effects, and the impacts on society, both in general through the development of social capital as well on the long-term commitment to engaged citizenship among students who participate in service-learning. While this agenda was subtitled as a research agenda for the next 5 years, it seems that no subsequent agendas have emerged. Indeed I might hypothesize that once a field of research gains its own momentum as this one has, there is much less need for collaboratively constructed agendas or research-based agendas outside of specific topics that have become differentiated in the field.

Community Engagement: A New Agenda: 2008

The title and the introduction of this chapter focus on service-learning and indeed it is noted above that this is a limit of such a focus. The journey to service-learning research grew out of a broader set of research agendas in the overarching area of experiential education and included internships, career development experiences, museum education and cooperative education. As part of its differentiation within and from experiential education, service-learning research took on a narrower focus. But the journey through service-learning research has broadened both for the field as well as for those of us who have traveled and are traveling through it. A good example is the evolution of the organization that is the sponsor of this volume. What began in 2001 as the first conference on service-learning research has now evolved into an organization called The International Association for Research in Service-Learning and Community Engagement (IARSLCE). While it is a debate for another forum about whether service-learning is a pedagogy that produces community engagement or if it is a form of community engagement, what is clear to this sojourner is that the field has broadened and our research questions have followed suit. One of the dimensions of this emphasis on community engagement grows out of faculty participation in service-learning and concerns the scholarship of engagement (Boyer, 1996) or scholarship as part of community engagement. In the last 4 years since the Carnegie Classification for community engaged campuses, there has been a dramatic increase in the literature on engagement. As with any emerging field, there has been a plethora of definitional variance or what Sandmann has called "definitional anarchy" (Sandmann, 2008). As a means to sort out the definitional confusion and differing and contested terms used in regard to engagement, I have recently proposed developing the same types of conferences and dialogue used for service-learning to develop a research agenda for the study of engaged scholarship in order to empirically illustrate its parameters, faculty involvement, and outcomes (Giles, 2008). It is my observation that many faculty who do engaged scholarship had their start by applying service-learning in their courses. As such, developing a research agenda to understand community engaged scholarship would in effect extend our knowledge of service-learning in terms of one the original research agenda categories: faculty.

ACCOMPLISHMENTS

Based on the criteria noted in the introduction I have selected works that reflect the key accomplishments of the overall journey to and through service-learning research for the field and some of my own steps and accomplishments in that journey. Clearly this is at base a set of subjective criteria, even though a case can made for widespread acceptance and citation of most of the milestone studies cited here. In choosing key research milestones, I have tried to be faithful to the primary categories of the research agendas, namely research on history, students, community, and faculty. In each category, in addition to studies in which I have played a role, I have selected other studies that were first or pioneering in terms of findings, answering important questions and, where applicable, were national in scope. Implied in these selection criteria is a judgment of impact and influence. In one area, I am able to cite a Delphi study that looked at how inquiries in a particular area have been valued and cited (Shumer, 2005). Still, this is not a literature review or a research bibliography. For a broader and more inclusive review of research studies, see Eyler, Giles, Stenson, and Gray (2000) and Howard et al. (2000).

Historical Research

One important dimension of the growth of a field such as service-learning is to have a sense of its origins and history, though not for slavish adherence to past principles or practices or a "presentist" approach to history. Rather, historical research reminds current practitioners of the core ideas, the struggles and the reasons for certain practices and positions. In a pedagogy such as service-learning that challenges many of the key practices and pedagogies of the academy, a historic sense of the movement's reform roots is crucial to maintaining its core values.

Out of this concern for the lack of historic consciousness due to the rapid growth of service-learning, several colleagues and I were able to conduct participatory research using oral history to capture the stories of the pioneers in the field (Stanton, Giles, & Cruz, 1999). As with any historical research, capturing and presenting the past is a value in and of itself. In the case of the pioneers we were able to collect oral histories as well as to compile their reflections on the motives for their work and their views on the practices and future policies for the field. In our discussions of definitions and terminology and our concerns about respective institutional roles, I think it is instructive to look at the 'birth' of service-learning and the rationale for its founding. Even though it has become largely an academic movement, its nursery in 1966 was not the academy but a community organization in Oak Ridge, Tennessee, namely, The Oak Ridge Institute for Nuclear Studies, University Relations Division. The purpose for establishing this program at a U.S. government funded scientific and regional development organization was to involve higher education in social and community problems. As one of the founders recalled in his interview for the study: "We decided to call it service-learning because service implied a value consideration that none of the other words we came up with did.... We were looking for something with a value connotation that would link action with a value of reflection on that action—a disciplined reflection" (Bill Ramsay, in Stanton et al., 1999, p. 67). One of the major outcomes of this research was having one of the founders, Bob Sigmon, codify and present his historical timeline, "An Organizational Journey to Service-Learning" (See Appendix B in Stanton et al., 1999). A less detailed list of highlights of the history of service-learning in the

**Exhibit 9.2.   Highlights of
Service-Learning History in the United States**

- 1966: Service learning Begins at Oak Ridge, TN
- 1969: First service-learning conference, Atlanta, Georgia
- 1972: University Year for Action signed by President Nixon
- 1979: National Center for Service-Learning
- 1985: Campus Compact established
- 1989: Wingspread Principles of Good Practice
- 1990: National & Community Service Act passed
- 1993: Service-Learning Listserve established
- 1994: *Michigan Journal of Community Service-Learning* established
- 2001: First Service Learning Research Conference in San Francisco

---

United States is found in Exhibit 9.2. Overall the historical picture that emerged was differing motives with regard to service and democracy, great hope, and times of struggle, as about half of the 33 who were interviewed lost their jobs or had their programs terminated.

Student Learning Outcomes

This was the first area of research and continues to be the largest arena for study because even though the founders envisioned service-learning as a way to engage higher education institutions in social and community problems, it rather quickly came to be viewed as pedagogy by educators, often under the umbrella of experiential education (Conrad & Hedin, 1991; Stanton et al., 1999). In all of the research agendas, the question of student learning remains central. In the annotated bibliography compiled by Janet Eyler and her colleagues, 7 of the 10 pages of summary findings are about research dealing with students and student learning (Eyler et al., 2000).

Even thought the focus of this research journey is on studies in postsecondary or higher education, it is impossible not to note the key influence of early studies in K-12 education that preceded any work in higher education service-learning. Indeed, I would argue that the early studies in K-12 research set the tone for the research agendas as well as the subsequent studies. One study in particular by Conrad and Hedin stands out not only because it was the earliest national study with data gathering taking place in the late 1970s,[2] but also because it established much of what we know about student learning outcomes even to this day. It also became the model for replication in higher education for Eyler and Giles's national study of higher education student learning outcomes undertaken in the mid 1990s (Conrad & Hedin, 1991; Eyler & Giles, 1999). Some of the key findings from Conrad and Hedin's national study were that experiential programs had impact especially on the social development of students, that reflection was key to academic learning and that there were elements of community settings that produced higher quality learning than others (Conrad & Hedin, 1991).

During the early- to mid-1990s, with major funding from the U.S. Department of Education's Fund for the Improvement of Post Secondary Education (FIPSE) and The Corporation for National Service, Eyler and Giles (1999) carried out two national studies. They were the first on higher education and combined mixed methods such as a pre- and post-national survey of 2,500 students, pre- and postproblem solving interviews, and interviews on best practices in reflection (Eyler & Giles, 1999). Centering on learning outcomes and following Conrad and Hedin's focus on program characteristics, they were able to identify fourteen areas of learning in response to the question of "Where's the Learning in Service-Learning?" that are listed in Exhibit 9.3.

This study also demonstrated, as did Conrad and Hedin, that program characteristics matter and were predictors of academic and other learning outcomes. As service-learning practitioners as well as researchers, they focused on how to strengthen the learning outcomes in service-learning.

Exhibit 9.3. The Learning in Service-Learning

- Deeper understanding of subject matter
- Understanding complexity of problems
- Applying class material to real problems
- Specific skills needed in the community
- Knowledge about community agencies
- Newfound natural curiosity about issues
- Connections to personal experience and people's lives
- New perspectives on social issues
- Enhanced problem analysis abilities
- Increased sense of importance of social justice
- Shift in understanding of locus of problems
- Greater valuing of public policy
- Personal perspective transformation
- Cognitive development

Source: Eyler and Giles (1999).

212   D. E. GILES, JR.

(See chapters 8 & 9 in Eyler & Giles, 1999). The most powerful predictors of learning outcomes they found were the application of content, placement quality, writing and discussion as forms of reflection, community voice in projects, service tasks and diversity. Another dimension of the two studies was to test and expand the idea of expert citizens developed by Batchelder and Root (1994). Borrowing the concepts of novice and expert from cognitive science and using pre- and post-problem-solving interviews with students who participated in service- learning and a comparison group who did not, they found that the students who participated in quality service-learning experiences were shown to exhibit greater civic knowledge and a higher ability to solve social and community problems (Eyler & Giles, 1999).

This research has been widely acknowledged, extensively cited and both authors have been recognized and have received multiple awards for this volume reflecting two national studies and 5 years of collaborative research. In a Delphi Study of the most influential K-12 service-leaning studies over the past 25 years, Shumer (2005) found that the Eyler and Giles study was rated by expert participants as the second most frequently cited. The context for the Eyler and Giles' study should be noted as well since FIPSE was willing to fund service-learning research for a brief window in the 1990s; this opportunity has not yet returned in the United States and other funds for large scale service-learning research seem to be lacking.

While the Eyler and Giles national study (1999) addressed the question of *where's the learning*, it did not really explore the question of the value added of service-learning as compared to community service. Also, the Eyler and Giles study was limited to being a cross sectional analysis with a pre and post time lapse of essentially one semester. As one of the foremost researchers in higher education for over 3 decades, Alexander Astin and his colleagues at the Higher Education Research Institute (HERI) at UCLA carried out a longitudinal study using a national sample of over 8,000 freshmen in 1994, surveying them again at graduation in 1998, and then 6 years after graduation (Astin et al., 2006; Vogelgesang & Astin, 2000). Some of the key findings include demonstration of the value added of service-learning over generic community service in terms of academic and civic outcomes, the key role of faculty in service-learning outcomes, and the centrality of reflection in establishing the impact of service-learning.

The topic of reflection will conclude our journey through the key accomplishments in research on student learning in service-learning. Reflection has been fundamental to service-learning practice and research for a variety of reasons. As noted above it was one of the major findings in the Conrad and Hedin study as a predictor of learning (Conrad & Hedin, 1991). Also many service-learning practitioners and researchers came from the broader fields of experiential education where reflection is a central theoretical concept. Much of this is derived from John Dewey's philosophy, where his linking of action and reflection is integral to a theory of learning in general and service-learning in particular (Giles & Eyler, 1994). One product of the Eyler and Giles' studies noted above was the development of an empirically based practitioner's guide to reflection. Based on interviews with over 60 students, this guide presents techniques and conceptual models such as those of David Kolb in utilizing reflection to produce learning outcomes (Eyler, Giles & Schmiede, 1996).

Several studies have shown that reflection is central and demonstrated the types of reflection most valued by students. One recent empirical study has shown not only that learning in service-learning depends on the integration of academic content with experience but also that reflection needs to have three characteristics, namely: (1) it must be structured; (2) regular; and (3) include clarification of values (Hatcher, Bringle & Muthiah, 2004). This refinement means that we have moved from Dewey's insistence on the importance of reflection in learning to an empirically grounded understanding of how to do effective reflection and what constitutes its characteristics (Eyler et al., 1996; Hatcher et al., 2004).

Community Impacts

This is arguably the area of least accomplishment in service-learning research and is somewhat ironic given the intent of service-learning to have students contribute to the community. Many would argue that paying attention to community is a moral demand given that we partner with community agencies through service-learning. I would certainly agree, but there is evidence that community participation is important in service-learning for learning's sake. For example, Eyler and Giles found that "Community voice, where students felt that the work they did was shaped by input from the community, did predict that students would feel more connected to the community" (Eyler & Giles, 1999, p. 47).

In an attempt to understand this puzzling lack of community research, Nadinne Cruz and I asked the question, "Where's the Community in Service-Learning Research?" (Cruz & Giles, 2000). One of the recommendations of the Cruz and Giles' piece was that given the difficulty, both methodologically and financially, of really studying community impacts and communitywide outcomes, it was a more realistic strategy and methodology to focus on community partnerships as the unit of analysis. This challenge to focus on partnerships has been taken up in a number of studies. Dorado and Giles (2004) examined thirteen service-learning partnerships in New England, focusing on the paths of engagement that occur over time. These are *tentative, aligned,* and *committed.* Each stage or path calls for a certain set of behaviors; those partnerships that reach the *committed* stage have a shared view of the student's learning and service outcomes. In each path of engagement, different forms of communication and partnership development are needed in order for the partnerships to succeed. In another analysis, the role of faculty in partnerships was examined in the context of whether there was a service- learning staff person coordinating the partnership (*delegated* partnerships) or whether the faculty member was responsible for developing and sustaining the partnership (*undelegated* partnerships). The findings were that

> Delegated partnerships—those with coordinators engaged only in coordinating duties—are likely to produce pre-defined outcomes while undelegated partnerships are likely to produce co-defined outcomes.... In undelegated partnerships there was no clear-cut division between coordination and participation.... In these partnerships outcomes were co-defined and tailored to the community partner, students' course work, and even students' profile and preferences. Interviewees discussed defining projects through negotiation and described excellent projects as those where "everybody's needs [were] being met." (Dorado, Giles & Welch, 2009)

Building on Dorado and Giles, and also using partnerships as the unit of analysis, Phillips examined the role of reciprocity in creating partnerships that transformed community and higher education partners.[3] He found that indeed reciprocity was crucial and that the elements that contributed to a truly transformational relationship included consistency in relationships and community-campus fusion (Phillips, 2007; Phillips & Ward, 2009). While community research in service-learning is still a largely neglected area, it is heartening to see more studies on community partnerships such as a recent book that notes that it was given the impetus from Cruz and Giles' (2000) call for more community research and to use the partnership as the unit of analysis (Stoecker & Tryon, 2009).

Faculty: Motivations and Rewards

Many practitioners have struggled with the challenge of how to get faculty involved in teaching service-learning. Indeed, the story of the evolution of service-learning might have a subplot of the many efforts to overcome faculty reluctance to participate in what Jeff Howard has characterized as a "counternormative pedagogy" (Howard, 1998).

Even though the inaugural issue of the *Michigan Journal of Community Service-Learning* had three articles on faculty involvement in service-learning, other published research on this topic has been sparse, probably only slightly less so than the dearth of articles on service-learning and community agencies. These three articles included a study by Hammond on how and why faculty get involved in service-learning, an analysis by Stanton on the effectiveness of a support seminar to generate faculty participation in applying service-learning, and Levine's reflective personal narrative of a faculty member's path to involvement in service-learning (Hammond, 1994; Levine, 1994; Stanton, 1994). From these studies we learned that faculty are motivated by the desire to provide better learning for their students, that campus support for teaching service-learning classes is critical, and that there are a number of steps for a faculty member to shift from traditional methods of teaching to service-learning.

The next major study in this domain of service-learning was published in 2000, based on the triennial national study of faculty administered by HERI at UCLA. which received more than 33,000 responses. The researchers added key questions on faculty's personal and professional involvement in service, including using it in courses. With such a large data set, the researchers were able to analyze the demographic and attitudinal predictors of faculty use of community service in a course. Among the key findings was that faculty with a humanistic orientation were most likely to use service in their courses and that women and faculty of color were more likely to engage in service-learning as part of their teaching (Antonio, Astin & Cress, 2000). A more recent study of faculty in Ohio showed that they were motivated to use service-learning by the belief that it deepened student learning and that many would continue to use this pedagogy even if it were not rewarded by their institution (Abes, Jackson & Jones, 2002).

In 2004, HERI added a significant number of questions about faculty involvement in service by turning to a national advisory board of service-learning researchers and practitioners, including myself. A major study was launched that surveyed over 40,000 faculty in 2004-05. Once again it was shown that women were more likely than men to use service-learning in their courses, as were faculty of color (Astin et al., 2006). The inclusion of engaged scholarship in this HERI faculty study is a further indicator of the shift or broadening of the field of service-learning. Other studies have focused on faculty engaged scholarship and the broader context of community engagement in higher education, including the influence of institutional roles in service-learning.[4] A recent major stimulus for this research in the United States has been the Carnegie Foundation's new elective classification of Community Engaged Institutions.

In 2006, the Carnegie Foundation awarded 76 campuses with its community engagement classification. Of those, five received the classification for curricular engagement, nine received the classification for outreach and partnerships, and 62 received the classification for both curricular engagement and partnerships. Of the 62 campuses that received both classifications, 33 answered the optional question indicating that they provided institutional rewards to encourage faculty involvement in service-learning. A database of these applications has provided the opportunity for a number of scholars to study faculty community engagement work in U.S. higher education, and several of these studies have recently been published in a single volume (Sandmann, Thornton, & Jaeger, 2009). Along with John Saltmarsh and several other colleagues, I have been involved in studying reward structures on the 33 campuses. The results of the first phases were published in last year's *Advances is Service Learning Research* volume (Saltmarsh et al., 2009) and indicate a very tentative picture of transformed policies and practices. In Phase 3 of this study, we are assessing seven campuses that meet our criteria for having transformed their faculty reward policies in favor of supporting engaged scholarship. Given that there was a 2008 round of classified institutions and that there will be another round in 2010, I and this group of colleagues will continue to study the question, "To what extent have higher education institutions that are committed to community engagement reshaped institutional reward policies in ways that create explicit incentives for faculty to undertake community engaged scholarship?"

ASPIRATIONS

In spite of the impressive body of service-learning research, much remains to be known and understood both in terms of basic knowledge and especially in terms of practice. While the list of aspirations below is nowhere near as long as the analysis of the agendas and accomplishments detailed above, I would argue that the breadth, scope, and vision of these aspirations is even larger than what we have already accomplished.

Reciprocity for Research and Practice

It is important to remember that the genesis and support for service-learning research arose largely out of a community of practice. With few exceptions, the early studies and even a large number of subsequent ones were done by those who had some connection to service-learning as a pedagogy and a field of educational endeavor. Only as the body of research has become known and accessible to scholars, especially doctoral students, has the more general research community taken up the topic for educational and other disciplinary research. But there is an irony in this phenomenon, rooted in the very nature of the effort to produce more and 'better' research, namely the drift away from practice. In addition to asking if the research has helped service-learning practice, we also need to consider the basic purpose of the research; as this conference theme asked, "Research for what?" Writing in the special research issue of the *Michigan Journal of Community Service Learning* a decade ago, Tim Stanton offered this observation: "Those who have been conducting service-learning research have also contributed to the practice-research-gap in this field. ...most service-learning research has tended to focus more on outcomes than on the methods needed to achieve these outcomes" (Stanton, 2000, p.120). My aspiration here is not only to raise and study questions that are relevant to practice but, as Shumer has argued, to do service-learning research in ways that are consistent with the values of participatory practices of service-learning (Shumer, 2000). Such truly participatory research approaches are related to maintaining the reciprocity of service-learning, as is proclaimed in the central claim that opens this chapter.

Reciprocity Between Campus and Community

Reciprocity is a given, or at least an espoused, value in the field of service-learning. In addition to the aspiration for more reciprocity between research and practice as presented in the preceding section, there is the core reciprocity between campus and community. The manifestations, challenges and techniques used to achieve this are perhaps the largest area for further research. While not to reiterate a detailed advocacy for more research in this area (Cruz & Giles, 2000), my aspiration is to do research with communities, to incorporate it in our service, and to have it represent an epistemology and way of knowing that we will come to accept and reward in the academy. In his argument for engaged scholarship, Ernest Boyer wrote: "I am convinced that ultimately, the scholarship of engagement also means creating a special climate in which the academic and civic cultures communicate more continuously and more creatively with each other...enriching the quality of life for us all" (Boyer, 1996). As engaged scholarship becomes more prevalent, as the Carnegie classification process for community engagement continues to develop in the United States, and as disciplines and campuses recognize more and more the role of higher education in solving community problems, we have a unique opportunity to study and encourage the reciprocity that the founders of the service-learning movement envisioned.

Global Inquiry

Even though this journey through service-learning research has focused on the United States, it does not represent an isolationist viewpoint. Indeed service-learning, like almost all endeavors at the present time, is affected by globalization. My aspiration is that this research area begin with the study of what happens to U.S. students who get involved in service-learning in non-U.S. settings. Even as more and more campuses invest in international service-learning, comparatively little is known about how this plays out for the students, the host countries, and the campuses. It is essential that international service-learning research not appear as justifying edutourism for privileged students. Our research needs to keep pace with this emerging area of practice, so as to understand its impact in comparison to locally-directed service-learning. While a thorough review of international manifestations of service-learning is beyond the scope of this chapter, there are enough studies on individual international initiatives to undertake broader analyses. For example, the *Michigan Journal of Service-Learning* has included studies in South Africa and Australia and conferences on service-learning have occurred in Asia, Australia, Canada, Europe, and Latin America. I recently gave a presentation on service-learning in Hong Kong, where several universities have established burgeoning service-learning programs, are doing research, hosting pan-Asian conferences and have recently published a special issue on service-learning (Chan, 2009). With internet social networking technologies, the aspiration of a global research enterprise in service-learning is imaginable, imperative, and doable.

Underlying all of these aspirations is the need to continually test the premise of service- learning, namely that it transforms both service and learning. For research this means big questions, bold designs, and reciprocal methods. It also means a diversity of epistemologies and ways of knowing. In summary, we need to inquire about long-term transformation of students who take service-learning courses, faculty who teach them and become engaged scholars, the communities that partner with campuses, institutions that become more community engaged, and finally, the extent to which we can determine the degree to which transformation occurs in global contexts.

NOTES

1. This organization later shortened its name to the National Society for Experiential Education (NSEE).
2. The results of this study are hard to find. It was never published as a research study because it came before the establishment of scholarly outlets for service-learning research. The earliest documents were a report to the funders and to the project base at the University of Minnesota. The 1991 reference is a summary of the work a decade later.
3. In the interest of disclosure, it should be noted that I was a member of Dr. Phillips' dissertation committee when he designed and carried out this research.

4. The Carnegie definition and assessment of *engaged campuses* includes curricular engagement as a key area of overall community engagement along with engaged scholarship.

REFERENCES

Abes, E. S., Jackson, G., & Jones, S. R. (2002). Factors that motivate and deter faculty use of service-learning. *Michigan Journal of Community Service Learning, 9*(1), 5-17.

Antonio, A. L., Astin, H. S., & Cress, C. M. (2000). Community service in higher education: A look at the nation's faculty. *Review of Higher Education, 23*(4), 373-398.

Astin, A. W., Vogelgesang, L. J., Misa, K., Anderson, J., Denson, N., Jayakumar, U., … Yamamura, E. (2006). *Understanding the effects of service-learning: A study of students and faculty.* Retrieved from http://www.heri.ucla.edu/PDFs/pubs/reports/UnderstandingTheEffectsOfServiceLearning_FinalReport.pdf

Batchelder, T. H., & Root, S. (1994). Effects of an undergraduate program to integrate academic learning and service: Cognitive, prosocial cognitive, and identity outcomes. *Journal of Adolescence, 17,* 341-355.

Boyer, E. L. (1996). The scholarship of engagement. *Bulletin of the American Academy of Arts and Sciences, 49*(7), 18.

Carnegie Foundation for the Advancement of Teaching. *Community Engagement Elective Classification.* Retrieved from http://classifications.carnegiefoundation.org/descriptions/community_engagement.php#2010

Chan, A. C. M. (Ed.). (2009). Special issue on service-learning. *New Horizons in Education, 57*(3).

Conrad, D., & Hedin, D. (1991). School-based community service: What we know from research and theory. *Phi Delta Kappan, 72*(10), 743-749.

Creswell, J. W. (2006). *Qualitative inquiry and research design: Choosing among five approaches.* Thousand Oaks, CA: Sage Publications.

Cruz, N. I., & Giles, D. E., Jr. (2000). Where's the community in service-learning research? *Michigan Journal of Community Service Learning, 7*(1), 28–34.

Dorado, S., & Giles, D. E., Jr. (2004). Service-learning partnerships: Paths of engagement. *Michigan Journal of Community Service Learning, 11*(1), 25-37.

Dorado, S., Giles, D. E., Jr., & Welch, T. C. (2009). Delegation of coordination and outcomes in cross-sector partnerships: The case of service-learning partnerships. *Nonprofit and Voluntary Sector Quarterly, 38*(3), 368.

Eyler, J., & Giles, D. E., Jr. (1999). *Where's the learning in service-learning?* San Francisco, CA: Jossey-Bass.

Eyler, J., Giles, D. E., J., & Schmiede, A. (1996). *A practitioner's guide to reflection in service-learning: Student voices and reflections.* Nashville, TN: Vanderbilt University.

Eyler, J., Giles, D. E. Jr., Stenson, C. J., & Gray, C. M. (2000). *At a glance: What we know about the effects of service-learning on college students, faculty, institutions, and communities, 1993-2000* (3rd ed.). Retrieved from http://servicelearning.org/filemanager/download/aag.pdf

Giles, D. E., Jr. (2008). Understanding an emerging field of scholarship: Toward a research agenda for engaged, public scholarship. *Journal of Higher Education Outreach and Engagement, 12*(2), 97-106.

Giles, D. E., Jr., & Eyler, J. (1994). The theoretical roots of service-learning in John Dewey: Toward a theory of service-learning. *Michigan Journal of Community Service Learning, 1*(1), 77-85.

Giles, D. E., Jr., & Eyler, J. (1998). A service learning research agenda for the next five years. In R. Rhoads & J. P. F. Howard (Eds.), *Academic service learning: A pedagogy of action and reflection* (pp. 65-72). San Francisco, CA: Jossey-Bass.

Giles, D. E., Jr., Honnett, E. P., & Migliore, S. (1991). *Research agenda for combining service and learning in the 1990s.* Raleigh, NC: National Society for Internships and Experiential Education.

Hammond, C. (1994). Integrating service and academic study: Faculty motivation and satisfaction in Michigan higher education. *Michigan Journal of Community Service Learning, 1*(1), 21-28.

Hatcher, J. A., Bringle, R. G., & Muthiah, R. (2004). Designing effective reflection: What matters to service learning. *Michigan Journal of Community Service Learning, 11*(1), 38-46.

Honnett, E. P., & Poulsen, S. (1989). *Principles of good practice for combining service and learning.* Racine, WI: The Johnson Foundation.

Howard, J. P. F. (1998). Academic service learning: A counternormative pedagogy. *New Directions for Teaching and Learning, 73*, 21-29.

Howard, J. P. F., Gelmon, S. B., & Giles, D. E., J. (2000). From yesterday to tomorrow: Strategic directions for service-learning research. *Michigan Journal of Community Service Learning, Special Issue, Fall 2000.* Retrieved from http://www.umich.edu/~mjcsl/volumes/2000contents.html

Levine, M. A. (1994). Seven steps to getting faculty involved in service-learning: How a traditional faculty member came to teach a course on "voluntarism, community, and citizenship." *Michigan Journal of Community Service Learning, 1*(1), 110-114.

Maxwell, J. A. (2004). *Qualitative research design: An interactive approach.* Thousand Oaks, CA: Sage.

Phillips, J. T. (2007). *Transformative campus-community service-learning partnerships.* Unpublished doctoral dissertation, Johnson & Wales University, Providence, RI.

Phillips, J. T., & Ward, C. V. L. (2009). Two-dimensional approach for assessing transformative campus/community service-learning partnerships. In B. E. Moely, S. H. Billig, & B. A. Holland (Eds.), *Creating our identities in service-learning and community engagement* (pp. 103-127). Charlotte, NC: Information Age.

Saltmarsh, J., Giles, D. E., Jr., O'Meara, K., Sandmann, L. R., Ward, E., & Buglione, S. (2009). Community engagement and institutional culture in higher education: An investigation of faculty reward policies at engaged campuses. In B. E. Moely, S. H. Billig, & B. A. Holland (Eds.), *Creating our identities in service-learning and community engagement* (pp. 3-29). Charlotte, NC: Information Age.

Sandmann, L. (2008). Conceptualization of the scholarship of engagement in higher education: A strategic review, 1996-2006. *Journal of Higher Education Outreach and Engagement, 12(*1), 91-104.

Sandmann, L., Thornton, C. H., & Jaeger, A. J. (2009). The first wave of community-engaged institutions. *New Directions for Higher Education, 147,* 6.

Shumer, R. (2000, Fall). Science or storytelling: How should we conduct and report service-learning research? [Special issue]. *Michigan Journal of Community Service Learning,* 76-83.

Shumer, R. (2005, November). *The Wisdom of Delphi: An investigation of the most influential studies in K-12 service-learning research in the past 25 years.* Presented at the Fifth Annual International Conference on Advances in Service-Learning Research, East Lansing, MI.

Stanton, T. (1994). The experience of faculty participants in an instructional development seminar on service-learning. *Michigan Journal of Community Service Learning, 1(*1), 7-20.

Stanton, T., Giles, D. E., Jr., & Cruz, N. I. (1999). *Service-learning: A movement's pioneers reflect on its origins, practice, and future.* San Francisco, CA: Jossey-Bass.

Stoecker, R., & Tryon, E. (Eds.). (2009). *The unheard voices: Community organizations and service learning.* Philadelphia, PA: Temple University Press.

Vogelgesang, L. J., & Astin, A. W. (2000). Comparing the effects of community service and service-learning. *Michigan Journal of Community Service Learning, 7,* 25-34.

Yelon, S. L., & Duley, J. S. (1978/1990). *Efficient evaluation of individual performance in field placement* (No. 14: Guides for the Improvement of Instruction in Higher Education). East Lansing, MI: Michigan State University Media Center.

ABOUT THE AUTHORS

Kay W. Allen is an associate professor in the College of Education at the University of Central Florida. She holds a PhD in psychological and sociological foundations of education. Her teaching and research interests are human development, adult learning, and teacher education.
E-mail: kallen@mail.ucf.edu

Inna Altschul is an assistant professor in the Graduate School of Social Work, University of Denver. Her scholarly work focuses on promoting well-being and positive development among low-income and immigrant youth. Combining ecological, sociological and psychological perspectives, she studies youth leadership development, as well as the impact of community, family, school and student factors on indicators of youths' well-being.
E-mail: inna@du.edu

Haiyan Bai is an assistant professor in the College of Education at the University of Central Florida. She holds a PhD in quantitative research methodology. Dr. Bai has conducted methodological and empirical research in education and published her work in both areas.
E-mail: hbai@mail.ucf.edu

Nicholas A. Bowman is a postdoctoral research associate in the Center for Social Concerns at the University of Notre Dame. He received his PhD in psychology and education, two master's degrees in education, and a graduate certificate in culture and cognition from the University of Michigan. His research interests include college diversity experiences and stu-

dent development, the assessment of college student outcomes, and the effects of college rankings on various higher education constituencies.
E-mail: nbowman@nd.edu

L. Richard Bradley is a consultant and trainer for Learn & Serve Ohio, The John Glenn Institute at The Ohio State University, and the Meharry State Farm Project.
E-mail: creativityrb@juno.com

Jay Brandenberger, a developmental psychologist, is director of research and assessment at the Center for Social Concerns at the University of Notre Dame. His research focuses on the development of moral judgment and purpose in the contexts of higher education.
E-mail: Jay.W.Brandenberger.1@nd.edu

Vilma D'Rozario is a subdean of student counseling and liaison and associate professor with the Psychological Studies Academic Group at the National Institute of Education, Nanyang Technological University. She is part of the team which implements service-learning for all student teachers at the institute. She also teaches preservice counseling and graduate group counseling courses. Her research interests include service-learning, master therapists, group counseling, and multicultural counseling. She is also actively involved in student life on campus as adviser to student clubs. She volunteers extensively in environmental and wildlife conservation projects in Singapore.
E-mail: vilma.drozario@nie.edu.sg

Janet Eyler, is a professor of the practice of education and director of undergraduate studies of the Department of Leadership, Policy and Organizations of Vanderbilt University.
E-mail: janet.s.eyler@Vanderbilt.edu

Dwight E. Giles, Jr. is a professor of higher education in the Graduate College of Education and a senior associate at the New England Resource Center for Higher Education at the University of Massachusetts, Boston. He is the 2009 Distinguished Research Award recipient from the International Association for Research on Service-Learning and Community Engagement as well as the winner of the 2003 Campus Compact Thomas Ehrlich Faculty Service-Learning Award.
E-mail: dwight.giles@umb.edu

Kim Chuan Goh is the head of the Office of Quality Management at the National Institute of Education in Singapore. He developed and man-

aged several of the teacher education initiatives at the NIE since 2004 and has been actively involved in creating innovative programs throughout Asia, including the First and Second International Conference on Service-Learning and Character Education, held in Singapore.
E-mail: kimchuan.goh@nie.edu.sg

Irwin Goldzweig is an assistant professor in the Department of Family & Community Medicine and program director of the Meharry–State Farm Alliance, Metropolitan Demonstration Project and the Teen Occupant Protection Project.
E-mail: igoldzweig@mmc.edu

Barbara A. Holland is professor and director of academic initiatives in social inclusion at the University of Sydney (Australia). She also maintains connection with Indiana University-Purdue University Indianapolis as a senior scholar in their Center for Service and Learning. An internationally recognized scholar and administrator with expertise in organizational change and community engagement, she is executive editor of *Metropolitan Universities* journal and coeditor of both the *Advances in Service-Learning Research series and* the *Australasian Journal of University-Community Engagement.*
E-mail: barbara.holland@sydney.edu.au

Paul Juarez is a professor of family and community medicine and vice-chair, Department of Family and Community Medicine at Meharry Medical College. He is principal investigator for a CDC funded teen seat belt study in Jackson, MS.
E-mail: pjuarez@mmc.edu

Jeff Keshen is a professor and chair of the History Department at the University of Ottawa. From 2004 to 2010, he served as director of the University of Ottawa's Experiential Learning Service, and now acts as senior academic advisor to the university's new "Au Service du Monde/In Service to Others" program.
E-mail: Jeffrey.Keshen@uOttawa.ca

Jihyun Kim is pursuing a PhD in adult education in the Department of Lifelong Education, Administration, and Policy at the University of Georgia. Her research interests include adult education for social change, transformative learning, and community-engaged scholarship. She received her masters of education from Seoul Nation University in South Korea.
E-mail: kim.jihyun235@gmail.com

Brandon Kliewer is a PhD candidate in the Department of Political Science at the University of Georgia. His research looks at the intersection between normative questions of political theory and the administration of higher education engagement. Kliewer holds a master's degree in political science from Virginia Tech.
E-mail: brandon.kliewer@gmail.com

Annie McKitrick is the manager of the Canadian Social Economy Hub, a 5-year funded research partnership between university researchers and practitioner organizations. Annie has a masters degree in education from the University of Victoria. She is a former school trustee and executive director of nonprofit organizations with an interest in civil society, governance and adult education.
E-mail: secoord@uvic.ca

Barbara E. Moely is professor emerita in psychology and research affiliate of the Center for Public Service at Tulane University in New Orleans. Her research is concerned with factors affecting service-learning outcomes for college students and the development of campus-community partnerships. She is senior associate editor of the *Michigan Journal of Community Service Learning*.
E-mail: moely@tulane.edu

Connie Nelson is director of the Food Security Research Network and has provided extensive leadership and support in the development of service-learning around a food security theme at Lakehead University. She contributes a strong and long-standing network of relationships with northern communities in areas of social capital, food security and community well-being that have been instrumental in building the network of partners for service-learning on campus.
E-mail: cnelson@lakeheadu.ca

Nicole Nicotera is an associate professor in the Graduate School of Social Work at the University of Denver. Her research focuses on measuring civic development in children, interventions to enhance civic leadership and positive youth development, the influence of neighborhood collective socialization and social cohesion on young people, and issues of unearned privilege and oppression in social work practice, education and research.
E-mail: Nicole.Nicotera@du.edu

Anthony Omerikwa is a senior researcher in the government of Kenya. He is also a PhD candidate in adult education in the Department of Lifelong Education, Administration, and Policy at the University of Georgia,

with research interests in community-based research, social learning theories, and qualitative research methods.
E-mail: omerikwe@uga.edu

Lorilee R. Sandmann is professor in the Adult Education Program, Department of Lifelong Education, Administration, and Policy at the University of Georgia. Her research focuses on leadership and organizational change in higher education with special emphasis on the institutionalization of community engagement, as well as faculty roles and rewards related to engaged scholarship. Her latest book is *Institutionalizing Community Engagement in Higher Education: The First Wave of Carnegie Classified Institutions* (Sandmann, Thornton, & Jaeger, 2009).
E-mail: sandmann@uga.edu

David Schlundt is an associate professor in the Department of Psychology at Vanderbilt University and an Adjunct Associate Professor in the Department of Family and Community Medicine at Meharry Medical College.
E-mail: d.schlundt@vanderbilt.edu

Andrew Schneider-Munoz is visiting associate professor at the University of Pittsburgh School of Education. where he leads practice education and research for youth work in after-school, national service, and other school and community-based youth development settings. He is editor of the *Journal of Child and Youth Care Work*. He was formerly chief operating officer at Search Institute and vice president for research and development at City Year, where he designed and implemented strength-based initiatives for high-risk populations.
E-mail: amunoz@pitt.edu

Robert Shumer is the former founding director of the National Service-Learning Clearinghouse and current lecturer at the University of Minnesota in curriculum and instruction and education policy and administration on topics related to service-learning, participatory evaluation, and experiential learning. He currently edits the research journal, *Information for Action: A Journal for Research on Service-Learning with Children and Youth*.
E-mail: drrdsminn@msn.com

Janel Smith is a former research coordinator for the Canadian Social Economy Hub and has a masters degree in dispute resolution from the University of Victoria. Janel is currently a doctoral student in international relations at the London School of Economics exploring the roles of "grass-roots" civil society in peace building.
E-mail: janels@uvic.ca

Trae Stewart is an assistant professor in the College of Education at the University of Central Florida. He holds a PhD in educational policy, planning, and administration from the University of Southern California. He specializes in service-learning and social foundations of education. He is a board member of the International Association for Research on Service-Learning and Community Engagement, and chairs the Early Career Network Steering Committee.
E-mail: pbstewar@mail.ucf.edu

Mirella Stroink conducts research on the psychology of human interaction with the natural environment, the factors underlying perceived food security, and the dynamics of cultural identity in a multicultural environment. Her service-learning initiatives include undergraduate courses in environmental and community psychology, as well as a directed studies graduate course in which students and First Nation communities are partnering in the development of an online toolkit supporting the development of sustainable local food systems.
E-mail: mstroink@lakeheadu.ca

Ben Webman is a senior data analyst at EdSource. He is responsible for data analysis and technical work and oversees data work done by other staff. He is working on the EdSource study of middle grades practices. He was formerly a senior planner at the Greater Miami Jewish Federation, the director of research at City Year, Inc. and senior analyst in the Institutional Research Department at Eastern Connecticut State University.
E-mail: bwebman@edsource.org